AN INTRODUCTION TO CONTEMPORARY EPISTEMOLOGY

Matthias Steup
St. Cloud State University

Prentice Hall, Upper Saddle River, New Jersey 07458

Library of Congress Cataloging-in-Publication Data

STEUP, MATTHIAS
  An introduction to contemporary epistemology / Matthias Steup.
    p. cm
  Includes bibliographical references and indexes.
  ISBN 0-13-037095-9 (alk. paper)
    1. Knowledge, Theory of. I. Title.
BD161.S6825 1996
121—dc20   95-19804

Acquisitions editor: *Ted Bolen*
Editorial assistant: *Meg McGuane*
Editorial/production supervision and interior design: *Edie Riker*
Cover design: *Wendy Alling Judy*
Cover photo illustration: *Magritte, Rene (Belgian 1898–1967), "La condition Humaine," 1933, Canvas/oil on canvas, 1.000 x .810 x .016 (39 3/8 x 31 7/8 x 5/8), National Gallery of Art, Washington, Gift of the Collectors Committee.*
Manufacturing buyer: *Lynn Pearlman*

To Carolina

©1998 by Prentice-Hall, Inc.
A Pearson Education Company
Upper Saddle River, NJ 07458

Printed in the United States of America

10 9 8 7 6 5 4 3 2 1

ISBN   0-13-037095-9

Prentice-Hall International (UK) Limited, London
Prentice-Hall of Australia Pty. Limited, Sydney
Prentice-Hall Canada Inc., Toronto
Prentice-Hall Hispanoamericana, S.A., Mexico
Prentice-Hall of India Private Limited, New Delhi
Prentice-Hall of Japan, Inc., Tokyo
Pearson Education Asia Pte. Ltd., Singapore
Editoria Prentice-Hall do Brasil, Ltda., Rio De Janeiro

CONTENTS

CHAPTER NINE: NATURALISTIC AND NONNATURALISTIC EPISTEMOLOGY   177

CHAPTER TEN: SKEPTICISM   203

PREFACE

This book presents a systematic, up-to-date account of the landscape of contemporary epistemology. To ensure that it is suitable for introductory epistemology courses, I have explained each issue from scratch, presupposed very little philosophical knowledge, and included an account of the logical and conceptual tools that are used for philosophical discussion and analysis. Numerous examples illustrate the problems, theories, objections, and rebuttals that make up the meat of each topic, and study questions and exercises at the end of each chapter review and reinforce the material covered in that chapter.

The writer of a textbook of limited length must make some kind of trade-off between breadth and depth, between including every important topic and doing full justice to every topic included. This book, I believe, offers a reasonable compromise. It contains chapters on all the central topics of epistemology—the analysis of knowledge, epistemic justification, foundationalism, coherentism, reliabilism, traditional versus naturalistic epistemology, and skepticism—and discusses each of these topics in depth. Thus it is of interest to both undergraduates and beginning graduate students who wish to familiarize themselves with the epistemological territory.

There are sections in this book in which, some will think, I unnecessarily digress from the main theme or pursue a particular issue for too long. Since diverging judgments about such matters can't be avoided, I propose that instructors simply choose from the table of contents to make up a menu of their own liking.

One epistemological topic conspicuously missing from this book is perception. I decided to omit this topic because including it would have meant either making the book too long for an introductory test or omitting some other topic I considered too important to leave out. I suggest that instructors who want to cover perception use supplementary course materials. Another feature of this book that needs explaining is the location of the chapter on skepticism. Since skeptical arguments are an excellent device for getting students excited about the study of epistemology, a discussion of them might reasonably be expected at the book's beginning. A satisfactory treatment of skepticism, however, requires a good grasp of what epistemology is about, plus a certain amount of skill at philosophical reasoning. For these reasons, I have placed the discussion of skepticism at the very end of the book.

I have tried, as far as possible, to link particular theories to the philosophers who advocate them because I think the best way to penetrate a philosophical issue is to look at the writings of philosophers who are widely regarded as representing opposing camps on that issue. Hence much of the book is devoted to discussing William Alston as a critic of the deontological concept of epistemic justification; Laurence BonJour and Keith Lehrer as advocates of coherentism; Alvin Goldman as a proponent of reliabilism; W. V. Quine, Alvin Goldman, and Hilary Kornblith as advocates of naturalized epistemology. Other contemporary philosophers whose writings either figure in, or have influenced this book are Robert Audi, Roderick Chisholm, Alvin Plantinga, and Ernest Sosa.

I don't believe that a textbook writer should attempt to adopt a neutral point of view. Concealing one's own stand on the issues under consideration usually results in a stale and lackluster product. Thus on occasion I have added my own two cents to the issues I discuss. Of course I have done my best to give each theory and point of view a fair hearing.

I am indebted to Ted Bolen for his encouragement and support, to my colleague Casey Swank for reading the entire manuscript and discussing it with me, to Noah Lemos for his helpful comments on several chapters, and to my reviewers, Mark Bernstein, Douglas C. Long, and Paul E. Tibbetts, for their comments and criticisms. I am especially grateful to a reviewer who would like to remain anonymous for generously providing me with a vast amount of critical comments.

CHAPTER ONE

KNOWLEDGE AND JUSTIFICATION

EPISTEMOLOGY

Epistemology is the study of knowledge and justified belief. To engage in this study is to seek answers to the following questions:

Q1   What is knowledge?

Q2   What do we know?

Q3   What is it for a belief to be justified?

Q4   Which of our beliefs are justified?

To answer question 1, we must define the concept of knowledge, while to answer question 2, we must determine the extent of knowledge. Question 3 calls for an analysis of the concept of justification, which involves stating criteria that tell us when beliefs are justified and when they are not. And if we wish to answer question 4, we must figure out the extent of what we are justified in believing. According to skeptics, the extent of what we know and what we are justified in believing is smaller than we ordinarily think. They reason that we have no way of ruling out that an evil demon is deceiving us without our being aware of the deception, or that a mad scientist has reduced us to unsuspecting brains in vats. According to nonskeptics, the claim that we have no way of ruling out such skeptical hypotheses is false. Nonskeptics believe, therefore, that the actual extent of knowledge and justified belief is, by and large, what we ordinarily think it is.

The four questions listed above are *theoretical* in nature. Epistemologists, however, are also interested in a *practical* question: What should we believe?[1] In order to answer this question, epistemologists must develop appropriate methodologies—methodologies that, if followed, help their practitioners to acquire justified beliefs, or even knowledge, and to avoid unjustified beliefs and error. Our focus in this book will be mostly theoretical. We shall discuss issues of practical epistemology only insofar as they bear on theoretical questions.

Many philosophers think there is a close conceptual connection between knowledge and justification. They hold that a belief cannot amount to knowledge unless it is justified. On that view, we cannot answer the two questions about knowledge without answering the two questions about justification. However, since the nature and extent of justified belief is an independently interesting issue, questions 3 and 4 would still remain central questions of epistemology even if these philosophers were wrong.

In this chapter, we will focus on the definition of knowledge and the role justification plays in that definition. In Chapter 2, we will consider precisely what we wish to accomplish when we attempt to analyze concepts such as knowledge and justification. In Chapters 3 through 8, we will consider various theories about the nature of justification. In Chapter 9, we will be concerned with issues of methodology, with *how* epistemology ought to be done. Finally, in Chapter 10, we will examine the extent of justified belief and knowledge and discuss skeptical and nonskeptical responses to questions 2 and 4.

PROPOSITIONAL KNOWLEDGE

When epistemologists concern themselves with knowledge, what they are interested in is the *propositional* meaning of the word "know," which must be distinguished from two other meanings. First, the word "know" can be used in the sense of "knowing *how*" to do a certain thing. For example, we may say: "He knows how to cook an omelet," or "She knows how to play the violin," or "They know how to pick good stocks." Second, the word "know" can be used in the sense of "being acquainted with." In this sense, knowing something, such as a place, a person, or a movie, involves becoming acquainted with it through a personal experience. I know Paris if I have been there and explored the city a bit; I know Arnold Schwarzenegger if I have met him; and I know the movie *Vertigo* if I have seen it.

Knowledge in the propositional sense, however, is knowledge of facts; it is knowing that so-and-so. This kind of knowledge is called "propositional" because the phrase "so-and-so" is to be replaced with a sentence expressing a proposition. For example, replacing "so-and-so" in "I know that so-and-so" with the sentence "The opossum is a nocturnal animal" results in "I know that the opossum is a nocturnal animal."

In order to ask the question, What is knowledge? in complete generality, let us use the letter S to stand for the subject to whom knowledge is attributed. Furthermore, instead of using the phrase "so-and-so" to represent the proposition known, let us use the letter p. This allows us to reformulate our question thus: What is it for S to know that p?[2] In contemporary episte-mology, the dominant approach to answering this question is to state a set of conditions that are both necessary and sufficient for a person S to know that p.

KNOWLEDGE AS JUSTIFIED TRUE BELIEF

There is an analysis of knowledge, often referred to as the *traditional* or *stan-dard account*, that holds that knowledge is justified true belief. We may state the conditions of the standard account of knowledge as follows:

> *The JTB Account*
> S knows that p if and only if (i) p is true; (ii) S believes that p; and (iii) S is justified in believing that p.

The first condition, the *truth condition*, requires that p be true. What is known must be true, or to put it the other way around, it is impossible to know a proposition that is false. Here are two examples. First, since it is false that there is a fax machine on my desk, I cannot know that there is a fax machine on my desk. Second, many people believe that there are space aliens who periodically visit earth and abduct humans to perform experi-ments upon them. Some people claim that they themselves have been the victims of such abductions. According to the truth condition, if it is false that these people were abducted by space aliens, then they do not know they were abducted, however strongly they believe it.

The second condition, requiring that S believe that p, is called the *belief condition*. There is, for example, the truth expressed by the 978th entry in the Chicago telephone book (assuming the possessor of the number listed in that entry hasn't disconnected service). Now, if I have got no idea what that number is and whom it belongs to, I don't have a belief about that matter, and thus don't know the truth contained in that entry.

According to the third condition of the JTB account, the *justification condition*, a true belief amounts to knowledge only if it is justified. This condition was first suggested by Plato. In his dialogue *Theatetus*, Socrates asks: What shall we say that knowledge is? Theatetus answers that knowl-edge is true opinion. Socrates is not pleased with this answer, and formu-lates an objection to it. In reply, Theatetus says:

> There is a distinction, Socrates, which I have heard made by someone else, but I had forgotten it. He said that true opinion, combined with reason, was knowledge, but that the opinion which had no reason was out of the sphere of knowledge: and that things of which there is no rational account are not knowledge.[3]

The distinction Theatetus alludes to is that between beliefs supported by reason and beliefs *not* supported by reason, and his proposal is that true beliefs qualify as knowledge only if they are supported by reason. In contemporary parlance, the distinction is that between justified and unjustified beliefs, and the condition Theatetus is proposing is that for a true belief to amount to knowledge, it must be justified.

What is the rationale for claiming that justification is necessary for knowledge? Many epistemologists would say that an unjustified true belief is no more than a *lucky guess*, and that a lucky guess falls short of being knowledge.

Here is an example of what is meant by calling a belief a "lucky guess." Consider a professor who enjoys full attendance in his logic class during the first week of the semester. On Monday of the second week, there does not appear to be an obvious drop in attendance, and the professor forms the belief: "And here we have full attendance once again." As a matter of fact, the professor's belief is true. However, he has no evidence to support his belief, for there are too many students taking his course for him to recognize how many are in attendance just by glancing around the classroom. Moreover, the fact that there was full attendance throughout the entire first week does not mean that there will be full attendance during the second week. Actually, after the first week of a course, a drop in attendance is to be expected. Hence, in order to be justified in believing that there is full attendance, the professor would have to count how many students are actually in his classroom. But he doesn't do that. Instead, he succumbs to *wishful thinking*. He is hoping for full attendance, and when he looks out on a nearly full classroom, he just can't help believing that *all* of his student are present. The professor's belief, then, is unsupported by evidence and triggered by wishful thinking. Though true, it is an unjustified belief—a lucky guess—and thus is not an instance of knowledge.

THE GETTIER PROBLEM

According to the standard account, knowledge is justified true belief. In his famous paper "Is Justified True Belief Knowledge?" Edmund Gettier demonstrated, however, that the three conditions of the standard account are not sufficient.[4] Let us consider one of the two counterexamples he presented in that paper.

Suppose Smith is justified in believing

(1)   Jones owns a Ford

because, as far back as Smith can remember, Jones has always owned a Ford, and he just got a ride in a Ford Jones claimed was his. As a matter of fact, Jones sold his old Ford and is currently driving a Ford he rented from Hertz. Hence (1) is false. Suppose further that Smith applies the laws of deductive logic to (1) and deduces the following three propositions about the whereabouts of his friend Brown:

(2)   Either Jones owns a Ford or Brown is in Boston.

(3)   Either Jones owns a Ford or Brown is in Barcelona.

(4)   Either Jones owns a Ford or Brown is in Brest-Litovsk.

By sheer coincidence, Brown happens to be in Barcelona. Hence (3) happens to be true. Smith, however, has no evidence at all for believing that Brown is in Barcelona. Nevertheless, according to Gettier, Smith is justified in believing (3). Gettier defends this claim by appealing to the following principle:

> If S is justified in believing p, and p entails q,[5] and S believes q because he deduces q from p, then S is justified in believing q.[6]

Although some philosophers have challenged this principle, it must be admitted that it is quite plausible. Its plausibility derives from the fact that there is no better way of expanding the stock of one's justified beliefs than through deduction.[7] If we apply this principle to our case, we can reason thus: Smith is justified in believing (1), he recognizes that (1) entails (3), and thus deduces (3) from (1); consequently, he is justified in believing (3). However, does he *know* that (3) is true? Since (1) is false, and Smith has no evidence at all for believing that Brown is actually in Barcelona, we'd have to say that he does not. Hence (3) is an example of a justified true belief that falls short of being knowledge.

In order to solve the Gettier problem, the definition of knowledge must be modified either by adding a fourth condition or by building an appropriate clause into the justification condition. Later in this chapter, we will return to this issue. In the meantime, let's briefly consider each of the three concepts that figure in the traditional account of knowledge: truth, belief, and justification.

TRUTH

There are several competing philosophical theories about the nature of truth: the correspondence theory, verificationism, and pragmatism.[8] Here is what these theories assert:

The Correspondence Theory
> The belief that p is true if and only if it corresponds with the fact that p.

Verificationism
> The belief that p is true if and only if it is an instance of (idealized) rational acceptability.[9]

Pragmatism
> The belief that p is true if and only if it is useful.[10]

Each of these theories has its shortcomings. The problem with the correspondence theory is that unless we know (i) what a fact is and (ii) what it is for a belief to correspond to a fact, the definition doesn't tell us much. Moreover, if we try to explain what a fact is, we will see that it is difficult to do so without using the concept of truth. Hence it is doubtful that the correspondence theory can provide us with a noncircular account of truth.

Next, consider verificationism. Since "rational acceptability" is just another term for "justification," what verificationism tells us is that a true belief in a certain area is one that enjoys ideal justification—the best kind of justification we can come by in that area. The problem with this view is that it's not so easy to explain why it shouldn't be possible for a belief to enjoy such justification and nevertheless be false. Take the belief that there is an external world of physical bodies. This belief is a good candidate for an ideally justified belief. Many philosophers believe, however, that it is logically possible for this belief to be false. Descartes, for example, took it to be a logical possibility that an evil demon was deceiving him into believing that there is a world of physical objects, and many contemporary philosophers think that it is logically possible to be a brain in a vat that is somehow kept alive and stimulated so that the illusion of a normal life is generated. But if it is possible to be deceived by an evil demon or to be a brain in a vat, then it is possible for ideally justified beliefs about physical objects to be false. Since verificationists can't allow for evil-demon deception and unsuspecting brains in vats, they face the uphill battle of having to show what precludes such things from being possible.[11]

Finally, let's consider pragmatism, which proposes that a true belief is a useful belief. It is doubtful that truth and usefulness are as closely linked as this theory supposes. It is easy to imagine true beliefs that are not useful at all. Suppose you are about to take an oral examination on a difficult subject. You believe—unfortunately, truly—that you are badly prepared. In all likelihood, this belief will not be useful to you; it might even make you more nervous than you would be anyhow, and thus lower your chances of passing the exam. Now suppose you believe—falsely—you are well prepared. This belief might be useful to you because it will make you more confident, and thus able to perform as well as your present level of ability allows. It would appear, therefore, that true beliefs can fail to be useful and useful beliefs can fail to be true.

In spite of their respective shortcomings, each of these views has its advocates. Since we cannot delve any further into these matters here, we shall take a neutral stance concerning the nature of truth. However, we shall presuppose that in doing epistemology, we should be guided by the following two points about the relation between truth and justification:

(i)   It is possible that *p* is true although there is no one who has a justified belief that *p*.

(ii)   It is possible for S to be completely justified in believing that p although p is false.

We will use the following example to illustrate the first point: Let p be a truth about what 999 is equal to. I don't have a justified belief that p for two reasons: first, I lack the requisite belief; and second, I didn't make any attempt to compute what that figure is equal to, so I have no justification for forming a belief about the matter.

To illustrate the second point, let us suppose that, unbeknownst to the public, Susan Rook, one of the anchors on CNN, has an identical twin sister, Sibyl Rook. Sometimes Sibyl, pretending to be Susan, reads the news, and except for a few people on the CNN staff, no one knows this is going on. Suppose you turn on CNN and believe yourself to be watching and listening to Susan Rook, when in fact Sibyl Rook is acting as the anchor on that occasion. Since you have no reason to suspect such a deception, your belief is justified. Nevertheless, it is false. Hence it is possible to have a justified false belief.

You may think that these two points are inconsistent with verificationism. Note, however, that verificationism doesn't identify truth simply with justification, but with *ideal* justification. Hence a verificationist could accommodate the first point by arguing that a true belief about what 999 is equal to is one that is capable of ideal justification, whether or not I actually hold that belief and whether or not I actually have justification for it. For example, she could say that the equation in question is a truth because the community of the best-trained mathematicians endorses it. Concerning the second point, she could argue that when you mistake Sibyl for Susan Rook, you are completely justified in that belief although it is not an instance of a belief that enjoys ideal justification.[12]

BELIEF

The standard view is that a belief is an attitude one can have toward a proposition.[13] Epistemologists distinguish among the following three propositional attitudes. One can:

(i)   believe that p (take p to be true);

(ii)   disbelieve that p (take p to be false);

(iii)   suspend judgment as to p (neither believe nor disbelieve p).

Of course, disbelief is just a special case of belief, for if you disbelieve that p, then you believe that the negation of p is true.

The concepts of theism, atheism, and agnosticism can be used to illustrate these three propositional attitudes. Let the proposition in question be that God exists. The theist believes that proposition, the atheist disbelieves it, and the agnostic neither believes nor disbelieves it, but suspends judgment on the matter of God's existence.

Note that, with regard to any proposition one considers, one cannot escape taking one of these three attitudes. If you wonder whether God exists—that is, if you consider the proposition "God exists"—then you must either believe that God exists, disbelieve it, or suspend judgment on the question.

Beliefs, of course, are held with various degree of intensity. You might be slightly inclined to believe that God exists, or you might be generally convinced that God exists although at times you have doubts, or you might feel so certain that he exists that there is no room in your mind for any doubt.

Before moving on to justification, let us consider one more distinction epistemologists make concerning the concept of belief: that between occurrent and standing beliefs. An occurent belief is one that is presently before your mind. For example, having just read about God's existence, your belief that God exists (or does not exist) might be one you are presently focusing on. If so, it is an occurent belief. Occurent beliefs can be either standing beliefs or beliefs that are newly formed. For example, that two and two equal four is a standing belief of yours that is not normally occurent. In contrast, a belief such as "The phone is ringing" is typically an occurent belief without being a standing belief.

JUSTIFICATION

According to the JTB account of knowledge, for a true belief to amount to knowledge, it must be justified. Now, if the JTB account were true, we should be able to characterize justification as that which "epistemizes" true belief—as that which turns true belief into knowledge. We have seen, however, that the three conditions of the JTB account are not sufficient for knowledge. What epistemizes true belief is justification plus something else, or "de-Gettiered" justification. But if justification is not what "epistemizes" true belief, how can we characterize it?

Epistemologists frequently answer this question by distinguishing between two kinds of true beliefs: those that are lucky guesses and those that are not. Recall the example of a lucky guess we considered above: A professor believes, without taking a head count,

(1)   And here we have full attendance once again

and he happens to be right. We assumed that his belief lacked justification because, instead of basing it on evidence acquired through counting, he simply succumbs to wishful thinking. The reason the professor's belief must be viewed a "lucky guess" is that he doesn't have evidence in support of (1). In fact, his knowledge that in the second week of the semester class attendance usually drops makes it likely that (1) is false. Thus he has no reason to think that (1) is true, and if subsequently he were to assess the situation, he'd have to say that it was mere luck that he got things right. Let us, then, define a lucky guess as follows:

> ### A Lucky Guess
> *S*'s belief that *p* is a lucky guess if and only if (i) *p* is true; (ii) *S* believes that *p*; (iii) *S* has no evidence for believing that *p* is true.

Note that we are not defining the concept of a lucky guess by simply saying: A lucky guess is a belief the truth of which is just a matter of luck. To do so would be misguided because, as Gettier cases illustrate, even a completely justified belief can be true as a result of sheer luck. Consider the Gettier case we stated earlier. Smith believes:

(2)   Either Jones owns a Ford or Brown is in Barcelona.

Smith's reasoning in support of (2) is impeccable. He has good evidence for believing that Jones owns a Ford, and he knows that (2) is entailed by the proposition that Jones owns a Ford. So as far as Smith's evidence and reasoning go, his belief is by no means a lucky guess. Yet, given that the first disjunct of (2) is false, there is a sense in which (2) is true by sheer luck. Brown just *happens* to be in Barcelona on the day Smith is ruminating about Jones's Ford. Had Brown changed his travel plans, he might have been somewhere else.

We must distinguish, then, between two kinds of lucky beliefs. First, a belief can be lucky because, in relation to certain relevant *facts*, its truth was not a likely outcome. Second, a belief can be lucky because, in relation to the subject's *evidence*, its truth was not a likely outcome. Let us call the former a lucky truth (for lack of a better name), and the latter a lucky guess. Justification is what prevents a true belief from being a lucky guess, but not from being a lucky truth.

We are now in a position to reevaluate the significance of the Gettier problem. What the Gettier problem shows us is that in order for a true belief to qualify as knowledge, it must satisfy two conditions: it must not be a lucky guess (that is, it must be justified), *and* it must not be a lucky truth. A true belief that isn't a lucky guess—like Smith's belief that (2) is true—may still be a lucky truth, and thus fall short of being knowledge. Hence in order to solve the Gettier problem, epistemologists have to figure out what kind of condition can prevent a true belief from being a lucky truth. Later in this chapter, we shall consider two proposals about what such a condition might look like. Before we can do that, however, we must examine a few more points about the nature of justification.

THE PROPERTY AND THE ACTIVITY OF JUSTIFICATION

It is important to distinguish between the *activity* of justifying a belief and a belief's *property* of being justified. When you engage in the activity of justifying a belief, you are explaining what evidence, or what reasons, you have in support of that belief. Your aim is to convince others—or perhaps yourself—that the belief in question is justified. About the logical relation between justification as a property and justification as an activity, two points must be made.

First, a belief of yours can have the property of being completely justified even if you have not engaged in the activity of justifying it. Consider your present belief that you are reading a book. Obviously, unless very odd circumstances obtain, this is a justified belief, even though (in all likelihood) you have not bothered to explain to anyone your evidence in support of that belief.

Second, it is possible for you to have no idea how to justify a certain belief although that belief is, as a matter of fact, justified. Suppose that on your first day in an epistemology class, the instructor asks you what your justification is for believing that you exist. Suppose further that the question completely dumbfounds you, so that you can't think how to respond to it. Does that mean you are not justified in believing you exist? Clearly not. Hence it is one thing for a belief to be justified, and quite another for the believer to be able to show that the belief is justified.

JUSTIFICATION AND EVIDENCE

There is a tight connection between one's justification for believing that p and one's evidence for p. According to some philosophers, we can even say that S is justified in believing that p if and only if believing p fits S's evidence.[14] Others would further tighten the connection between justification and evidence; they would say that one is justified in believing that p if and only if one has adequate evidence for p and believes that p *because* of that evidence.[15]

Traditionally, philosophers have recognized four sources of evidence: perception, introspection, reason, and memory. Perceptual evidence comes from our five senses: we have visual, auditory, olfactory, tactile, and gustatory experiences that provide us with evidential clues about the properties of physical objects. Introspection allows us to "look" inside ourselves, to know what mental states we are in: whether we are hungry, tired, excited, thinking about unicorns, worried about the future, and so on. Reason is the faculty that permits us to recognize such propositions as the following: p follows from q, p and q cannot both be true, p could not possibly be false, and p and q make r probable. Finally, memory permits us to retain knowledge that is derived from one of the other sources.

A reliable authority is one more commonly recognized source of evidence. Evidence based on a reliable authority can be acquired from an expert in a certain subject, an encyclopedia, an article in a trustworthy magazine, or the like. It should be noted, however, that evidence based on a reliable authority can be fully explained in terms of the other categories. Consider how you would acquire knowledge in Biology 101. The learning process in the classroom involves your senses: you hear the professor's voice, and you see what she writes on the board. Moreover, the professor's lectures and the textbook for this course convey a body of knowledge that was gained through cognitive processes and research methods combining perceptual observation, reason, and memory.

CONCLUSIVE AND NONCONCLUSIVE EVIDENCE

Justification comes in degrees: some beliefs are more justified than others. Examples of beliefs that are justified to the highest degree are beliefs in the elementary truths of arithmetic and axioms of logic, as well as simple beliefs about one's own conscious states. Beliefs that are justified to lesser degrees are those about the physical world, the past, the future, and things that are presently unobserved.

The degree to which a belief is justified depends, among other things, on whether that belief is supported by conclusive or nonconclusive evidence. Conclusive evidence guarantees the truth of the belief it supports, and thus affords complete certainty to the possessor of such evidence. Nonconclusive evidence, on the other hand, does not guarantee the truth of the belief it supports. Thus, if one has nonconclusive evidence for a proposition p, one's justification for p is of a lower degree than complete certainty.

Consider the belief "I exist." As Descartes argued in the first of his *Meditations*, if I didn't exist, then I couldn't be thinking about my own existence. Consequently, it is impossible to mistakenly believe oneself to exist. My evidence for believing that I exist—introspective awareness of the fact that I am thinking about the question whether I exist—is conclusive: it guarantees that my belief that I exist is true, and thus provides me with complete certainty.

In contrast, my evidence for believing that there is a desk in my office is nonconclusive. I presently have the experience of seeing that desk in front of me. However, it is logically possible that I who am having that experience am a brain in a vat whose sensory experiences are the result of direct stimulation through a computer.[16] If I were such a brain in a vat, then *ex hypothesi* I would not be in Brown Hall 109 but in a mad scientist's laboratory. Consequently, having the perceptual evidence I am currently having does not provide me with a logical guarantee that the belief that evidence supports is true.

The distinction between conclusive and *nonconclusive* evidence is an epistemological one. Do not confuse it with the distinction between conclusive and *inconclusive* evidence that is part of our ordinary language. When I'm in my office looking at my desk, then my evidence for believing that there is a desk there is certainly not inconclusive in the sense in which that term is ordinarily used. That is to say, outside of the context of epistemology, we would take my evidence to be conclusive—to leave no doubt whatsoever as to the presence of my desk. However, in the sense in which we shall use the term here, my evidence is nonconclusive since it does not guarantee my belief's truth.

One way of expanding one's stock of justified beliefs is to use deduction. Consider the following argument:

(1)   I exist.

Therefore:

(2)   Someone exists.

Premise (1) is certain, and it is certain that (2) follows deductively from (1). Thus the deductive link between (1) and (2) transmits certainty from (1) to (2). In general, because deduction is truth-preserving, it allows us to start out with premises for which we have conclusive evidence and to end up with conclusions for which we have conclusive evidence.[17] Conclusive evidence for a conclusion cannot be achieved with nondeductive types of derivation. For example, if p does not entail q but only makes q probable, then I cannot have conclusive evidence for q even if my evidence for p is conclusive.

It should be noted that a deductively derived conclusion cannot enjoy a higher degree of justification than the premise (or premises) from which it is derived. To illustrate this, we will consider another argument:

(1)   My wife is presently at home.

Therefore:

(2)   Presently, someone is at home.

Suppose I am justified in believing (1) because I know that at the present time my wife is normally at home. Clearly, though, this kind of evidence does not provide me with certainty for (1). After all, she might be out on an errand. Hence, although the deductive step from (1) to (2) is certain, the argument's conclusion is not because the premise from which it is derived is not.

JUSTIFICATION AND DEFEASIBILITY

One's justification for believing a proposition p is sensitive to changes in the total body of one's evidence. As one's evidence changes, one can gain, lose, and regain justification for believing something. Suppose S sees a sheet of paper that looks blue to him. S believes

(1)   This sheet of paper is blue

on the perceptual evidence that

(2)   The sheet of paper looks blue to S.

Suppose further that S is informed that

(3)   Blue light is shining on that sheet of paper.

If what S has to go on is no more than (2) and (3), S is not justified in believing (1) because (3) defeats (2) as S's justification for believing (1). We can define the concept of evidential defeat as follows:

Evidential Defeat
> d defeats e as evidence for p if and only if e is evidence for believing that p, but e in conjunction with d is not evidence for believing that p.

S's justification for believing a proposition p is defeated if S has evidence for another proposition that defeats S's evidence for p. This can happen in two ways: (i) S can acquire evidence that justifies S in believing that p is false; or (ii) S can acquire evidence that destroys S's justification for believing that p is true, without, however, justifying S in believing that p is false. Let us call defeaters of the former type *contradicting* defeaters and those of the latter type *undermining* defeaters.[18] (3) is an example of an undermining defeater. It destroys S's justification for believing that (1) is true, but it does not justify S in believing that (1) is false.

The following is an example of a contradicting defeater. Suppose again that S believes (1) on the basis of (2). Suppose further that S is informed of the truth of the following two propositions:

(4)   This sheet of paper is a grade-change form.

(5)   Grade-change forms are always pink.

In this case, S has an explanation of why the sheet of paper looks blue—namely (3)—and has further evidence indicating that it is in fact not blue but rather pink. In this situation, S is justified in believing that (1) is false. The conjunction of (4) and (5), therefore, functions as a contradicting defeater.

A defeater for p can, in turn, be defeated. If this happens, then the justification S originally had for p is restored. Suppose, once again, that S believes (1) on the basis of (2). S is informed that (3) is true, and thus his justification for believing (1) is defeated. However, subsequently S is informed of the following two propositions:

(6)   This sheet of paper is a grade-appeal form.

(7)   Grade-appeal forms are always blue.

This information provides S with further relevant evidence indicating that (1) is true after all. Since this evidence is not perceptual in nature, it is not affected by the fact that blue light is shining on the sheet of paper. After all, a sheet of paper that is blue to begin with will still look blue when illuminated by blue light. Hence, as soon as S learns of the facts expressed by (6) and (7), he is again justified in believing that the sheet of paper he is looking at is blue.

DEFEASIBILITY AND THE GETTIER PROBLEM

In the last section, we saw that justification can be defeated because some elements of S's evidence can defeat other elements of S's evidence. In this section, we shall see that—as is illustrated by Gettier cases—justification can also be defeated by certain *facts*: facts that bear evidentially on, but are not part of, S's evidence and defeat S's justification for believing that p in the sense that his justification for p remains intact but fails to give him knowledge of p. Let us keep these two types of defeat separate by distinguishing between *evidential* and *factual* defeat of justification. The following two definitions specify how these concepts differ:

> *Justificational Defeat*
>   d evidentially defeats S's justification for believing that p if and only if (i) S has evidence e for believing that p; (ii) S has also evidence e' for a proposition d that defeats e as evidence for p.

> *Factual Defeat*
>   d factually defeats S's justification for believing that p if and only if (i) S has evidence e for believing that p; (ii) there is a proposition d such that d is true, S does not have evidence for d, and d defeats e as evidence for p.

Suppose some elements of my evidence support p in such a way that, if I had no further relevant evidence, I would be justified in believing that p. Suppose further that other elements of my *evidence* defeat the evidence I have for p. In that case, I am not justified in believing that p. However, if there is a fact that is hidden from me—hidden in the sense that I don't have evidence for it—that defeats my evidence for p, then although I remain justified in believing that p, I am not in a position to *know* that p.[19]

To keep these two types of defeat properly distinct, we shall distinguish between *epistemizing* and *nonepistemizing* justification. Epistemizing justification is justification that is both evidentially and factually undefeated; it turns true beliefs into knowledge. Nonepistemizing justification is justification that is factually defeated without being evidentially defeated. Nonepistemizing justification's shortcoming is that, for reasons beyond S's ken, it is undermined by certain facts about S's situation, and thus fails to epistemize S's belief that p—that is, to turn it into knowledge.

In light of these considerations, it is clear that the phrase "S's justification for believing that p is defeated" is an ambiguous one. It might refer either to evidential or to factual defeat. Let us avoid this ambiguity by adopting the following convention: When S's justification for p is evidentially defeated, we shall simply say that S's justification for p is defeated. If, on the other hand, S's justification for p is factually but not evidentially defeated, we shall say that the *epistemizing potential* of S's justification for p is defeated.

Let us see how this convention works in a concrete case. Consider again the Gettier case we discussed earlier. Smith is justified in believing

    (1)   Jones owns a Ford

and deduces

    (2)   Either Jones owns a Ford or Brown is in Barcelona.

Since Brown happens to be in Barcelona, (2) is true. But Smith doesn't know (2) because there is (or so let's suppose) the following fact about his situation that is hidden from him:

    (3)   The Ford Jones drives is a Hertz rental car.

(3) is a contradicting defeater for (1): if Smith had evidence for believing (3), then he would be justified in believing that (1) is false. However, (3) is hidden from Smith; he has no evidence at all for (3). Consequently, (3) does not defeat Smith's justification for believing (2); it merely defeats the epistemizing potential of his justification for (2), and thus prevents Smith from knowing (2). Hence, in spite of (3), Smith is fully justified in believing (2). Indeed, it is an essential element of Gettier cases in general that the subject's justification remains intact. Gettier cases, after all, are cases of *justified* true belief.

A FAILED ATTEMPT AT SOLVING THE GETTIER PROBLEM

In the next section, we shall discuss how the concept of defeasibility can be exploited for the purpose of solving the Gettier problem. In this section, we shall consider a different solution, one that has turned out to be a dead end.[20] The gist of this solution is expressed by the following condition:

    C1 S's justification for p does not depend on any falsehood.

This condition gives us the right result for Gettier's original case about Smith and his ruminations about Jones's Ford. When Smith deduces (2), he uses (1) as a premise. But (1) is false, and thus his justification for believing (2) depends on a falsehood. So S does not meet condition C1, and hence does not know (2).

Nevertheless, supplementing the JTB account with C1 does not solve the Gettier problem. There are other Gettier-type cases in which a justified true belief meets C1, yet does not qualify as an instance of knowledge. Let's consider a case of that type.

Suppose you look out your window and see your cat in your yard. Naturally, you believe, "My cat is in the yard." But what you take to be your cat isn't a cat at all but a hologram so perfect that, by vision alone, it cannot be distinguished from an actual cat. Unbeknownst to you, your neighbor has acquired the equipment to project holograms, and he is playing a trick on you. Furthermore, suppose that your cat is in your yard, but is lying right underneath the window, where you cannot see her from your present point of view. Your belief that your cat is in your yard, then, happens to be true. Furthermore, you are completely justified in believing that your cat is in the yard because your cat can be found there quite frequently, the hologram bears a striking resemblance to your cat, and you have no grounds whatever to suspect your neighbor of projecting cat-holograms into your yard.

In this case, the proposition you are justified in believing—my cat is in the yard—is not deduced from anything. Rather, you have a certain perceptual experience (that of seeing what seems to you to be your cat), and that experience triggers in you the belief that your cat is in the yard. Your justification for your belief is not, therefore, inferred from a further proposition that is false, and hence does not depend on any falsehood. Hence, if the JTB account is supplemented with C1, we get the wrong result for cases like this one.

A DEFEASIBILITY SOLUTION TO THE GETTIER PROBLEM

Since Gettier examples involve the factual defeat of S's justification for believing the proposition in question, many epistemologists attempt to solve the Gettier problem by formulating conditions that require that S's justification remain undefeated.[21] There are, of course, rival proposals, among which this defeasibility approach is just one contender. Indeed, it would be fair to say that what is conspicuous about the literature on the Gettier problem is, first, the multitude of approaches and, second, the lack of a settled solution. Unfortunately, for reasons of space, we cannot go beyond a discussion of the defeasibility approach here.

The defeasibility approach is based on the idea that the full range of relevant facts must not defeat—in the factual sense of the word—S's justification for believing that p. The following condition captures the idea behind this approach:

C2   There is no proposition d such that d factually defeats S's evidence for believing that p.

C2 gives us the right result for the Gettier case we have considered. In Gettier's case about Smith and Jones's Ford, we assumed the following proposition is true:

(1)   The Ford Jones is currently driving is a Hertz rental car.

(1) defeats the epistemizing potential of Smith's justification for believing that either Jones owns a Ford or Brown is in Barcelona. Hence, although Smith is justified in believing that either Jones owns a Ford or Brown is in Barcelona, he does not know it.

In the case about your cat in the yard, this is a true proposition:

(2)   What you are looking at is a hologram that looks like a cat.

(2) is a factual defeater for the evidence you have for believing that your cat is in the yard. Hence you don't know that your cat is in the yard.

It is important to note that when we apply C2 to particular cases, we must take into account the total body of S's evidence. The following case illustrates this. Suppose S is justified in believing

(3)   This sheet of paper is blue

because the sheet of paper looks blue to him and he knows that

(4)   This sheet of paper is a grade-appeal form and all such forms are blue.

Suppose further that the following proposition is true:

(5)   Blue light is shining on it.

(5) defeats S's perceptual evidence for believing (3). Nevertheless, C2 is met because (5) does not defeat S's evidence for (3) in its *totality*. Part of S's evidence is his knowledge of (4), which by itself is sufficient to justify S's belief. Hence, although there is a true proposition that defeats one element of S's justification for (3), S has nevertheless knowledge of (3).

AN AMENDED JTB ACCOUNT OF KNOWLEDGE

According to the traditional account, knowledge involves three ingredients: truth, belief, and justification. The Gettier problem demonstrates that a further ingredient is needed. Advocates of the defeasibility approach propose that this missing ingredient is the absence of factual defeat. Thus they would add a fourth condition to the traditional account:

S knows that p if and only if
(i) p is true;
(ii)   S believes that p;
(iii)   S has justifying evidence for believing that p;

(iv)   there is no proposition *d* that factually defeats *S's* evidence for believing that *p*.

Note, however, that condition (iv) makes the truth condition redundant.[22] Whenever *p* is false, there will be a true proposition *d* that defeats whatever justification *S* may have for *p*: the negation of *p*, and any proposition that entails the falsehood of *p*. Hence condition (iv) fails to be met whenever *p* is false. To see why this is so, recall our definition of evidential defeat:

> *d* defeats *e* as evidence for *p* if and only if *e* is evidence for believing that *p*, but *e* in conjunction with *d* is not evidence for believing that *p*.

Suppose *p* is false, and *S* has evidence *e* in support of *p*. Since *p* is false, the negation of *p*, *not-p*, is true. We must ask, therefore, whether *e* in conjunction with *not-p* is evidence for *e*. And the answer is that it is not, for nothing is evidence for *p* if it is conjoined with the negation of *p*.

Let us consider a simple case of believing a false proposition. Suppose that, while taking a walk in the countryside, you believe

(1)   There is a sheep in the field

because you see an animal that looks like a sheep to you. In fact, it is a dog that, because of some bizarre features, looks from your point of view exactly like a sheep. Thus the following proposition is true:

(2)   What you are looking at is actually a dog that looks like a sheep.

This proposition factually defeats your evidence for believing (1). If you were to acquire evidence for (2), you would no longer be justified in believing (1). So condition (iv) of the amended JTB account of knowledge is not met, and we get the result that you don't know there is a sheep in the field.

As you can see, then, adding condition (iv) to the traditional account makes condition (i) superfluous.The amended account, therefore, can be stated in three conditions only:

S knows that *p* if and only if
(i)   *S* believes that *p*;
(ii)   *S* has justifying evidence for believing that *p*;
(iii)   there is no proposition *d* that factually defeats *S's* evidence for believing that *p*.

STUDY QUESTIONS

1. According to the traditional account of knowledge, what three conditions must S meet in order to know that *p*? What is the rationale for each of these conditions?
2. What is the Gettier problem?
3. How does a belief's property of being justified differ from the activity of justifying a belief?
4. What is the difference between conclusive and nonconclusive evidence?
5. What is meant by calling evidence "defeasible"?
6. In Gettier cases, in which sense is S's justification for believing that p defeated?
7. Why does the condition *S's justification for believing that p must not depend on any falsehood* fail to solve the Gettier problem?
8. How can the concept of defeasibility be exploited to solve the Gettier problem?

EXERCISES

1. Construct your own case in order to argue that knowledge does not entail belief, and then explain how an advocate of the belief condition could try to accommodate that case.
2. Construct your own example of a Gettier case.
3. The following is a Gettier case proposed by Ernest Sosa:

   Someone, S, is about to release a nail and predicts its fall. Unknown to him, however, there are powerful magnets overhead and underfoot such that the nail will fall as usual but under the influence of the magnets, next to which gravity is negligible. Surely S's prediction that the nail will fall does not amount to knowledge, but why not? What goes wrong?[23]

   Try to answer the question Sosa asks at the end of this passage. Do you think the defeasibility solution to the Gettier case as described in this chapter can accommodate Sosa's case?

NOTES

[1] According to Roderick Chisholm (1989), the practical purpose of epistemology can be put thus: "We want to do our best to improve our set of beliefs—to replace those that are unjustified by others that are justified and to replace those that have a lesser degree of justification with others that have a greater degree of justification" (p. 1). For an elaboration of the theoretical and practical dimensions of epistemology, see Sosa (1991), essay 14.

[2] An expression of the form "S knows that *p*" is called a "schema." A schema is a formula that is neither true nor false, but can be transformed into a sentence that is true or false by making appropriate replacements. Thus, if we replace "S" with "Socrates" and "*p*" with "Courage is a virtue," the result is: "Socrates knows that courage is a virtue." Since strict adherence to the "that" clause can result in awkward formulations, we shall also use the phrase "S knows *p*," taking it to be understood that substituting a proposition for "*p*" will call for adding a "that."

[3] *Theatetus* 200d—-201d. Quoted from *The Dialogues of Plato*, 4th ed., trans. Benjamin Jowett (Oxford: The Clarendon Press, 1953).

4 See Gettier (1963).

5 By saying that p entails q, we mean that it's not possible for p to be true and q to be false.

6 This principle asserts that justification is transmitted from one proposition to another through recognized entailments. It is also referred to as the "closure" principle because it tells us that moving from one proposition to another on the basis of a recognized entailment does not get us outside of the closed area of justified beliefs. See Dancy (1985), pp. 10f.

7 The reason for that is that deduction is *truth-preserving*. If p is true and q can be deduced from p, then it is impossible that q is false. See Klein (1992), p. 460.

8 For a brief account of these views, see Horwich (1992).

9 For a defense of this view, see Putnam (1981).

10 For a classical account of this view, see James (1909).

11 Thus Putnam, who advocates verificationism (or antirealism, as this view is often called), has proposed an elaborate argument according to which one could not possibly be a brain in a vat. See Putnam (1981), chap. 1.

12 Obviously, under ideal conditions, you would have evidence revealing the true identity of the woman you mistakenly believe to be Susan Rook.

13 There are alternative theories that compete with the standard view, but here we don't have the space to review them. For brief account, see Heil (1992).

14 This view is defended in Conee and Feldman (1985).

15 For a discussion of this view, see ibid., sect. IV. See also Armstrong (1973), pp. 150f, and Pollock (1986), pp. 36f.

16 Although there are some philosophers who deny this possibility, even they would probably concede that I might suffer from a hallucination so vivid that I believe I am in my office looking at my desk when, in fact, I am in a laboratory where a mad scientist is inducing the hallucination.

17 Of course, a deductive argument whose premises are certain results in a certain conclusion only if each step in the derivation is certain as well.

18 For an account of these two types of defeat, see Pollock (1986), pp. 37ff.

19 The term "hidden fact" comes from Hetherington (1992), p. 115.

20 For a comprehensive discussion of various solutions to the Gettier problem, see Shope (1983). For a brief discussion of the solution discussed in this section, see Dancy (1985), pp. 27f.

21 The approach was first developed in Lehrer and Paxson (1969). See also chap. 7 in Lehrer (1990). For brief but useful accounts of the defeasibility approach, see Dancy (1985), pp. 29f, Moser (1992), and Shope (1992).

22 See Dancy (1985), p. 29.

23 See Sosa (1986).

CHAPTER TWO

EPISTEMOLOGY AND PHILOSOPHICAL ANALYSIS

CONCEPTS AND PROPOSITIONS

In this chapter, we shall distinguish between two ways of analyzing concepts. However, before we take up the topic of conceptual analysis, a few remarks about how we use the term "concept" are in order. Concepts, as we shall use the term, are properties.[1] Thus we shall take the concept of knowledge to be the property of knowing, pertaining to persons, and the concept of justification to be the property of being justified, pertaining to the attitudes persons take toward propositions.

Concepts, in the sense in which we shall use the term, must not be confused with either words or ideas in the mind. When in Chapter 1 we discussed the analysis of knowledge, our concern was not with the English word "knowledge", but rather with the concept that this word denotes (and that synonymous words in countless other languages denote). Words are particulars, concrete items belonging to specific languages. Concepts, however, are universals: properties that can be exemplified by many individual objects. Thus we may speak of concepts as having "instances", which are the individual objects that exemplify them. For example, my neighbor's cat is an instance of the concept of catness, and your knowing that cats have four legs is an instance of the concept of knowledge.

Since we view concepts as universals, we must not confuse them with ideas in people's minds, which are particulars. When we engage in a philosophical examination of such things as knowledge and justification, then, what we are interested in is not what ideas of knowledge and justification people carry in their heads, but rather what people have in common when they know something and when they are justified in believing something.

Parallel to the distinction between concepts and words is the distinction between *propositions* and *sentences*. The constituents of sentences are words; therefore, just like words, sentences are particular items belonging to particular languages. In contrast, propositions are the things that are expressed by sentences (that is, by sentences that are either true or false). For example, the two sentences

(1)   Two and two is four

(2)   Zwei und zwei ist vier

belong to different languages: (1) is English and (2) is German. But what they express is one and the same thing: the proposition that two and two equal four. Sentences are particulars; they have a location in space and time, and since they are physical in nature, they can be perceived. Sentences (1) and (2), for example, are located wherever your copy of this book is located. They came into existence when this book was printed, and if, after reading it, you decide to burn it, they will cease to exist. However, the proposition (1) and (2) express is an abstract object; it does not have a location in space and time, and since it is not physical in nature, it will not cease to exist if you burn this book.

If we view the relation between sentences and propositions in this way, we may say that a sentence is true or false depending on the truth value of the proposition it expresses. Propositions, then, are the primary bearers of truth, whereas sentences have their truth values only derivatively: by expressing propositions. Note that this view is not uncontroversial. Some philosophers object that, since propositions are supposed to be abstract objects, they are inaccessible to human experience. Sentences, on the other hand, are concrete physical entities, and thus are accessible through perception. Printed sentences can be seen, and spoken sentences heard. It might be argued, therefore, that we ought to prefer sentences over propositions for the role of truth bearers.

Let us briefly consider two replies to this argument. First, friends of propositions would argue that while it is true that propositions cannot be perceived, it is false that they are altogether inaccessible to the human mind. After all, we can understand propositions and consider whether they are true or false. Second, friends of propositions would point out that if we were to prefer sentences to propositions as the bearers of truth, we would encounter a serious difficulty. Consider this box:

> Caesar was killed by Brutus.
> Caesar was killed by Brutus.

How many sentences are in the box? In order to answer this question, we must distinguish between sentence *types* and sentence *tokens*, which enables us to say this: There are two tokens of the same sentence type in this box. Sentence tokens are particular physical inscriptions: patterns of ink on paper or chalk on a board. Sentence types, in contrast, are abstract forms that are instantiated by sentence tokens. Now, when critics of propositions maintain that we ought to take sentences as the bearers of truth, what they have in mind can't be sentence types, for sentence types are abstract objects, just like propositions. When you look at the box, what you see (and thus what is accessible to your experience) is two sentence tokens. The sentence type of which these two tokens are instances is something you can comprehend, or grasp, but you can't perceive it, just as you can't perceive the proposition that is expressed by the two sentence tokens in the box.

The critics of propositions, then, claim that the sorts of things that are true or false are sentence tokens. But now we may wonder whether there are enough true sentence tokens to express all the truths there are. Just consider the infinite series $2 + 1 = 3, 2 + 2 = 4, 2 + 3 = 5, 2 + 4 = 6$, and so on. At some point, this series will reach truths that, if printed, would be several miles long and, if spoken, would take days to formulate. There is an infinite number of similar series. Obviously, the infinite number of truths of arithmetic is not, and for practical reasons cannot be, matched by an infinite number of corresponding sentence tokens.[2] It would appear, therefore, that a theory that identifies the bearers of truth with sentence tokens is not very plausible.[3]

NECESSITY AND POSSIBILITY

In this section, we will distinguish among four different types of propositions. To begin with, there are propositions that are *necessarily true.* We may refer to them as "necessary truths." Here are some examples:

> All bachelors are unmarried.
>
> Whatever is red is colored.
>
> If there are more than three quarters in my wallet, then there are more than two quarters in my wallet.
>
> If Royce is as tall as Gabelli and Gabelli is as tall as Berger, then Royce is as tall as Berger.

Each of these propositions is such that it could not be false. The sense of "could not" here is logical: it is logically impossible for any of these propositions to be false. There are also propositions that are *necessarily false.* Examples of such propositions are:

> Smith has a colorless red car.
>
> There are more than three but fewer than two quarters in my wallet.
>
> Royce is as tall as Gabelli and Gabelli is as tall as Berger, but Royce is shorter than Berger.

Each of these propositions is a necessary falsehood: such that it could not possibly be true.

Third, there are *contingent* propositions: propositions that are neither necessarily true nor necessarily false. Consider the following three examples:

(1)   The forty-second president of the United States is George Bush.

(2)   The forty-second president of the United States is Bill Clinton.

(3)   If Bill Clinton is married to Hilary Clinton, then Hilary Clinton is married to Bill Clinton.

(1) is contingently false, and (2) is contingently true. (3), however, is not a contingent proposition, for it is necessarily true.

Fourth, there are propositions that are not necessarily false. Such propositions are *possibly true*. The three propositions displayed above all belong to this category. (1) is actually false, but possibly true. (2), on the other hand, is actually true, and hence is possibly true. Finally, (3) is necessarily true, and thus possibly true. To generalize: Any false proposition that isn't necessarily false is possibly true, and every true proposition, be it necessarily or contingently true, is possibly true.

In thinking about matters of necessity and possibility, it is important not to confuse *logical* and *physical* necessity. The laws of nature tell us what is physically possible and what is not. For example, it is physically impossible for humans to cross the Atlantic by flapping their arms or to stay alive for ten years without eating any food. However, as far as logic is concerned, if something is not outright contradictory—as, for example, a round square or a married bachelor—then it is possible, however far-fetched it may strike us. Hence we shall consider propositions such as

> Jones crossed the Atlantic by flapping his arms;
>
> Gabelli didn't eat anything for ten years and didn't lose a pound;
>
> Through an act of sheer will, Berger lifted himself from his chair and floated in midair;

as merely contingently false. Though as far as the laws of nature are concerned, they are bound to be false, from the point of view of logic, they are not. Although actually false, they are possibly true.

ENTAILMENT AND NECESSARY COEXTENSION

In the next section, we shall concern ourselves with the nature of philosophical analysis. But first we need to consider two ways in which concepts and propositions can be related to each other. We shall define these relations as follows:

Entailment

A concept A entails a concept B if and only if, necessarily, whatever is an instance of A is also an instance of B.

A proposition p entails a proposition q if and only if it is impossible that p is true and q is false.

Equivalence

Two concepts A and B are equivalent if and only if, necessarily, whatever is an instance of A is also an instance of B, and vice versa.

Two propositions p and q are equivalent if and only if it is impossible that p and q have different truth values.

Here are some examples to illustrate these definitions. The concept of being a mother entails the concept of being female, and is equivalent to the concept of being a female who has at least one child. The concept of triangularity entails, and is equivalent to, the concept of three-sidedness. The proposition "Smith and Brown know that Jones owns a Ford" entails the proposition "It is true that Jones owns a Ford" and is equivalent to the proposition "Brown and Smith know that Jones own a Ford." Finally, the proposition "It is true that Smith has three quarters is his wallet" entails the proposition "It is possible that Smith has three quarters in his wallet," which in turn is equivalent to the proposition "It is not necessarily false that Smith has three quarters in his wallet."

If two concepts are equivalent to each other, they are *necessarily coextensive*. A concept's extension is the collection of all instances of that concept. For example, the extension of the concept "goat" is the collection of all goats. The extension of the concept "being a member of the Supreme Court of the United States" is a collection of exactly nine justices, and the extension of the concept "being the president of the United States" is (in 1994) Bill Clinton. For two concepts to be necessarily coextensive, they must mutually entail each other: it must be logically impossible for there to be an object that is an instance of one concept without being an instance of the other. The two concepts we considered above, "being a mother" and "being a female who has at least one child," are an example of such a pair of concepts. Concepts that are necessarily coextensive have the same instances in all possible worlds. For example, there is no possible world in which an object that is three-sided fails to be an object with three angles, and vice versa; and there is no possible world in which a person is a brother without being a male sibling, and vice versa.

For an example of two concepts that are coextensive, but not necessarily coextensive, consider the two concepts "being president of the United States" and "being the commander-in-chief." The U.S. Constitution stipulates that the president and the commander-in-chief are one and the same person. But there is nothing necessary about what the Constitution stipulates. An amendment putting an end to this tradition might get passed, which means that it is logically possible for the president and the commander-in-chief to be two different people. Another example of two concepts that are coextensive without being necessarily coextensive are "x is an animal with a heart" and "x is an animal with a liver."[4] As far as the laws of nature go, whatever is an instance of one must also be an instance of the other concept; logically, however, there is nothing necessary about that. Nature might change, which is to say that, although this is difficult to conceive, in the future creatures might evolve that have hearts but not livers.

CONCEPTUAL ANALYSIS

In many cases, when we attempt to solve a philosophical problem, we try to analyze what a certain concept *means*. For example, the questions

>   What is a person?
>   What is a cause?
>   What is an action?
>   What is knowledge?

call for the analysis of concepts. Concepts, however, can be *simple* or *complex*. While a complex concept can be analyzed by uncovering its constituent elements, no such thing can be done with a simple concept. Rather, in order to convey what we mean by a simple concept, we can do no more than give a definition by relating it to other concepts that we take to mean the same thing. We shall, therefore, distinguish between (i) defining a simple concept by stating synonyms and (ii) defining (or analyzing) a complex concept by breaking it down into its constituent elements.

The concept of necessity, for example, is a simple one. A conceptual analysis of it, in the sense of identifying its constituent elements, cannot be given. However, we can define what we mean by the concept of necessity by relating it to the concept of possibility. We can define the concept of a necessary proposition by saying this: A proposition is necessary if and only if it is not possible for it to be false. A parallel point can be made regarding the concept of possibility. Since it cannot be broken down into constituent elements, we cannot give an analysis of it. We can, however, define a possible proposition by saying that a proposition is possibly true if and only if it is not necessarily false.

Another example of a simple concept is that of moral rightness. Rightness does not have any constituent parts, and therefore is not accessible to conceptual analysis. However, we can define the concept of rightness by relating it to other normative concepts. For example, we may say this:

Doing *x* is morally right if and only if it is not morally obligatory to refrain from doing *x*. And the concept of obligation can in turn be defined by the concept of permissibility: Doing *x* is obligatory if and only if refraining from doing *x* is not permissible.

Unlike simple concepts, complex concepts have parts that are constitutive of their meaning. Thus, in order to convey what we mean by a complex concept, we can analyze its constituent elements. For example, the concept of a mother is complex: it contains the two constituents "being female" and "having at least one child." In order to formulate an analysis of that concept, we can put down a biconditional of the following form:

> *Sample Analysis #1*
> For every x, x is a mother if and only if (i) x is female and (ii) x has at least one child.

We shall call the left-hand side of an analysis the *analysandum* (that which needs to be analyzed) and the right-hand side the *analysans* (that which does the analyzing). For an analysis to be correct, the analysans must specify conditions that are individually necessary and jointly sufficient for the analysandum. Our sample analysis does just that. The two conditions it lists are individually necessary: a person can't be a mother without being female, and a person can't be a mother without having at least one child. Furthermore, the two conditions it lists are jointly sufficient: whoever satisfies both (i) and (ii) is a mother.

The same point can be made by saying that for an analysis to be correct, the analysandum must entail each of the conditions in the analysans, and the analysans must entail the analysandum. Again, our sample analysis satisfies this requirement. The concept of a mother entails "being female" as well as "having at least one child," and these two concepts taken together entail "being a mother." In short, then, a correct analysis is one in which the analysandum and the analysans entail each other—that is, are equivalent, or necessarily coextensive. Thus if an analysis is correct, there is no possible world in which an object is an instance of the analysans but fails to satisfy the conditions stated in the analysans, and vice versa. The following two analyses do not satisfy this requirement.

> *Sample Analysis #2*
> For all *x*, *x* is a mother if and only if (i) *x* has at least one child.

> *Sample Analysis #3*
> For all *x*, *x* is a mother if and only if (i) *x* is female and (ii) *x* has at least one son.

Our second sample analysis fails because the analysandum does not entail the analysans, for there is a *counterexample*: a person who has at least one child but is not a mother—that is, a person who is a father. This means the analysis is too broad; it *includes* too much. In contrast, the third sample analysis is too narrow; it *excludes* too much. Although its analysans implies the analysandum, it is not the case that the analysandum implies the analysans. That this is so can again be illustrated with a counterexample: a mother who does not satisfy condition (ii)—that is, a mother who has one or several daughters, but no sons. A general requirement for an analysis of a concept, then, is that there be no counterexamples to it, which is the case if and only if it is neither too broad nor too narrow.

The point of the last paragraph can be restated as follows: For an analysis to be correct, the analysandum and the analysans must be equivalent, or necessarily coextensive. It would be a mistake to think, however, that any biconditional relating two equivalent concepts amounts to an analysis. For example, the following analysis

> *Sample Analysis #4*
> For all *x*, *x* is a mother if and only if *x* is a mother of at least one child

meets the equivalence requirement. Nevertheless, it fails because it is *circular*: the concept that needs to be analyzed occurs in the analysans. For an analysis to be successful, it must be illuminating, which it cannot be if it is circular. An analysis also fails to be illuminating if the concept used in the analysans is as much in need of analysis as the analysandum itself. For example, the following analysis

> *Sample Analysis #5*
> For all *x*, *x* is a triangle if and only if *x* is three-sided

does not admit of any counterexamples, for triangularity and three-sidedness are necessarily coextensive concepts. Nevertheless, if fails to be illuminating because when we are told that all triangles are three-sided and vice versa, we are not really being told what a triangle is.

CRITERIOLOGICAL ANALYSIS

A definition of a simple concept conveys that concept's meaning by relating it to other concepts. An analysis of a complex concept conveys that concept's meaning by breaking it down into its constitutive elements. In this section, we shall see that when we are concerned with evaluative (or normative) concepts, there is yet another type of analysis.

When *nonevaluative* concepts are applied to an object, nothing is asserted to the effect that there is some way in which that object is good or bad, worthy of our praise, or just the way it ought to be. In contrast, when *evaluative* concepts are applied to an object, the object is being evaluated as in some respect good or bad, as being, or not being, the way it ought to be. In ethics, some central evaluative concepts, to be applied to human acts, are: obligatory, permissible, right, forbidden. And in epistemology, some central evaluative concepts, to be applied to either beliefs or propositions, are: justified, certain, probable, reasonable, evident, unreasonable, improbable, doubtful, unjustified.[5]

What matters with regard to the analysis of these concepts is this: they are all simple. They can be defined in terms of other evaluative concepts belonging to the same family, but they cannot be broken down into constituent parts. From this we should not, however, draw the conclusion that philosophical investigations of these concepts are restricted to offering definitions. Rather, philosophers have traditionally been engaged in *two* projects concerning the evaluative concepts of ethics and epistemology: conveying what these concepts mean by giving definitions of them; and stating *criteria* for the application of these concepts. In addition to definition and conceptual analysis, there is, then, a third philosophical project: *criteriological analysis*.

To see what criteriological analysis amounts to, consider hedonistic utilitarianism, according to which an action's moral status is determined by the effect it has on the overall balance of pleasure over pain. According to hedonistic utilitarianism, moral rightness is to be analyzed thus:

Hedonistic Utilitarianism
>   An action x is right if and only if x maximizes the balance of pleasure over pain.

The right-hand side of this biconditional does not tell us what we *mean* by rightness. Rather, it provides us with a *criterion* for the application of the term *right*: it tells us when an action is morally right by specifying a condition that is supposed to be both necessary and sufficient for moral rightness. It asserts, then, that the concept of maximizing the balance of pleasure over pain entails, and is entailed by, the concept of moral rightness.

Of course, we might have objections to hedonistic utilitarianism. However, the point here is not to debate which analysis of moral rightness is correct, but rather to illustrate that when philosophers set forth an analysis of rightness—be it a version of utilitarianism or some other theory—they attempt to specify what are sometimes called "right-making characteristics." According to hedonistic utilitarianism, there is one, and only one, right-making characteristic: the maximization of the balance of pleasure over pain. Other ethical theories offer alternative right-making characteristics. But however these theories differ, they typically share a common objective: to pin down what it is that makes an action right and, most importantly, *to do so without using evaluative terms*.

A striking feature of hedonistic utilitarianism is this: while its analysandum—rightness—is a normative term, no such term occurs in the analysans. The key notions of the analysans are those of pleasure and pain. But these concepts are nonnormative—or, as we might say, naturalistic, or descriptive. When we state, for example, that Jones is in pain, we are not *evaluating* Jones in any way whatever, but merely *describing* a condition Jones is in. If we were to state that it is a *bad* thing for Jones to be in pain, or that Jones is *deserving* of the pain he is experiencing, or that we are *obligated* to alleviate Jones's pain, then we would be making an evaluative statement. But if we state simply that Jones is in pain and say no more than that, we are not at all making a normative judgment.

Hedonistic utilitarianism, then, offers us a descriptive criterion for an evaluative term; it states the necessary and sufficient conditions of moral rightness in nonnormative terms. In *epistemology*, criteriological analyses of normative concepts are supposed to do the same: they are expected to state criteria for the application of such terms without using any evaluative language.6 With regard to the concept of justification, Alvin Goldman puts this point thus:

> The term "justified" ... is an evaluative term, a term of appraisal. Any correct definition or synonym of it would also feature evaluative terms. I assume that such definitions or synonyms might be given, but I am not interested in them. I want a set of substantive conditions that specify when a belief is justified. [Consider] the term "right." ... Normative ethics tries to specify non-ethical conditions that determine when an action is right.... Analogously, I want a theory of justified belief to specify in non-epistemic terms when a belief is justified.7

Notice that Goldman distinguishes here between defining the concept of epistemic justification and offering what we are calling a criteriological analysis of that concept. Both are, of course, legitimate projects of epistemology.8 Note further that Goldman demands of his analysis that it be carried out in *nonepistemic* terms. By this he means terms that do not share the evaluative character of the concepts of epistemic appraisal we mentioned earlier, concepts such as certainty, probability, reasonableness, justification, and the like.

SUPERVENIENCE IN EPISTEMOLOGY

Why is it the aim of a criteriological analysis of epistemic justification to specify when a belief is justified in nonevaluative terms? One answer to this question has been proposed by Jaegwon Kim. He writes:

> A justified belief cannot be a brute fundamental fact unrelated to the kind of belief it is. There must a reason for it, and this reason must be grounded in the *factual* descriptive properties of that particular belief.9

The same can be said about the moral status of an action. If a particular action is the right thing to do, then there must be a reason for its rightness—that is, there must be something about this action that *makes* it a right action. Its rightness, Kim would say, cannot be a "brute" fact that is inaccessible to an explanation in terms of nonevaluative right-making characteristics. Likewise, a belief's epistemic status—the degree to which it is justified or unjustified—must be explainable by reference to certain characteristics of the belief, characteristics that confer on it its epistemic status.

This thought motivates a doctrine that has in recent years gained much prominence: the doctrine that normative properties *supervene* on nonnormative properties.[10] To say that normative properties supervene on nonnormative properties means, roughly, that whether an object does or does not have a certain normative property *depends on*, or is *determined by*, its nonnormative properties. Another way of making the same point is to say that things have their normative properties *by virtue of* their nonnormative properties. Yet another way to state the same point is to say that what *makes* an object have the normative properties it has are its nonnormative properties. Applied to ethics, the supervenience doctrine tells us that an action's moral status is determined by its nonnormative properties; applied to epistemology, the doctrine tells us that a belief's epistemic status is determined by its nonnormative properties. Our ground for making these claims is the belief that things don't just happen to have the properties they have; rather, there are *reasons* they have certain properties and lack others.

Let us apply the supervenience doctrine to the concept of justification as that concept is used in epistemology. Suppose that, while taking a walk in a park, you see a dog running across the lawn, and thus you believe "There is a dog over there." Let us stipulate that the conditions of observation are excellent: it is broad daylight, your vision is excellent, and the dog is close enough to you to be clearly discernible. We may safely assume, then, that your belief is justified. According to the supervenience doctrine, your belief's epistemic status—its being justified—supervenes on your belief's epistemically relevant nonnormative properties. In this case, some of these properties are: its being a perceptual belief, its being a belief formed during daylight, and its being a belief about a medium-sized object that is not very far away.

WEAK AND STRONG SUPERVENIENCE

To understand the significance of supervenience in epistemology, it is necessary to distinguish between weak and strong supervenience. According to the weak version of the supervenience doctrine, it would be incoherent to say that your belief is justified, but another belief just like yours is not. Suppose a friend of yours joins you on your walk. She sees the dog, too, and thus believes, just as you do, that there is a dog over there. Let us suppose that her belief and your belief share all the relevant nonnormative characteristics. Given this assumption, it would be capricious to say that your belief is justified while hers is not, or vice versa. Given that the two beliefs are alike in all their relevant nonnormative features, either both are justified or neither is.

This point can be stated by saying that epistemic judgments must be *universalizable*, which means that, when we judge a belief B to be justified, there must be a reason for doing so that is equally applicable to *all* beliefs that are just like B. In short, we must judge like beliefs alike; they must be either all justified or all unjustified. The doctrine of weak supervenience, then, expresses the requirement that epistemic judgments must be universalizable.[11] It asserts that if two beliefs are alike in their nonnormative properties, they must also be alike in epistemic status—there can't be an epistemic difference without a corresponding nonepistemic difference.

We will define the concept of weak supervenience as follows (letting J stand for the property of being justified, and N for the family of nonnormative base properties on which J supervenes):[12]

Weak Supervenience
> J weakly supervenes on N if and only if, necessarily, whenever a belief has property J, there is a property P in N such that whenever a belief has P, it has J.

The concept of weak supervenience must be distinguished from the *assertion* of weak supervenience. Let the term "WS thesis" refer to the assertion that the property of being justified weakly supervenes on nonnormative properties. When we apply the WS thesis to our example of a justified belief, it tells us this: Given that your belief that there is a dog over there is justified, there must be a nonnormative property (or set of properties) such that *all* beliefs having it are justified. Consequently, it can't be that two beliefs share this property, and yet one of them is justified while the other one is not. Put differently: There can't be a difference in epistemic status without a corresponding nonepistemic difference.

Some philosophers would argue that the WS thesis is too weak. They would maintain that although the WS thesis goes a long way toward providing us with an adequate understanding of epistemic normativity, it falls short of satisfying a further important intuition about the nature of epistemic evaluation. This intuition will become clear if we digress into ethics. The ethical equivalent to the WS thesis asserts that, necessarily, whenever an act has a moral property M, there is a nonnormative property P such that any act having P has M. Let us apply this principle to Jeffrey Dahmer's horrible crimes: acts of kidnapping and killing boys and young men for the sake of gratifying a perverse lust for murder and domination. The ethical version of the WS thesis, expressing the requirement of universalizability, asserts that we must judge any act like that, irrespective of who commits it, in the same way we judge Jeffrey Dahmer's acts. However, it does not tell us *how* we must judge Jeffrey Dahmer's acts. Thus, if we were perverted enough to call his acts noble, and if we were to call noble all acts like his, then we would meet the requirement of universalizability. Philosophers who consider the ethical version of the WS thesis too weak would say, however, that surely we believe acts like Dahmer's are *necessarily* wicked, and thus could not possibly be noble. They would deny that there is a possible world in which someone commits acts like Dahmer's and does something noble. The WS thesis, however, allows for such a world. It merely tells us that if in any world W in which Dahmer's acts are noble, all like acts in W are noble as well.

In epistemology, the WS thesis raises a parallel problem. Consider again your and your friend's belief that there is a dog over there. The WS thesis tells us that if we call your belief justified, then we must call your friend's belief—and indeed all beliefs that are like your belief in their relevant features—justified. Likewise, it tells us that if we call your belief *unjustified*, then we must call your friend's belief unjustified, and indeed all beliefs that share their relevant nonnormative properties with your belief. The WS thesis does not tell us, however, that the beliefs in question, given their nonepistemic properties, *must* be justified. Rather, it allows for possible worlds in which such beliefs are unjustified. According to those who think the WS thesis is too weak, this is objectionable, for they take it that given the descriptive properties of these beliefs, they could not possibly be unjustified.

If we wish to modify the definition of weak supervenience so as to ensure this result, we must add the modal operator "necessarily" before the last clause. Thus we get a special case of what Kim calls "strong supervenience":

Strong Supervenience
> J strongly supervenes on N: necessarily, whenever a belief has property J, there is a property P in N such that, necessarily, whenever a belief has P, it has J.

Let the term "SS thesis" stand for the claim that the property of being justified strongly supervenes on nonnormative properties. The SS thesis tells us this: Whenever a belief is justified, there must be a nonnormative property that entails the property of justification. A belief that has this property could not possibly fail to be justified. Thus, if the SS thesis is true, there is no possible world in which a belief has the same nonnormative features as your belief that there is a dog over there and yet is unjustified.

Consider again the ethical analogy. The ethical equivalent to the SS thesis, according to which moral properties strongly supervene on nonmoral properties, asserts that whenever an action has a moral property

M, there must be a nonnormative property P that *entails* M. When we apply this thesis to the Jeffrey Dahmer example, it tells us that the wickedness of his acts supervenes on a nonnormative property that is a necessitating ground of wickedness. Put differently, the thesis that moral properties strongly supervene on natural properties tells us that there are no possible worlds in which acts like those committed by Jeffrey Dahmer fail to be wicked.

Back to epistemology: Let's consider the example involving your justified belief that there is a dog over there. Regarding that belief (let's call it B), the SS thesis asserts that the conjunction of its nonnormative properties entails that it is justified. There is no possible world in which a belief B* shares its descriptive characteristics with B and fails to be justified. Thus the SS thesis is considerably stronger than the WS thesis. Whereas the WS thesis merely asserts that in any possible world in which B is justified, all beliefs like it are justified, the SS thesis tells us that beliefs like B are justified in *all* possible worlds.

THE CASE FOR STRONG SUPERVENIENCE

Should we accept the doctrine that a belief's justification supervenes on its nonnormative properties? If we were to reject this doctrine, then we would have to deny either the WS thesis or the SS thesis. Let us see what such denials would involve.

In order to discuss what it means to deny the WS thesis, consider again the example in which you and your friend see a dog run across the lawn, and thus both of you believe that there is a dog over there. We stipulated that this belief is a paradigm example of what we would consider a justified belief. We also stipulated that there is no relevant difference between your believing that there is a dog over there and your friend's believing that there is a dog over there. According to the WS thesis, your belief's epistemic status of being justified must be accompanied by a nonnormative property P such that any belief having P is justified.

This claim can be attacked in two ways. First, it might be asserted that it's possible that your belief is justified while your friend's is not, and vice versa. But if that were possible, then it would be possible for two beliefs to differ in epistemic status for no reason whatever. If we were to ask, Why do they differ in epistemic status? there would be no other answer than: Well, they just do. Certainly this would not be a very appealing view of epistemic normativity.

Second, the WS thesis might be attacked by asserting that while a difference in epistemic status requires a nonepistemic difference, this difference need not be nonnormative. For example, it could be argued that differences in epistemic status are grounded in differences in moral status. The problem with this suggestion is that a difference in moral status, being a normative difference itself, is just as much in need of an explanation as the difference in epistemic status it is supposed to explain. Ultimately, we are seeking a nonnormative difference that explains the difference in epistemic status. We must conclude, therefore, that there are good reasons for endorsing a supervenience thesis that is *at least* as strong as the WS thesis.

Let us now see what is involved in denying the SS thesis. If we were to accept the WS thesis, but not the SS thesis, then we would have to accept that there are pairs of possible worlds W1 and W2 such that although there are no relevant nonnormative differences between them,

(i)   all beliefs that are justified in W1 are unjustified in W2;

(ii)   in W1, all beliefs are justified, while in W2 all beliefs are unjustified;

(iii) in W1, all beliefs formed in the hour of 12:00 to 1:00 p.m., and no other beliefs, are justified, while in W2 all beliefs formed in the hour of 12:00 to 1:00 p.m., and no other beliefs, are unjustified.

Advocates of the SS thesis would say that such possibilities are absurd: there are no possible worlds that correspond to these descriptions. The WS thesis, however, allows for such worlds, for the WS thesis does not demand that the nonepistemic property on which a belief's justification supervenes be such that it *entails* the property of being justified. Consequently, the WS thesis permits possible worlds in which epistemic properties are linked to nonepistemic properties in the most bizarre ways.[13]

Opponents of the SS thesis might wonder whether we shouldn't concede that there are possible worlds as bizarre as those mentioned above. Such worlds are certainly crazy, but why should that mean they don't exist? The weakness of this objection becomes apparent as soon as we expand our view to include morality. If we were to assert that moral properties supervene only weakly on nonnormative properties, then we would have to accept that there are pairs of possible worlds W1 and W2 such that although there are no relevant nonnormative differences between them,

(i)   all acts that are right in W1 are wrong in W2;

(ii)   in W1, all acts (no matter how cruel) are right, while in W2, all acts (no matter how beneficent) are wrong;

(iii) in W1, all acts performed in the hour of 12:00 to 1:00 P.M., and no other acts, are right, while in W2 all acts performed in the hour of 12:00 to 1:00 P.M., and no other acts, are wrong.

Anyone who denies strong supervenience for moral properties must be prepared to assert that it is possible for an act of unspeakable cruelty to be right simply because it was performed during the hour between 12:00 and 1:00 p.m. Such an assertion, however, seems absurd. The property of being performed in the hour between 12:00 and 1:00 p.m. is not a right-making characteristic: it is not possible for such an act to be right simply because it was performed at that time. If, however, we are prepared to accept, on the basis of such considerations, that moral properties strongly supervene on nonnormative properties, it would seem to follow that we should accept the strong supervenience thesis for epistemic properties as well.

ANALYTICAL MONISM AND PLURALISM

If we agree that a belief's epistemic status supervenes on certain of its nonnormative properties, obviously we would like to know what these properties are. Thus if we accept the supervenience doctrine, we have a good reason to conceive of the analysis of epistemic justification in the way Alvin Goldman suggests in the passage cited earlier: as the task of specifying the nonnormative properties that are both necessary and sufficient for epistemic justification.[14] Such a project can be carried out in two ways. First, it might be argued that there is one, and *only* one, nonevaluative property on which the property of being justified supervenes. Second, it might be argued that there are *many* such properties. We shall call examples of the first approach "monistic" theories, and examples of the second "pluralistic" theories.

In ethics, the difference between these two types of theories is nicely illustrated by utilitarianism, on the one hand, and W.D. Ross's theory of prima facie duties, on the other.[15] As G. E. Moore aptly puts it, utilitarianism is an answer to the following question: "What characteristic is there which belongs to *all* voluntary actions which are right, and *only* to those among them which are right?"[16] According to utilitarianism, the characteristic in question is the maximization of utility. Utilitarians believe that there is one unique property all right acts have in common: that of maximizing utility.[17] W.D. Ross, however, rejects the idea that there is just *one* "right-making" characteristic; he believes that there are many different ones—gratitude, justice, and beneficence, for example.

In epistemology, a prominent example of the monistic approach is reliabilism, according to which there is one unique nonnormative property that makes beliefs justified: the property of being produced by a reliable cognitive process.[18] Reliabilism, in its simplest form, asserts the following:

SR S is justified in believing that p if and only if S's belief that p is produced by a reliable cognitive process.

Roderick Chisholm champions the pluralistic approach. According to him, the project of analyzing the concept of justification must be carried out by producing a list of *epistemic principles.*[19] An epistemic principle is a conditional that (i) is supposed to express an entailment and (ii) may not contain any normative terms in the antecedent. Thus the antecedent of an epistemic principle is meant to state a nonnormative base property that entails the property of being justified. Any belief having such a property would be a justified belief.

Consider the following three nonnormative base properties—being grounded in (i) introspection, (ii) perception, and (iii) memory—and assume that these are just some among many properties on which epistemic justification supervenes. The following is a simplified version of a criteriological analysis of epistemic justification:

P1   If a belief is grounded in introspection, then it is justified.

P2   If a belief is grounded in perception, then it is justified.

P3   If a belief is grounded in memory, then it is justified.

We shall refer to this analysis as a "Chisholm—type" analysis because it is a simplified model of the kind of theory Chisholm has proposed. Now since none of these three base properties on our list entails the property of justification, P1—P3 are all false. However, here we are not concerned with which principles are correct, but only with how the monistic and the pluralistic approaches differ from each other, and what they have in common.

The chief difference between our simplified Chisholm—type list of epistemic principles and a monistic analysis such as SR is this: According to SR, there is one, and only one, nonevaluative property. According to the Chisholm—type list, however, there are three. Furthermore, SR tells us both what is sufficient and what is necessary for justification. Our Chisholm—type list provides us with three properties that are sufficient for justification, but it doesn't tell us what is necessary for it. After all, a belief might be justified because it has a property that is not on the list. It does not, therefore, amount to an equivalence.

Suppose, however, that besides the three base properties we introduced above, there are no other properties on which justification supervenes. In that case, our list would tell us both what is sufficient and what is necessary for justification, and we could state the criteriological analysis of justification expressed by P1—P3 in the form of a biconditional:[20]

CA   *S* is justified in believing that *p* if and only if *S's* belief that *p* is grounded in either introspection, perception, or memory.

As a matter of fact, Chisholm does not aspire to state a complete list; he does not intend to make a claim about what is necessary for justification.[21] His analysis, therefore, falls short of asserting what epistemic justification is equivalent to.[22]

Some philosophers object to the project of criteriological analysis because they think that the analysis of epistemic justification ought to avoid what has been called the "scatter problem." Suppose CA is true: being grounded in introspection, perception, or memory are the three nonnormative properties that make beliefs justified. Critics of analytical pluralism would argue that it is unsatisfactory to list several distinct properties as entailing grounds of epistemic justification without being able to say what these three properties have in common or what unites them.[23]

Why, however, should we assume that there *is* a unique characteristic that is shared by all instances of justified belief? There is no obvious reason in support of this assumption. Of course, the existence of such a property could be established by demonstrating the truth of a particular monistic analysis. For example, if reliabilism could be proven true, then we could know that perceptual, introspective, and memorial beliefs are ultimately justified, not because they are grounded in perception, introspection, or memory, but rather because they are reliably produced.

What, however, if no monistic theory from among the various competing analyses proposed emerges as the clear winner? In that case, we may suspect that the advocates of analytical monism have set their expectations too high. And as a matter of fact, in contemporary epistemology, no undisputed monistic theory has emerged. Perhaps, then, to assume that there is one unique base property, without having at hand a theory to demonstrate the existence of such a property, is to be unduly optimistic about what criteriological analysis can achieve. Indeed, it is quite optimistic even to assume that a Chisholm—type pluralistic analysis of justification can be found, as we shall see in the next two sections.

PRINCIPLES OF PRIMA FACIE JUSTIFICATION

The doctrine that the property of being justified strongly supervenes on nonnormative grounds tells us this: whenever a belief is justified, there is a nonnormative property P (where this property may be a conjunction of several distinct properties) such that, necessarily, any belief having P is justified. This is a doctrine of metaphysics: a doctrine about how the property of justification is related to certain other properties. It entails nothing with respect to our ability to pin down what these other properties are. It is, therefore, entirely consistent to maintain that epistemic status strongly supervenes on nonnormative base properties and at the same time to doubt that the project of criteriological analysis can meet with success.

Since reliabilism will be discussed in a separate chapter, let us discuss the prospects of criteriological analysis focusing on the Chisholmian project of listing epistemic principles. Consider the second of the epistemic principles we stated above:

P2   If a belief is grounded in perception, then it is justified.

It is easy to see that this principle is false. Recall the standard example of a defeated belief that was explained in Chapter 1: You are looking at a white sheet of paper that appears blue to you because it is illuminated by blue light. Although you have evidence for suspecting that the sheet of paper is thus illuminated, you still believe it to be blue. Your perceptual evidence for your belief is defeated, and thus, though grounded in perception, your belief is unjustified.

In order to repair P2, we could add a clause to the effect that, for a perceptual belief to be justified, one may not be in possession of further evidence that defeats one's perceptual evidence. This would give us the following modified principle:

> P2a   If a belief is grounded in perception and is not defeated by further evidence, then it is justified.

To be sure, P2a is a good candidate for a true epistemic principle. It tells us that undefeated perceptual evidence is a source of justified belief. Indeed, it provides us with a criterion of justification: the property of *being grounded in undefeated perceptual evidence* is arguably a property that entails the property of being justified. However, P2a is not the kind of principle criteriological analysis is supposed to establish, for its antecedent makes use of the concept of evidential defeat, which is an epistemically evaluative term.

To see why the notion of evidential defeat is epistemically evaluative, we need only consider its definition:

> *d* defeats *e* as evidence for *p* if and only if *e* is evidence for believing that *p*, but *e* in conjunction with *d* is not evidence for believing that *p*.

The right-hand side of this definition makes use of the term "is evidence for," which is a term of epistemic evaluation. Hence the concept of defeat is itself epistemically evaluative.

P2a, then, contains an epistemic concept in its antecedent and thus falls short of satisfying the objective of criteriological analysis. This does not mean, though, that it is worthless. Indeed, as mentioned above, it tells us something interesting: undefeated perceptual evidence is an entailing ground of epistemic justification. There are no possible worlds in which beliefs grounded in such evidence fail to be justified. But since we could render P2a true only by adding a normative qualifier in its antecedent, it must be said that it is not the kind of principle we seek when we are trying to set forth a criteriological analysis of epistemic justification.

Is there any way of modifying P2 so that it remains true, yet its antecedent stays nonnormative? There is indeed: we can weaken the principle's consequent. Instead of saying that beliefs grounded in perception are justified, we can say that they are *prima facie* justified. When we call perceptual beliefs prima facie justified, we mean that such beliefs are justified in the absence of defeating evidence. Compare perceptual beliefs with beliefs that are instances of wishful thinking. Such beliefs are not prima facie justified, for we can't say that they are justified in the absence of further evidence. Suppose you take yourself to be perceiving a dog in front of you. Unless there is further evidence undermining your perceptual evidence, you are justified in believing there is a dog in front of you. On the other hand, if wishful thinking induces you to believe that tomorrow's weather will be good, we can't say that, unless there is further undermining evidence, you are justified in believing that tomorrow's weather will be good. The difference between the two beliefs is that the first is based on evidence that, in the absence of further countervailing evidence, justifies your belief.

A prima facie justified belief might or might not be *ultima facie* justified. An ultima facie justified belief is justified *all things considered*. Consider again the counterexample to P2. Since the sheet of paper appears blue to you, we may say that although you are prima facie justified in believing that it is blue, you are not ultima facie justified in believing this because you are in possession of defeating evidence. So, *de facto*, your belief is unjustified. Of course, beliefs that are prima facie justified need not be unjustified. Typically, prima facie beliefs are also ultima facie justified beliefs.

Let us compare the notion of prima facie justification in epistemology with that of a prima facie duty in ethics. According to W. D. Ross, telling the truth is merely a prima facie *duty*: a duty that can be defeated by other duties. For example, if you could save a person's life by telling a lie, then the duty to save that person's life would defeat your duty to tell the truth. In this particular situation, telling the truth is your *prima facie* duty, but not your *ultima facie* duty. All things considered, it is your duty to tell a lie. Typically, however, telling the truth is not only your prima facie duty but also your ultima facie duty. Truth telling, we may say, *tends* to be one of our duties, which is to say that typically it is our duty to tell the truth. Likewise, perceptual evidence tends to justify our beliefs, which is to say that, neglecting exceptions, beliefs grounded in perception are justified.

The maneuver of weakening the consequent of P2 by turning it into a principle about prima facie justification gives us the following result:

> P2b If a belief is grounded in perception, then it is prima facie justified.

Unlike P2, P2b is an excellent candidate for a true epistemic principle. However, just like P2a, it is not the kind of principle we seek when we are interested in producing a criteriological analysis of epistemic justification. For what we want to find out in pursuing such an analysis is what *nonnormative* base properties make beliefs ultima facie, not prima facie, justified. Thus, if all we can achieve is to formulate principles such as P2b, our analysis would fall short of accomplishing its objective.

In order to see why this is so, note that P2b marks no real improvement over P2a because it is logically equivalent to it. Given our understanding of prima facie justification, we may reformulate P2b thus:

P2b* If a belief is grounded in perception, then it is justified unless it is defeated by further evidence.

P2b tells us the same as P2b*, which tells us the same as P2a. Consequently, if P2a is not what we aspire to in analyzing the concept of epistemic justification, then neither is P2b. So whichever way we go—modifying the antecedent of P2 by adding a "no defeat" clause or weakening the consequent by turning P2 into a principle about prima facie justification—we don't get the result we intended to get: a principle that specifies a nonnormative base property on which justification supervenes.

Parallel reasoning can be applied to epistemic principles about the other two nonnormative base properties we introduced: being grounded in introspection and being grounded in memory. The question arises, therefore, whether it is at all possible to find the kind of principles criteriological analysis seeks.

EPISTEMOLOGICAL PESSIMISM

Let us call *epistemological pessimism* the view that although there are nonnormative properties on which epistemic justification supervenes, we can't pin down what these properties are. Ernest Sosa refers to this view as "skepticism about our ability to comprehend the principles that underlie [the supervenience of epistemic on descriptive properties], perhaps because they are infinite in number or degree of complexity."[24] If epistemological pessimism is correct, we must give up the hope of identifying which nonnormative base properties entail the property of justification. Instead, we must be content with formulating principles of prima facie justification: principles telling us which nonnormative properties *tend* to make beliefs justified.

According to a theory of prima facie justification, there are several sources of justification—for example, introspection, perception, and memory. Beliefs grounded in any of these sources are prima facie justified, or justified unless defeated by further evidence. Consider again perceptual beliefs. Whether a particular perceptual belief is justified depends on the specifics of the situation: does the subject, or does she not, have further evidence that defeats her perceptual evidence for the belief? Epistemological pessimists would say that we cannot find general criteria that, when applied to particular situations, tell us whether the subject has further defeating evidence, and thus whether the belief in question is justified or not. Rather, they would say that we must, for each individual case, consider all the relevant data that are available and then judge the belief's epistemic merits.

Let us compare epistemological pessimism with its counterpart in ethics: W. D. Ross's theory of prima facie duties. According to Ross, our moral duties spring from sources such as fidelity, reparation, gratitude, justice, beneficence, self-improvement, and nonmaleficence. Each of these sources provides us with a sufficient ground of prima facie duty. Thus Ross would say that if doing x were an act of gratitude, then doing x would be a prima facie duty; and if doing x were an act of injustice, then refraining from doing x would be a prima facie duty. But he does not propose what we have called a criteriological analysis. For, first of all, some of the items on Ross's list are *normative*: justice and beneficence, for example. And second, he does not claim that the properties on his list *entail* that acts instantiating these properties are acts one has a duty to perform (or refrain from performing).

Obviously, different duties can come into conflict with one another. For example, justice and beneficence notoriously conflict with each other. In a situation in which they do, there is a prima facie duty to be just and a prima facie duty to be beneficent. The problem is deciding which of these duties would take precedence all things considered. Ross does not believe that there are general principles that tell us when considerations of justice outweigh considerations of beneficence, or vice versa. Rather, he believes that each case in which these considerations come into conflict must be judged individually. Ross, then, is a pessimist about criteriological analysis in ethics. Though his view is compatible with the supervenience doctrine—in each case of a particular act's being a moral duty, there is a base property on which the act's moral status supervenes—it entails that we cannot pin these properties down by formulating general principles of ultima facie duties.

In epistemology, conflicting bodies of evidence are analogous to the phenomenon of conflicting duties. For example, perceptual evidence about an object's color can be undermined by further evidence about the conditions of observation. If the object appears blue, then there is prima facie justification for believing it to be blue. But if we know that blue light is shining on the object, there is also prima facie justification for refraining from believing that it is blue. The question about such cases is this: Which body of evidence is stronger, the evidence that supports believing the object is blue or the evidence that supports refraining from believing this? In other words, what would be our ultima facie duty: to believe, or not to believe, that the object is blue? The answer to this question depends, of course, on the specific features of the situation. Perhaps there is further evidence suggesting that the sheet of paper is actually blue or further evidence supporting the belief that it is actually white. Epistemological pessimists would say that because there are too many different ways in which evidence can be defeated, there are no general principles that tell us, for all such cases, what we are ultima facie justified in believing. All we can know, in the way of general principles, is that an object's looking blue provides us with prima facie justification for believing it to be blue, and that evidence to the effect that blue light is shining on the object provides us with prima facie justification for refraining from believing that the object is blue.

Is epistemological pessimism a plausible view? Of course we should not dogmatically rule out the possibility that an ingenious epistemologist could generate a list of epistemic principles with nonnormative antecedents or even an equivalence with a nonnormative analysans. However, advocates of epistemological pessimism could argue that as long as there is neither a monistic nor a pluralistic theory that is clearly acceptable, epistemological pessimism is at least indirectly confirmed.[25]

STUDY QUESTIONS

1. What is the difference between concepts and words? Between propositions and sentences?
2. What is the difference between a coextension of two concepts that is necessary and one that is not?
3. How do logical and physical necessity differ?
4. How do defining a simple concept and analyzing a complex concept differ?
5. What's the difference between a conceptual analysis of the concept of knowledge and a criteriological analysis of the concept of epistemic justification?
6. What's the difference between weak and strong supervenience?
7. On what grounds would an advocate of the SS thesis argue that the WS thesis is not strong enough?
8. How do analytical monism and analytical pluralism differ?
9. What is the difference between prima facie and ultima facie justification?
10. What is epistemological pessimism?

EXERCISES

1. Describe what you take to be an evil act. Discuss which nonnormative properties make that act evil and whether these properties are such that, *necessarily*, any act that exemplifies them is evil.
2. Describe what you take to be an utterly unjustified belief. Discuss which nonnormative properties make that belief unjustified and whether these properties are such that, *necessarily*, any belief that exemplifies them is utterly unjustified.
3. Consider the following epistemic principle: If *S* has perceptual evidence for believing that *p*, and *S* is not in possession of further evidence that defeats his perceptual evidence for *p*, then *S* is justified in believing that *p*. First, discuss whether there are any counterexamples to this principle. Second, discuss whether a philosopher seeking a criteriological analysis of justification would find this principle satis-

factory. Third, discuss whether, from your own point of view, this principle is illuminating or not.

NOTES

1 For a brief account of the nature of concepts, see Bradley and Swartz (1979), pp. 87ff.

2 In order to generate such series, we don't have to restrict ourselves to arithmetic. For example, there is an infinite number of things that are not in my office: elephants, vending machines, nuclear missiles, aircraft carriers, and so on. Thus we can easily form extremely long and cumbersume truths about my office that are certainly not matched by any existing sentence tokens.

3 See Bradley and Swartz (1979), pp. 73f.

4 In order to avoid a counterexample provided by modern medical technology, the concepts in question should be taken to refer to animals whose proper genetic design involves a heart and animals whose proper genetic design involves a liver.

5 For definitions of various epistemic terms, see Chisholm (1989), chap. 2.

6 See Goldman (1979) and Kim (1988), p. 382.

7 Goldman (1979), p. 1.

8 It would be a mistake to think that the project of defining epistemic concepts and the project of providing a criteriological analysis are mutually exclusive. In fact, the former is necessary for the latter. After all, how can we determine what the criteria for a given epistemic concept are if we are not clear on what we mean by that concept? For an example of the project of defining epistemic concepts, see Chisholm (1977); chap. 1, and (1989); chap. 2. For a discussion of various ways to define the concept of epistemic justification, see Alston (1989), pp. 81—114.

9 Kim (1988), p. 399 (my italics).

10 For an excellent discussion of the concept of supervenience, see Kim (1984); and for a useful collection of articles on the topic, see Horgan (1983).

11 The *locus classicus* for the weak supervenience thesis in ethics is the following statement by Richard Hare (1952): "Suppose that we say 'St. Francis was a good man.' It is logically impossible to say this and to maintain at the same time that there might have been another man placed exactly in the same circumstances as St. Francis, and who behaved in exactly the same way, but who differed from St. Francis in this respect only, that he was not a good man." (p. 145).

12 The following definition is a special case of what Kim calls "weak supervenience." See Kim (1984), pp. 157ff.

13 See Kim's analysis of weak supervenience in his 1984 paper, pp. 159f. For a brief consideration of the implications of denying the SS thesis, see Van Cleve (1985), pp. 98f.

14 This is not to say that this reason is decisive. As we shall see later in this chapter, there are also good reasons to doubt that the attempt to set forth a criteriological analysis of epistemic concepts can succeed.

15 For a statement of Ross's theory, see Ross (1988), chap. 2.

16 G. E. Moore (1912), p. 13.

17 Another example of a monistic analysis is ethical egoism, which asserts that an act is right if and only if it maximizes the agent's self-interest. Yet another example is the divine command theory, according to which an act is right if and only if it is commanded by God.

18 Reliable cognitive processes are those whose belief output enjoys a high ratio of true beliefs. For further elaboration, see Chapter 8.

19 For a statement of Chisholm's epistemic principles, see this *Theory of Knowledge*, 2nd ed. (1977), pp. 73—84, and 3rd ed. (1989), chap. 7, as well as his 1990 article, "The Status of Epistemic Principles." For an excellent brief account of Chisholm's epistemology, see Foley (1992).

20 The underlying metaphysical phenomenon here is this: if the property of being justified strongly supervenes on a set of normative properties, then there is a necessary coextension between that property and a set of normative properties. See Kim (1984), pp. 169f, and Van Cleve (1990), pp. 230f. In case of monistic theories, necessary coextension is obvious. According to the SS thesis, in every instance of a justified belief, the belief's justification is entailed by a nonnormative property N. Now, if there is one, and only one, such property N, it is clear that the property of being justified is equivalent to the property N. In the case of a Chisholm—type pluralistic theory, there is a necessary coextension as well. If there is a finite number of nonnor-

mative base properties {N1, N2, Nn}, the property of being justified will be necessarily coextensive with the disjunctive property "*N*1 or N2 or Nn." If the number of base properties is infinite, the property of being justified will be necessarily coextensive with an infinite disjunction of base properties.

[21] See Chisholm (1977), p. 84.

[22] In the current literature, reliabilism is often viewed as an example of the naturalistic approach to epistemology, whereas the Chisholmian approach is considered the epitome of nonnaturalism. See, for example, Maffie (1990). Such views are mistaken. Both reliabilism and the Chisholmia approach are examples of what we have called "criteriological analysis," and thus share significant metaphysical assumptions. In fact, reliabilism, as an instance of analytical monism, is committed to a more daring metaphysical claim than the endeavour of listing a variety of different nonnormative base properties.

[23] For statements of this objection, see Pollock (1986), p. 94, and Sosa (1991), pp. 128 and 187.

[24] Sosa (1991), p. 154.

[25] Above, we referred to Chisholm's project of listing epistemic principles as an example of pluralistic criteriological analysis. Interestingly, though, Chisholm's principles, with one exception, are all prima facie principles: they all have epistemic qualifiers in their antecedents. In *Theory of Knowledge* (1989), Chisholm begins his list of ten epistemic principles (which he calls "material epistemic principles") with this one:

> MP1   If the property of being F is self-presenting, if S is F, and if S believes himself to be F, then it is certain for S that he is F.

Assuming that the concepts of self-presentation and belief are nonnormative, MP1 would be an example of criteriological analysis, having a descriptive antecedent and an epistemic term in its consequent. However, Chisholm's second principle,

> MP2   Accepting h tends to make h probable

does not tell us what is probable, but only what is *prima facie* probable. And his third principle

> MP3   If S accepts h and if h is not disconfirmed by S's total evidence, then h is probable for S

is similar to our principle P2a. Although it does provide us with a condition that entails the epistemic status of being probable, it specifies this condition using a concept of epistemic evaluation: that of a proposition's being *disconfirmed* by S's total evidence. The same holds for the remaining seven principles: they all contain epistemic concepts in their antecedents. It would appear, therefore, that, with the exception of MP1, Chisholm's principles are a version of epistemological pessimissm.

CHAPTER THREE

A PRIORI KNOWLEDGE

KANT'S DEFINITION OF APRIORITY

In this chapter, we shall concern ourselves with the following topics: (i) the concept of apriority, (ii) the distinction between analytic and synthetic propositions, and (iii) skepticism about a priori knowledge.

The terms *a priori* and *a posteriori* were introduced into philosophy by the German philosopher Immanuel Kant, marking a distinction that had already been drawn by Descartes, Leibniz, and Locke. In his *Critique of Pure Reason*, Kant defined a priori knowledge in terms of independence of experience.[1] According to Kant, a priori knowledge is knowledge that is prior to, or gained *independently* of, experience, whereas a posteriori knowledge is knowledge gained *through* experience. The point of his definition may be illustrated by the following two propositions:

(1) If Yuri lives in Alma-Ata and Alma-Ata is the capital of Kaza-khstan, then Yuri lives in the capital of Kazakhstan.

(2) Yuri lives in Alma-Ata.

In order to see that (1) is true, you need only think about what it is that (1) asserts. Thought alone, without the aid of any information drawn from experience, is sufficient to determine whether (1) is true or false. In contrast, thought alone is not sufficient to determine whether (2) is true or false. Rather, in order to find out the truth value of (2), you must have the kind of experience needed to acquire the relevant information. For example, Yuri might tell you he lives in Alma-Ata, or you might hire a private investigator to find out where Yuri lives, or you might watch a report about Yuri on *60 Minutes*. Obviously, no such experiences are necessary in order to see that (1) is true. Thus Kant would say that while you know *a priori* that (1) is true, knowledge of (2) would have to be *a posteriori*.

The notion of a priori *knowledge* is closely related to that of a priori *justification* because what makes an instance of knowledge a priori is the way in which it is justified. Justification through experience is one mode of justification; justification that is independent of experience is another. A priori knowledge, then, can be defined as the kind of knowledge whose justification is a priori. Of course, this definition is not very illuminating, for it doesn't tell us what makes justification a priori. If we were to apply Kant's suggestion, we could say that a belief is justified a priori if and only if its justification is independent of experience. This definition raises two issues. First, precisely what do we mean by the concept of *experience*? Second, what do we mean by the concept of *independence* of experience?

SENSORY AND NONSENSORY EXPERIENCE

Suppose by "experience" we mean *sense* experience: experience that is either visual, auditory, olfactory, tactile, or gustatory. In that case, we would have to formulate Kant's definition thus:

D1   *S* is justified a priori in believing that *p* if and only if *S's* justification for believing that *p* does not depend on sense experience.

But this definition is not satisfactory, for there are beliefs such that their justification does not depend on sense experience, but they are not justified a priori. Suppose I believe "This morning I was thinking about having steak for dinner." This belief is not a priori, for its justification depends on the memorial experience of clearly recalling what dinner plans I was making this morning. But a memorial experience is not a form of *sense* experience, and thus my justification for believing that I was thinking about having steak for dinner does not depend on sense experience. Hence D1 yields the wrong result that I am justified a priori in believing that I was thinking about having steak for dinner.

A parallel argument can be made about introspection. My justification for believing that I would like to eat a bar of chocolate right now does not depend on any sense experience. Thus D1 implies that my belief is justified a priori. But this is the wrong result; my belief is not justified a priori because it depends for its justification on my experiencing desire for a piece of chocolate. If I did not have such an experience, I could not justifiably believe that I would like a piece of chocolate. So, D1 proves wanting again.

These two examples show that when a priori justification is defined as justification that is independent of experience, the relevant concept of experience includes not only sense experience but memorial and introspective experiences as well. However, just as we must take care to note what the relevant concept of experience includes, we must also consider what it *excludes*. Now in order to see what kind of experience a priori justification need not be independent of, ask what it intellectually *feels* like to consider the following two propositions:

(2) $2 + 2 = 4$
(3) $2 + 2 = 5$

Alvin Plantinga would say that while (2) feels right, (3) feels wrong. (2), he suggests, feels "compelling," while (3) "off-putting and eminently rejectable."[2] Following Plantinga, let us say that there are experiences such as intellectual compulsion and repulsion. Many a priori beliefs are accompanied by an experience of intellectual compulsion. Some philosophers would even say that a priori beliefs can be justified by such an experience.

When a priori justification is said to be independent of experience, what is meant, then, is not that it must be independent of an experience such as intellectual compulsion. Hence in defining a priori justification as justification that is independent of experience, the relevant concept of experience includes memorial and introspective experience, but excludes the experience of intellectual compulsion. We shall stipulate, therefore, that in the following definition the term "experience" is to be understood in precisely this sense.

D2   *S* is justified a priori in believing that *p* if and only if *S's* justification for believing that *p* does not depend on any experience.

Does D2 imply that if you believe

(1)   If Yuri lives in Alma-Ata and Alma-Ata is the capital of Kazakhstan, then Yuri lives in the capital of Kazakhstan

you are justified a priori? Since your justification for believing (1) depends neither on sense nor on memorial or introspective experience, the answer is that it does.

A PRIORI JUSTIFICATION AND CONCEPT LEARNING

It could be objected, however, that your justification for believing (1) depends on experience after all. You couldn't be justified in believing (1) unless you understood what the proposition means, and you couldn't understand what the proposition means unless you knew what the relevant concepts mean. So in order for you to be justified in believing (1), you must understand the concepts of city, nation, and capital. It would be impossible to learn what these concepts mean without undergoing a vast array of experiences. Typically, learning such concepts involves complex social interactions between parents and children, and between teachers and students, and thus a succession of innumerable experiences. Indeed, for any proposition *p*, the justification you might have for believing p could not possibly be independent of the experiences necessary for learning the concepts out of which p is composed. So it would appear that your justification for believing (1) does depend on a vast number of experiences, and thus is not a priori.

In reply to this objection, we would have to admit that the experiences you had when you learned the concepts occurring in (1) were necessary for the justification you have for believing (1). Had you not had those experiences, you would not understand (1), and thus could not be justified in believing (1). However, when you are now justified in believing (1), experiences that you had many years ago when you learned certain words surely do not *now* play a justificatory role. That is, although you could not be justified in believing (1) without having had those experiences, they are not what generates your justification for believing (1) at the present time. And this is precisely the point when the expression "S is justified a priori in believing that p" is defined by appeal to the concept "independence of experience": that which generates $S's$ justification for believing p, or makes $S's$ belief that p justified, must not be experience. When you are justified a priori in believing a proposition p, then whatever it is that generates your justification must be something other than experience—which is entirely compatible with the fact that had you not had certain experiences, you could not be justified in believing p at all.

Let us distinguish between two ways in which something can depend on something else. First, an event x can depend on an event y because had y not happened, x would not have happened. Second, an event x can depend on an event y because y makes x the kind of event it is. For example, my thinking about tonight's dinner depends on my breathing a sufficient amount of oxygen. Without breathing a sufficient amount of oxygen, I couldn't be thinking about tonight's dinner. My thinking about tonight's dinner also depends on my hunger. If I were not hungry, then I wouldn't be thinking about tonight's dinner. There is, however, a big difference between these two examples of dependence. For certainly it is not my breathing oxygen, but rather my hunger, that makes me think about tonight's dinner. My justification for believing (1) depends on my having learned certain concepts in the same way in which my thinking about tonight's dinner depends on my breathing oxygen. This is not the kind of dependence that matters in D2; rather, the kind of dependence that matters is the second kind: what *makes* you justified in believing (1)—whatever it is—must be something other than experience. Hence it is true after all that, according to D2, your justification for believing (1) is a priori.

In the next two sections, we shall consider two alternative ways of characterizing a priori justification. In discussing them, we shall sometimes use the phrase "a priori propositions" instead of the cumbersome expression "propositions that are knowable or justifiable a priori." Similarly, we shall substitute the term "apriority" for the "the property of being knowable or justifiable a priori."

APRIORITY AND NECESSITY

Our first approach to the analysis of apriority—what makes justification a priori is independence of experience—tells us what does *not* generate a priori justification, but it doesn't tell us what does. Thus we are still left with the question of how it can it be possible to determine a proposition's truth value without relying on any experience. One answer to this question appeals to the concept of necessity. Consider the following examples of propositions that, according to a long-standing philosophical tradition, are examples of a priori knowledge:

    (a)   The sum of two and two is four.

    (b)   Two is an even number.

    (c)   Whatever is square is rectangular.

    (d)   Whatever is red is colored.

    (e)   Whatever is blue all over doesn't have green spots.

    (f)   For any two propositions p and q, if p is true and q false, then the conjunction of p and q is false.

    (g)   Either it's raining or it's not raining

Propositions (a) and (b) are truths of mathematics, (c) is a truth of geometry, (d) and (e) are examples of what we might call "conceptual" truths, and (f) and (g) are logical truths. What all of these propositions have in common is that they are *necessary*. According to a second conception of a priori justification, that is precisely what makes a priori justification possible. If a proposition is necessarily true, then simply *thinking* about it will be sufficient for recognizing its truth—assuming, of course, the proposition isn't so complicated that it cannot be known at all.

Consider the proposition "Whatever is red is colored." If you understand what it is for an object to be red and what it is for an object to be colored, then you can understand as well that there couldn't possibly be an object that is red without being colored. Put differently, you can come to see that the property of being red *includes* the property of being colored, and thus that the proposition "Whatever is red is colored" is *necessarily* true.[3] Thus one might propose to explain apriority by saying the following: What makes the proposition "Whatever is red is colored" a priori is that you can *grasp its necessity*. Consider a second example: Nothing that is square is circular. If you know what a square is (a rectangle with four equal sides), then you know that the property of being square *excludes* the property of being circular: whatever is square *cannot* also be circular. This is why thought alone enables you to see that there couldn't possibly be a nonrectangular square—why you don't need experience in order to know that all squares are rectangular. Again, so the proposal goes, what makes your justification for believing this proposition a priori is that when you consider that proposition and reflect on it, you can grasp its necessity.

In order to evaluate this proposal, it is important to examine what relation exists between apriority and necessity. To begin with, let us consider the following definition:

> D3   S is justified a priori in believing that *p* if and only if *S* believes that *p* and *p* is a necessary truth.

This definition fails for two reasons. First, it fails because it does not place any constraints on the *manner* in which *p* is believed; it does not demand that *S* form the belief that *p* in a way that makes *S's* belief *justified*.[4] Suppose you believe a complicated logical theorem (i.e., a necessary truth) because you think you proved it. In constructing this proof, though, you were quite sloppy. You were preoccupied with other matters, and thus didn't concentrate very well. Your proof, therefore, is of dubious value. Its validity would be no more than a lucky accident. Surely, such a proof does not *justify* you in believing the theorem. However, since you *believe* a proposition that, ex hypothesi, is a necessary truth, D3 yields the wrong result that you are justified a priori in believing it. The fact of the matter is that you are not at all justified in believing it. The general lesson to be drawn from this case is that since it is possible to believe a necessary proposition without any justification at all, it is not sufficient for a priori justification that the proposition believed be necessary.

A POSTERIORI JUSTIFICATION FOR NECESSARY TRUTHS

The second reason D3 fails is that it implies the following: *Whenever* you believe a necessary truth, your justification for it is a priori. However, isn't it possible to be justified *a posteriori* in believing a necessary truth? If a famous and eminent logician were to tell you that a certain theorem is true, wouldn't you be justified in believing it to be true? It's plausible to say that you would be. But if you are justified in believing a proposition on the basis of authority, then your justification for believing that proposition is a posteriori. So if trusting an authority can justify you in accepting a necessary proposition, then it's possible to be justified a posteriori in believing necessary truths. D3 does not allow for this possibility, and thus must be rejected.[5]

Against this argument, the following objection could be raised. When we consider a particular proposition, we must distinguish between the sentence expressing that proposition and the proposition it expresses. Let's call a sentence that expresses a logical theorem a "formula." When you learn from an authority on logic that a certain formula is true, then what you are justified in believing—so the objection goes—is that the formula expresses a truth. You are not, however, justified in believing that truth itself. According to the objection, you are not justified in believing the truth itself because you don't really *understand* it.

Now, it must certainly be admitted that there are logical formulae whose truth master logicians can see, whereas ordinary mortals can't even begin to understand them. And if we were to take a master logician's word that such a formula is true, then indeed we would be justified, not in believing the truth that formula expresses, but only in believing that a certain formula expresses a truth. However, it is implausible that this is so *whenever* we believe a formula to be true on the basis of authority. The objection does not, therefore, rule out the possibility of a posteriori justification for believing a necessary truth.

Consider, for example, the Goldbach conjecture: Every even number greater than two is the sum of two prime numbers.[6] If the Goldbach conjecture is true, it is necessarily true, and if it is false, it is necessarily false.[7] As a matter of fact, however, we don't know whether the Goldbach conjecture is true or false; no one has proven or disproven it. Suppose a famous mathematical genius proves that the Goldbach conjecture is true, his proof is well publicized, and the community of mathematical experts agrees the proof is sound. The question we must answer is whether under these circumstances we would be justified in believing the Goldbach conjecture itself—or only in believing that

(1)   The sentence "Every even number greater than two is the sum of two primes" expresses a truth.

It could reasonably be argued that someone who knows what an even number, a prime number, and a sum of two numbers are, understands perfectly well what the Goldbach conjecture means. If so, then we would (in the case we are imagining) be justified in believing not only (1) but the Goldbach conjecture itself. Thus, if we were to learn from an authority that the Goldbach conjecture is true, then we would be justified *a posteriori* in believing a necessary truth. D3 does not allow for this possibility, and thus must be rejected.

D3, then, fails for two reasons: first, it is too liberal regarding the manner in which p is believed, and second, it doesn't allow for the possibility of being justified a posteriori in believing a necessary truth. The following definition suffers from neither of these problems:

D4 S is justified a priori in believing that p if and only if S grasps that p is necessarily true.

D4 requires that S grasp that p is necessarily true, and thus places a constraint on the manner in which p is believed. Furthermore, it permits a posteriori justification for believing necessary truths, for if one believes a necessary truth on the basis of authority, then one believes that truth without *grasping* that it is necessarily true. If you were to believe the Goldbach conjecture because an authority told you that it was a necessary truth, then you would believe a necessary truth without grasping its necessity. Hence, according to D4, your justification for believing the Goldbach conjecture would be a posteriori.

THE TRUTH VALUE AND MODAL STATUS OF PROPOSITIONS

Unfortunately, the proposal to define a priori justification in terms of the grasp of necessity raises another kind of problem. Consider again the proposition

(1)   Whatever is red is colored.

Probably you have formed the belief that (1) is necessarily true. However, we must distinguish between two different beliefs:

B1   (1) is true.
B2   (1) is necessarily true.

Since B1 is a belief about the *truth value* of (1) and B2 a belief about the *modal status* of (1), B1 and B2 are two very different beliefs.[8] It is possible for a person to believe a proposition to be true without giving any thought to the question of what the proposition's modal status is. This means it's possible to believe that *p* is true without simultaneously believing that it is *necessarily* true.

   Suppose you believe that (1) is true—say, because you experience a feeling of "intellectual compulsion"—without, however, having considered the question of whether (1) is necessarily true. You have grasped that (1) is true, but you have not grasped that it is necessarily true because you didn't even ask yourself whether (1) is necessarily true. D4 implies that, in this case, you would not be justified *a priori* in believing (1). Hence, if it is true that you would be, then D4 is false.

   The point of this objection is this: Grasping that *p* is necessarily true involves, minimally, *believing* that *p* is necessarily true. However, it seems possible to be justified a priori in believing a proposition *without* believing that that proposition is necessarily true. Consequently, if we define a priori justification in terms of grasping a proposition's necessity, our definition would appear to be too narrow.

THE FALLIBILITY OF A PRIORI JUSTIFICATION

A second problem afflicting D4 arises from the possibility of having a priori justification for believing a proposition to be necessarily true although that proposition is in fact *false*. If there is such a possibility—that is, if a priori justification is *fallible*—then D4 is false, for according to D4, a priori justification for p involves *grasping* that p is necessarily true. Can you grasp that a proposition p is necessarily true when p is in fact false? You cannot, for if p is false, then you mistakenly believe, but do not *grasp*, that p is necessarily true. So, grasping that p is necessarily true entails that p is true. Thus D4 tells us that one can't be justified a priori in believing a false proposition.

Is it possible, however, to be justified a priori in believing a falsehood to be true? Here is an argument for answering this question with "yes": Ask yourself whether you believe that when you take away from a heap of sand a single grain, what's left is still a heap of sand. If you believe that, then, on reflection, you should believe as well the following assumption:

(A) If two collections of grains of sand differ in number by just one grain, then either both collections are heaps of sand or neither is.

Is your justification for (A) a priori? It's plausible to say it is. The issue of whether (A) is true or false is not one that calls for an empirical investigation of heaps of sand. Rather, it is a conceptual issue, raising problems having to do with "heapness." Unfortunately, (A) leads to the paradoxical result that there are heaps of sand consisting of one grain only.[9] Once you become aware of this paradox, it is questionable whether you are any longer justified in believing (A).[10] However, it could be argued that *before* you become aware of the paradox, your justification for believing (A) was untarnished. And if this is right, then prior to discovering the paradox you were justified a priori in believing (A)—a proposition that is arguably false.[11]

Thus far, we have examined two approaches to the analysis of a priori justification: according to the first, a priori justification can be analyzed in terms of necessity; according to the second, it can be analyzed in terms of grasping necessity. We have seen that there are obstacles to both approaches. We should not, however, completely dismiss the possibility that, with appropriate refinements, one of these approaches might succeed. In the next section, we shall examine yet another approach.

Before moving on, however, let's briefly summarize what has emerged from our discussion. An adequate definition of a priori justification for a proposition p should: (i) place constraints on the manner in which p is believed; (ii) permit a posteriori justification for necessary truths; (iii) allow for the possibility of being justified a priori in believing a proposition to be true without believing it to be necessarily true; and (iv) make a priori justification fallible.

A THIRD WAY OF DEFINING APRIORITY

Some philosophers attempt to define apriority by saying the following: The reason justification for a priori propositions does not require experience is that in order to recognize an a priori proposition's truth, *understanding* it is all that is necessary. For example, the proposition "Whatever is red is colored" is such that, once you understand it, you are justified in believing it. Can this idea be turned into a satisfactory definition of a priori justification? Consider the following try:

D5 S is justified a priori in believing that p if and only if, necessarily, if S understands p, then S is justified in believing that p is true.

The problem with D5 is that it is too narrow. Suppose you are justified a priori in believing a proposition p on the basis of a simple proof.[12] Now, if in order to see that p is true you need to prove p, then we can't say that, necessarily, if you understand p, then you are justified in believing that p. For prior to proving p, you understood it without being justified in believing it. So, D5 implies that if your justification for p is based on a proof, it isn't a priori. However, if your proof for p is a priori itself—if experience is necessary neither for knowing its premises nor for knowing that the premises imply the conclusion—then, so the objection to D5 goes, you are justified a priori in believing that p.

We must distinguish, then, between a priori justification in a narrow and a broad sense. In the narrow sense, a priori propositions are restricted to propositions that are such that understanding them is sufficient for being justified in believing them. Let us call propositions that are a priori in the first sense "axioms." An axiom is a necessary truth that is incapable of proof in the sense that there is no other proposition that is "better known" than it is.[13] Recognition of an axiom's truth is derived not from other propositions, but simply from understanding it.

In the broad sense of apriority, a proposition that is known a priori is either an axiom or known on the basis of a proof. Though D5 fails as a definition of a priori justification in this broad sense, it succeeds as a definition of an axiom. We can, therefore, use the definiens (i.e., the defining condition after the "if and only if") of D5 to define the concept of an axiom.

D6 p is an axiom for S if and only if, necessarily, if S understands p, then S is justified in believing that p is true.

The proposition "Whatever is red is colored" is, according to D6, an axiom. It is not possible to understand it without being justified in believing it. In contrast, D6 implies, as it should, that the Goldbach conjecture is not an axiom, for understanding this conjecture is not sufficient for being justified in believing it to be true. D6 implies the same about the sand-heap assumption:

(A)   If two collections of grains of sand differ in number by just one grain, then either both collections are heaps of sand or neither is.

Although it is possible to be justified in believing (A), it is false that, necessarily, if one understands (A), one is justified in believing it. For as soon as one notices the paradox it involves, one's initial justification for it is undermined.

D6, however, defines merely axiomatic a priori justification. Thus we still need a definition of a priori justification in the broad sense—that is, of the kind of justification one can have for nonaxiomatic a priori propositions. The general idea for such a definition is expressed by D7.

> D7   S is justified a priori in believing that *p* if and only if either *p* is an axiom for S or S believes that *p* on the basis of a proof that is axiomatic for S.[14]

For D7 to be satisfactory, we would have to give an account of what it means, first, to believe a proposition on the basis of a proof and, second, for a proof to be axiomatic. However, even assuming that these phrases could be defined in turn, it is still far from clear that D7 is satisfactory. The problem is that there are many examples of propositions that are not a priori according to D7, but could reasonably be claimed to be a priori. For example, many epistemologists would agree that the proposition

> (1)   If there is an object that looks red to S, then S is *prima facie* justified in believing that that object is red

is a necessary truth that is knowable a priori. However, (1) is not axiomatic, for skeptics understand perfectly well what (1) means, but they would say that (1) is false. Perhaps, then, our justification for either accepting or rejecting (1) is a function of our reasons either for or against (1). But whatever the form of the reasoning in favor or against (1), philosophers hardly ever claim that it takes the form of an axiomatic proof. In fact, typically the arguments for or against principles such as (1) are long and complicated. It follows that, according to D7, philosophers who believe (1) are not justified a priori in believing it, and that philosophers who reject (1) are not justified a priori in rejecting it. Now, this wouldn't be a problem for D7 if we could simply conclude that when philosophers are justified in accepting, or rejecting, (1) their justification is *a posteriori*. Many philosophers, however, would refuse to draw that conclusion. They would say that *if* one is justified in accepting (or rejecting) a proposition such as (1), then one's justification is a priori.[15]

It could be objected, then, that D7 is too narrow. However, not every philosopher would agree with the objection's premises. Also, it might be possible to modify D7 in such a way that it captures those examples of apriority that it arguably leaves out. In any case, it seems safe to say that D7 provides us with a *sufficient* condition of apriority: if a proposition is either an axiom or such that it can be established on the basis of an axiomatic proof, then that proposition is knowable a priori.

A FOURTH WAY OF DEFINING APRIORITY

We have examined three ways defining a priori justification, and none of them has proven satisfactory. Let us return, therefore, to the Kantian definition and see whether we can develop it further. According to the Kantian approach to apriority, a priori justification is justification that does not depend on perceptual, introspective, or memorial experience. One objection to this definition is that instead of telling us what a priori justification is, it merely tells us what it is not: it is not justification that depends on certain experiences. However, if we classify experiences accordingly, perhaps we can modify the Kantian approach in such a way that we can get a definition telling us what a priori justification *is*.

Recall that, according to Alvin Plantinga, there are such experiences as intellectual attraction and repulsion. When you consider the proposition "2 + 2 = 4" you have strong, even irresistible, experience of intellectual attraction, and when you consider the proposition "2 + 2 = 5," you have an an irresistible experience of intellectual repulsion. Let us use Plantinga's proposal for the purpose of distinguishing between two kinds of experiences: purely intellectual ones and those that are not purely intellectual. Let us say that when you consider a proposition p and have the experience of being convinced of p's truth, and that experience does not involve perception, introspection, or memory, then you have a *purely intellectual* experience that p is true.

A purely intellectual experience that p can be mediate or immediate. In the case of simple truths of arithmetic, simple conceptual truths, and axioms of logic, such experiences are immediate: understanding them is sufficient for generating such an experience. In the case of more complicated propositions, an informal line of reasoning, or a technical proof, may be necessary for generating an intellectual experience that p is true.

If you have a purely intellectual experience that p is true, but you have also evidence for believing that p is false, then your experience is *defeated* and you are not justified believing that p. Suppose you are taking a logic class and you construct a proof that you take to demonstrate that a first formula, F1, entails a second formula, F2. Each step in the derivation strikes you as valid, and thus you are convinced that

(1)   F1 entails F2

is true. However, as soon as your professor sees the proof, she tells you that it is invalid. In this case, your conviction that (1) is true *fails* to justify you in believing (1) because it is defeated by your professor's verdict.

Perhaps, then, we may define a priori justification using the concept of an undefeated purely intellectual experience that p is true:

D8 S is justified a priori in believing that p if and only if S has an undefeated purely intellectual experience that p is true.

Before moving on, let us consider an objection to D8 that might be raised. Suppose, so an objector might argue, that S is a bit crazy and thus has an undefeated purely intellectual experience that *p* is true when *p* is an obvious falsehood such as

(2) $1 + 1 = 3.$

D8 implies that S is justified in believing (2). However, since (2) is an obvious falsehood, it is *false* that S is justified in believing (2).

In reply to this objection, two things could be pointed out. First, it is not so clear that what we are asked to suppose is really possible. Could S's purely intellectual experience that *p* is true really be undefeated? Second, even if we grant the possibility of this, it is not clear that we would have to agree with the objector. We could argue that while it is obvious to *us* that (2) is false, it is not obvious to S. After all, we are imagining S to be a bit crazy, and crazy people are often strongly convinced of rather strange things. Given that S does indeed have an undefeated purely intellectual experience that (2) is true, we can insist that S is justified in believing (2). But of course S doesn't *know* (2) because (2) is false. So while S has indeed a priori justification for (2), he doesn't have a priori knowledge of (2).

THE ANALYTIC-SYNTHETIC DISTINCTION

In the history of philosophy, there are two traditions that differ in their attitudes toward a priori justification: empiricism and rationalism. Though empiricists and rationalists often agree on what propositions are knowable a priori, they disagree on how to interpret these propositions. Sometimes, however, empiricists advance arguments to the effect that there is no such thing as a priori knowledge. Later in the text, we shall examine how a priori knowledge can be defended against such arguments. In the meantime, we will examine a more moderate empiricist claim: the doctrine that all a priori knowledge is *analytic*. In order to discuss this term, we must first turn to the analytic-synthetic distinction.

Empiricists—at least those who don't deny the possibility of apriority altogether—would by and large agree with rationalists on which propositions are a priori. For example, empiricists would classify

(1)   Whatever is red is colored

as a priori. However, rationalists and empiricists would disagree on what (1) is about. Empiricists tend to view (1) as trivial, as a mere tautology that is not really about the physical world but rather about our use of language. Rationalists, on the other hand, would insist that (1) does state a fact about the world of physical objects: any object that is an instance of "redness" is as well an instance of "coloredness." They would claim that, by virtue of what is sometimes called the "light of reason," we can apprehend that there are certain necessary facts about the physical world, facts that are accessible a priori. Empiricists deny this. They maintain that a priori propositions express either linguistic or logical truths, and thus are empty of factual content. We can distinguish, then, between a rationalist and an empiricist account of apriority. According to the rationalist account, a priori propositions describe necessary properties and relations of the physical world: red objects must be colored, square objects must be rectangular, odd-numbered sets of objects cannot be divided by two, and so on. And these properties and relations, rationalists would say, are recognizable through reason. Hence rationalists would say that through thought alone, we can recognize, not only what the world *is* like, but indeed what it *must* be like. According to the empiricist account, however, thought alone can't reveal anything about the physical world. Without the aid of experience, we can only know conceptual and logical truths.

In order to express their disagreement with rationalists, empiricists distinguish between analytic and synthetic propositions. *Analytic* propositions are not about the physical world but merely state truths of language and logic, and thus are trivial. *Synthetic* propositions, on the other hand, are about the physical world, and thus enjoy empirical significance. Analytic and synthetic propositions are mutually exclusive, and there is no middle ground between them. If a proposition is not analytic, then it is synthetic (and vice versa), and there are no propositions that are neither analytic nor synthetic. According to empiricists, analytic propositions are knowable a priori, synthetic propositions are not.

Empiricists employ the analytic-synthetic distinction with two objectives in mind. The first objective is to *deflate* apriority by establishing that all a priori propositions are analytic: not really about the physical world, but only about language and logic. The second is to replace what empiricists perceive as a *mysterious* account of apriority with one that is not. How, empiricists would ask, could it be possible to learn facts about physical objects without deriving information from experience? They criticize rationalists for assuming an ability somehow to "intuit," or to "see" in a nonperceptual way, truths about the physical world. Since we don't have any such mysterious ability, they would argue, it's impossible to know anything a priori about matters pertaining to the physical world. However, there is nothing mysterious about our ability to comprehend truths of logic and truths about the way we use words. So, from the empiricist point of view, what makes apriority digestible is the thesis that it is nothing but analyticity.

Next, we shall examine some of the ways in which analyticity has been defined and investigate whether these definitions imply that all a priori propositions are analytic.

KANT'S DEFINITION OF ANALYTICITY

Let us begin with Immanuel Kant's definition of analyticity, which can be found in the introduction to the *Critique of Pure Reason*.

> A1   *p* is analytic if and only if *p* is a proposition whose predicate is conceptually contained in its subject.

Many propositions adhere to what may be called the "subject-predicate form." For example, the proposition

(1)   All bachelors are unmarried

attributes the predicate "unmarried" to the proposition's subject: bachelors. Now, the concept of a bachelor can be defined as "unmarried adult male." Thus the predicate (1) ascribes to its subject—unmarried—is conceptually contained in its subject—bachelor. So A1 implies, as it should, that (1) is analytic. Furthermore, A1 implies that the proposition "All cyclists are lean" is synthetic, since the predicate "lean" is not contained in the concept of a cyclist.

A1 succumbs to the problem that not all a priori propositions are of the subject-predicate form. For example, empiricists would classify

(2)   Either it's raining or it's not raining

as a priori. And since they hold that all a priori propositions are analytic, they would have to say that (2) is analytic. However, since (2) does not adhere to the subject-predicate form, it has no predicate that is contained in its subject, and thus A1 implies that (2) is synthetic. So, A1 doesn't yield the result that all a priori propositions are analytic, and hence is not a satisfactory definition of analyticity from the empiricist point of view.[16]

A second problem with A1 is that it doesn't even work for all of those propositions that do adhere to the subject-predicate form. Consider

(3)   Whatever is red is colored

which is a standard example of an a priori proposition. (3) is of the subject-predicate form. It ascribes the predicate "colored" to its subject, redness. However, is its predicate really *conceptually contained* in its subject?

A first concept is contained in a second if and only if the first concept is part of an analysis of the second. An analysis of a concept breaks that concept down into its constituent elements. For example, the constituent elements of the concept of a bachelor are: unmarried, male, adult. Each of these predicates is contained in the concept of a bachelor.[17]

Is the concept of being colored contained in the concept of redness? To ask this question is to ask whether there is an analysis of the concept of redness that includes the concept of coloredness as a constituent part. Rationalists would say that since the concept of redness is simple, no such analysis exists.[18] Put differently, there is no way of verbally teaching anyone what the word "red" means. Rather, in order to know what it is for an object to be red, one must actually *perceive* a red object.[19] Other examples of qualities that can be perceived, but not analyzed, are sweetness, saltiness, tartness, sourness, softness, roughness. Each of these is a simple, unanalyzable concept.

It follows that there are many propositions of the subject-predicate form that are a priori but not, according to A1, analytic; for example: Whatever is sweet has a taste; whatever is rough has a surface; whatever is soft is extended. This outcome is unacceptable to empiricists. A1, then, fails to achieve the deflationary result empiricists wish to establish: that all a priori knowledge is analytic.

THE FREGEAN DEFINITION OF ANALYTICITY

Unlike Kant's definition of analyticity, Frege's, to which we turn next, is not restricted to propositions of the subject-predicate form:[20]

A2   *p* is analytic if and only if either *p* is a truth of logic or *p* is reducible to a truth of logic by substituting synonyms for synonyms.

In order to apply A2, it is necessary to define the concept of a logical truth. Here are two examples of logical truths:

L1   If it is raining, then it is raining
L2   Either it is raining or it is not raining.

The logical form of L1 is "If *p*, then *p*," and that of L2 is "Either *p* or not-*p*." Both of these forms are such that, whatever proposition we choose as a substitution for *p*, the result will be true. A logical truth, then, is a proposition whose logical form is such that all of its substitution instances are true.

We are now ready to examine how A2 is to be applied. Consider again the proposition

(1)   All bachelors are unmarried.

Since the concept of a bachelor can be defined as "unmarried adult male," substituting synonyms for synonyms results in

(1*)   All unmarried adult males are unmarried

which is an instance of the form

(4)   All FGH are F.

Any instance of (4) is true. So, by substituting "unmarried adult male" for "bachelor," (1) is transformed into a logical truth, and thus is analytic according to A2. Furthermore, unlike A1, A2 allows empiricists to classify logical truths such as L1 and L2 as analytic. Thus it would appear that by proposing A2 as a definition of analyticity, empiricists succeed in achieving the objective of showing that all a priori propositions are analytic.

TWO OBJECTIONS TO THE FREGEAN DEFINITION

Rationalists, however, would reject A2 for two reasons. First, they would object that A2 does not meet the empiricist objective of making *all* a priori truths analytic. Consider again the proposition

(3)   Whatever is red is colored.

According to A2, (3) is analytic if and only if substituting synonyms for synonyms turns (3) into a logical truth. Thus for A2 to give us the result that (3) is analytic, we need an appropriate synonym for "red." Replacing "red" with that synonym should turn (3) into an instance of the logical form "Whatever is FG is G"—that is, into a logical truth (since any instance of that logical form is true). However, since the concept of redness is simple (i.e., cannot be broken down or analyzed), no such synonym is available, which means that (3) cannot be turned into a logical truth. Hence A2 implies that (3) is synthetic.

To this argument, empiricists might reply that (3) can legitimately be translated as

(3*)   Whatever is colored red is colored.

Since (3*) is an instance of the form "All FG are F," and thus a logical truth, empiricists could argue that (3) is analytic after all.

For this proposal to work, "colored red" must be synonymous with "red." In reply to the empiricist move, rationalists could deny that these two terms are synonymous. They could reason that for a first expression to be synonymous with a second, it must mean *no more and no less* than the second. "Colored red," however, means more than "red," for "colored red" is a conjunction of two distinct concepts—coloredness and redness. So, "colored red" is not strictly synonymous with "red." Hence the transition from (3) to (3*) cannot be achieved by substituting synonyms for synonyms, and thus cannot be achieved in the way A2 requires. Consequently, A2 implies that (3) is synthetic.

Second, rationalists could deny that A2 provides us with an explanation of how apriority is possible. A2 defines analytic propositions as logical truths or propositions that can be turned into logical truths. What, however, is the status of logical truths themselves? According to the empiricist account of apriority, logical truths are knowable a priori because they are analytic. Unfortunately, if we apply the concept of analyticity as defined by A2 to the statement

> Logical truths are knowable a priori because they are analytic

we get

> Logical truths are knowable a priori because they are either logical truths or reducible to logical truths

which is not exactly an illuminating insight. So, if empiricists propose A2 as an analysis of analyticity, they succeed in explaining the a priori status of propositions that are *reducible* to logical truths, but they fail in explaining the a priori status of logical truths themselves.[21]

A LINGUISTIC DEFINITION OF ANALYTICITY

Thus far, the attempt to equate apriority with analyticity has turned out to be remarkably unsuccessful. It is no surprise, therefore, that empiricists have tried to exploit an altogether different gambit. In order to discuss it, we must distinguish between a sentence and the proposition the sentence expresses, for the following definition of analyticity is intended to define analyticity as a property of *sentences*:[22]

> A4   *p* is analytic if and only if *p* is true solely by virtue of meaning.

It's important to see that if it were not for the word "solely," the definiens of A4 would not mark any significant difference at all. Consider the synthetic sentence

> (7)   Snow is white.

Obviously, if "snow" meant grass, or if "white" meant green, (7) would be false. So what's responsible for the truth of (7) is not only that snow is, as a matter of fact, white, but also that the words "snow" and "white" mean what they mean. Sentences such as (7) have, so to speak, two truth makers: meaning and fact. That is, synthetic sentences, if true, are true partially by virtue of meaning, and if false, are false partially by virtue of meaning. Hence, if it were not for the word "solely," the definiens of A4 would apply to any sentence whatever, be it synthetic or analytic, and thus would be utterly unsuitable as a definition of analyticity. However, given the presence of "solely," A4 makes the significant claim that analytic sentences, unlike synthetic ones, have one, and only one, truth maker: meaning. For example, empiricists who favor A4 would say that

(3)   Whatever is red is colored

is analytic because it is true solely by virtue of the meaning of the words in (3). On the other hand, they would say that (7) is synthetic, for (7) is true not only by virtue of meaning but also by virtue of the fact that snow is white.

What could rationalists say in reply to A4? They could reply that *nothing* is true solely by virtue of meaning, and that, consequently, A4 gives us the result that all a priori propositions are synthetic. What is it that makes (3), understood as a *sentence*, true? First of all, what makes (3) true is that the words in (3) mean what they mean. Second, however, what makes (3) true is the fact that the property of being red includes the property of being colored. Hence it is false that (3) is true solely by virtue of meaning.

Put differently, rationalists would argue thus: When empiricists claim that (3) is true solely by virtue of meaning, they are, in effect, saying that there is one, and only one, condition that must be satisfied for (3) to be true: that the words in (3) mean what they mean. There is, however, a *second* condition that must be satisfied:

(8)   The property *being red* includes the property *being colored*.

If (8) were false, (3) would be false as well. So, the truth of (8) is a necessary condition for the truth of (3), and thus (3) is *not* true solely by virtue of meaning. Hence, rationalists would conclude, A4 implies that (3) is synthetic, and thus fails to accomplish what it is supposed to accomplish.[23]

As we have seen, none of the definitions of analyticity we have examined can be used successfully to establish the doctrine that all a priori knowledge is analytic. So, with respect to these definitions, we may conclude that there is synthetic a priori knowledge. It would be a mistake, however, to assume that an examination of a limited number of attempts to define analyticity is sufficient to dismiss once and for all the empiricist attempt to show that there isn't any synthetic a priori knowledge. For empiricists, there will always be the option to redefine analyticity once again, and then to reiterate that all a priori knowledge is analytic. Of course, each time the debate is reignited with a new proposal, rationalists may then try to show that, as with previous proposals, there is still some a priori knowledge left that cannot be classified as analytic.

SKEPTICISM ABOUT APRIORITY
AND THE NATURE OF ARGUMENTATION

Thus far, we have discussed the nature of apriority, and in doing so, we have simply assumed that there is such a thing as a priori knowledge. In the remainder of this chapter, we shall discuss how this assumption can be defended against total skepticism about a priori knowledge—that is, against arguments to the effect that there is no a priori knowledge at all.

Suppose a skeptic were to advance an argument whose premises are supposed to imply the conclusion that a priori knowledge cannot exist. Advocates of apriority could reply that they need not concern themselves with the particular content of the argument's premises, but instead need only make a counterargument about the nature of argumentation in general.

An Argument for the Existence of A Priori Knowledge
(1) Sometimes we grasp an argument's validity.
(2) Grasping an argument's validity is a form of a priori knowledge.
Therefore:
(3) Sometimes we have a priori knowledge.

Let us evaluate the first premise. To philosophize is to attempt, through argumentation, to establish the reasonableness of certain philosophically controversial beliefs and convictions. Thus those who believe that we don't ever successfully distinguish between valid and invalid arguments would have to view philosophy, and indeed any attempt at argumentation, as a pointless exercise. Philosophers, therefore, are hardly in a position to challenge the first premise.

The second premise is more controversial than the first. Is an *a posteriori* grasp of an argument's validity possible? Advocates of apriority would argue that it isn't. They would concede that you can come to *know* a posteriori that a certain argument is valid. For example, an expert logician could tell you that a certain argument is valid. If you had enough reason to trust his verdict, then you would come to know that that argument is valid. However, as long as your knowledge of the argument's validity depended on the expert logician's verdict, you would not come to *grasp* that argument's validity. For in order to grasp that the argument is valid, you would have to see and understand *yourself* that it is impossible for the premises to be true and the conclusion false. Thus, while it is possible to come to know an argument's validity on the basis of authority, it is impossible to *grasp* an argument's validity on that basis. Rather, to grasp an argument's validity is to recognize that its conclusion must be true if its premises are true. And how could such a recognition be anything but a priori?

Having made a case for the existence (and thus the possibility) of at least some a priori knowledge, advocates of apriority (apriorists, for short) could then go on to argue that total skepticism about the possibility of a priori knowledge is self-defeating. Consider a philosopher who claims that a priori knowledge is impossible. Either he intends to produce an argument whose conclusion follows from its premises or he does not. If he does not, his argument need not be taken seriously, for he is not really attempting to argue for anything. If he does intend to produce a valid argument, however, he is implicitly assuming that the validity of his argument is recognizable, and thus that a priori knowledge is possible. Consequently, either his argument need not be taken seriously or it is self-defeating.[24]

Producing an a priori argument against the possibility of a priori knowledge would be self-defeating in the most blatant way possible. Hilary Putnam, however, has suggested that an argument against the possibility of a priori knowledge, if based on *empirical* premises, is not self-defeating.[25] Apriorists could agree with Putnam that if the argument's premises are empirical, then it isn't self-defeating in the way it would be if they were a priori. But against Putnam, they could point out that even an empirical argument against the possibility of a priori knowledge is self-defeating in the sense explained above: it rests on the implicit presupposition that its validity is recognizable a priori.

It might be objected that it is possible to formulate an empirical argument against the possibility of apriori knowledge *and* to recognize the argument's validity on empirical grounds. To this objection, the apriorist will reply that it is possible to acquire about such an argument an empirically justified belief that it is valid. But acquiring such a belief would not be the same as *recognizing*, or *grasping*, its validity. And there's the rub: the apriorist's point is that there is no such thing as an empirical recognition of an argument's validity. Consequently, one cannot argue against the possibility of apriority without undermining the possibility of grasping validity. Hence to formulate an *argument* against the possibility of apriority is self-defeating. For to do so is, in effect, to argue that it is not possible to recognize whether that argument itself is valid or not.

There are, then, good reasons to assume that a general argument against the possibility of a priori knowledge can't even get off the ground. However, it should also be seen that a cogent argument in support of the possibility of a priori knowledge is equally difficult to produce, for producing such an argument would be question begging. It would rest on the implicit assumption that its validity is recognizable a priori, and thus would assume the existence of the very phenomenon whose existence it is supposed to prove. It seems reasonable to conclude, therefore, that the possibility of a priori knowledge must simply be presupposed by anyone who engages in the practice of argumentation.

STUDY QUESTIONS

1. What is wrong with defining a priori justification in terms of independence of *sense* experience?
2. Does your justification for believing "All triangles are three-sided" depend on the sense experience that was necessary for acquiring the concepts of triangularity and three-sidedness?
3. What is objectionable about defining a priori justification as the kind of justification one has when one believes a proposition that is necessarily true?
4. What is objectionable about defining a priori justification in terms of grasping a proposition's necessity?
5. What is wrong with the following definition of a priori justification: S is justified a priori in believing that p if and only if, necessarily, if S understands p, then S is justified in believing that p is true?
6. What are the shortcomings of Kant's definition of analyticity?
7. What are the shortcomings of the Fregean definition of analyticity?
8. How would an advocate of apriority object to the linguistic definition of analyticity?
9. What is the connection between a priori justification and argumentation?

EXERCISES

1. Find a proposition p such that: (i) you understand what p means; (ii) p is necessarily true; (iii) it is possible for you to have a posteriori justification for believing that p. Explain under what circumstances you would have a posteriori justification for believing that proposition.
2. Construct a case in which you are justified a priori in believing a proposition that is false. Explain where your justification for believing that proposition comes from.
3. Suppose that some time ago when you took a logic class you learned that P is a logical truth. At that time, your logical intuitions were well trained, and you could "see" that P had to be true; you *grasped P's* necessity. However, when you now consider P, you still remember that P is a logical truth, but you don't grasp that P is logically true. Is your justification for believing P now a priori or a posteriori?

NOTES

[1] See the Introduction to Kant (1781). For a criticism of Kant's definition of apriority, see BonJour (1992).
[2] See Plantinga (1993b), p. 104.
[3] A property F includes a property G if and only if, necessarily, whatever has F has G. For example, the property *being triangular* includes the property *being three-sided*. In contrast, the property *being a mother* does not includes the property *having a son*.
[4] See Casullo (1992), p. 2.

5 See Kripke (1972), p. 35. Kripke maintains that if one comes to know a necessary truth using a computer (for example, that such and such a number is prime), then that knowledge would be a posteriori.

6 Using the Goldbach conjecture as an example in this context was suggested to me by Noah Lemos.

7 This is so because numbers have their mathematical properties necessarily. For instance, the number five is necessarily odd, which is to say it could not possibly be even. And the number five is necessarily prime, which is to say it couldn't possibly be divisible without a remainder (except by itself or by one). See Kripke (1972), pp. 36f.

8 The importance of this distinction is pointed out in Casullo (1992).

9 Take a collection of grains of sand large enough to qualify as a clear-cut case of a heap. Create a second collection by removing exactly one grain. By virtue of (A), the second collection qualifies as a heap of sand. Now create a third collection by removing exactly one grain from the second, and continue creating further collections in the same way until you are left with one, and only one, grain of sand. By virtue of (A), heapness is transmitted from the first collection, via the intermediate collections, all the way down to the final one-grain collection. Hence (A) implies that there are heaps of sand containing only one grain. See R. M. Sainsbury (1988), pp. 25ff.

10 However, this is not to say that (A) ceases to feel intellectually compelling. It's quite difficult actually to believe that (A) is false—which is precisely why (A) presents us with a paradox.

11 A one-grain collection of sand couldn't possibly be a heap. So (A) implies a proposition that is false—that there are heaps of sand consisting of one grain only. But propositions that imply what's false are false themselves.

12 If a proof is long and complicated instead of short and simple, then deriving its conclusion involves the use of memory, in which case one doesn't know a priori that the conclusion follows from the premises. See Chisholm (1989), p. 30.

13 In one sense of the word, there is a "proof" for every axiom. After all, a necessary truth is implied by any proposition whatever. However, a good proof proceeds from what's more obvious to what's less obvious. If a proof's conclusion is at least as obvious as its premises, or if it is even more obvious than its premises, then the proof is pointless because it fails to be illuminating.

14 For an example of an approach to analyzing apriority along these lines, see Chisholm (1989), chap. 4.

15 Philosophical issues in general appear to pose this problem. If our beliefs about such things as the nature of the mind, personal identity, and freedom and determinism are justified, then presumably our justification is a priori. If so, however, then our justification is not a priori in the sense of D7, for our beliefs about such matters are almost never axiomatic.

16 In fairness to Kant, it must be pointed out that he himself did not mean to establish that all a priori knowledge is analytic. To the contrary, he went to great lengths to try to explain how a priori knowledge of synthetic propositions is possible. For a criticism of Kant's account of apriority, see BonJour (1992).

17 For more information on conceptual analysis, see Chapter 2.

18 Could "redness" be defined in terms of wavelength? It is true, of course, that light reflected from a red surface has a certain wavelength, which distinguishes it from light reflected from surfaces that have a different color. However, the connection between redness and its corresponding wavelength is contingent, and thus not suitable for a definition of redness. See Chapter 20.

19 Thus it is sometimes said that the meaning of "redness" can be conveyed only *ostensively:* by pointing to a red object.

20 Gottlob Frege (1848—1925) was a German mathematician and philosopher.

21 This argument can be found in BonJour (1985), p. 200.

22 For an account of the distinction between propositions and sentences, see Chapter 2.

23 See Chisholm (1977), p. 54.

24 An argument of this kind is suggested in Russell (1912), pp. 71f, and explicitly stated in BonJour (1985) pp. 194f.

25 See Putnam (1983), p. 98.

CHAPTER FOUR

THE CONCEPT OF EPISTEMIC JUSTIFICATION

EPISTEMIC JUSTIFICATION AND TWO KINDS OF NORMATIVITY

In Chapter 2, we distinguished among (i) defining a simple concept, (ii) analyzing a complex concept, and (iii) stating criteria for the application of a concept, and we discussed the problems that arise when we try to state criteria of epistemic justification. In this chapter, we shall focus on defining the meaning of that concept.[1]

The concept of epistemic justification, most philosophers would agree, is a normative one.[2] When a belief is said to be justified, it is positively appraised, evaluated as the kind of belief we favor vis-à-vis the epistemic end: the end of seeking truth and avoiding error, which is ultimately the end of acquiring knowledge.[3] What, however, do we *mean* by saying that a belief is appropriate, or favorable, vis-à-vis the epistemic end?

Answers to this question fall into two basic categories: deontological and nondeontological. According to *deontological* views, the meaning of the concept of epistemic justification is to be defined in deontic terms, terms such as "duty," "obligation," "permission," and "freedom from blame." The deontological view we shall discuss in this chapter asserts that whether a particular belief is justified is a function of meeting epistemic duties, duties that arise from aiming at the end of seeking truth and avoiding falsehood.

According to *nondeontological* views, a belief's being justified is a *normative* status, but the normativity in question here is simply one of goodness, or appropriateness, without involving anything having to do with duty, blame, or responsibility. For example, when a particular pig wins first prize at a county fair in rural Iowa, it is being appraised as excelling in a number of relevant respects, such as fatness and rosy skin. Obviously, the pig's normative status as a prize pig has nothing to do with its fulfilling any duties. In like fashion, we regularly evaluate, in a nondeontological way, things such as cars, tennis rackets, and bicycles as good or bad, or appropriate or inappropriate, vis-à-vis a certain end. Advocates of the nondeontological approach would say that when beliefs are evaluated as epistemically justified or unjustified, they are simply being appraised as good or bad, or appropriate or inappropriate, vis-à-vis the end of having true beliefs and avoiding false beliefs. William Alston formulates the possibility of nondeontological epistemic evaluation as follows:

> One can evaluate S's believing that p as a good, favorable, desirable, or appropriate thing without thinking of it as fulfilling or not violating an obligation . . . it could simply be a matter of the possession of certain good-making characteristics.[4]

Alston's own theory is an example of this nondeontological approach. Here is how he defines the concept of epistemic justification:

> *Alston's Nondeontological Concept of Justification*
>   S is epistemically justified in believing p if and only if S's believing p, as S did, was a good thing from the epistemic point of view, in that S's belief p was based on adequate grounds and S lacked sufficient overriding reasons to the contrary.[5]

Later we shall discuss in detail what Alston means by "adequate grounds." For now, what matters is that his definition makes no use of the concept of epistemic duty or any other deontic concepts. Justified beliefs are nondeontologically defined as beliefs that, by virtue of having certain characteristics, are good beliefs vis-à-vis the epistemic end. Later in the chapter, we shall discuss some of Alston's objections to the deontological approach. First, however, we must consider the view according to which the meaning of epistemic justification must be understood in terms of duty.

THE DEONTOLOGICAL APPROACH

The deontological concept of epistemic justification has its origin in the works of Descartes and Locke.[6] In the fourth of his *Meditations*, Descartes explains erroneous judgment as a misuse of intellectual freedom. He argues that it is up to us whether or not to believe a given proposition, and that we ought to believe it only when we perceive its truth clearly and distinctly. To believe a proposition in the absence of a clear and distinct perception of its truth is an intellectual failing, a failing for which we are fully responsible and may justly be blamed.

In his *Essay Concerning Human Understanding*, Locke discusses the subject of intellectual responsibility in the same fashion. He writes:

> He that believes, without having any reason for believing, may be in love with his own fancies; but neither seeks truth as he ought, nor pays the obedience due his maker, who would have him use those discerning faculties he has

given him, to keep him out of mistake and error. He that does not this to the best of his power, however he sometimes lights on truth, is in the right but by chance; and I know not whether the luckiness of the accident will excuse the irregularity of his proceeding. This at least is certain, that he must be accountable for whatever mistakes he runs into: whereas he that makes use of the light and faculties God has given him, and seeks sincerely to discover truth, by those helps and abilities he has, may have this satisfaction in doing his duty as a rational creature, that though he should miss truth, he will not miss the reward of it. For he governs his assent right, and places it as he should, who in any case or matter whatsoever, believes or disbelieves, according as reason directs him.[7]

In this passage, the idea of epistemic duty is clearly formulated. To seek the truth as we *ought* is to meet one's *duties as a rational creature*. Our intellectual faculties enable us to meet these duties; therefore, we are to be held accountable—that is, subject to criticism and blame—for their violation.

In contemporary epistemology, Roderick Chisholm is the most prominent advocate of this approach.[8] In his book *Theory of Knowledge*, he writes this on the topic of intellectual responsibility:

We may assume that every person is subject to a purely intellectual requirement—that of trying his best to bring it about that, for every proposition *h* that he considers, he accepts *h* if and only if *h* is true. One might say that this is the person's responsibility or duty *qua* intellectual being.[9]

Locke speaks of duties we have as "rational creatures," Chisholm of a requirement we have as "intellectual beings." According to Locke, it is our duty to seek the truth to the best of our power; according to Chisholm, it is intellectually required of us to do our best to believe the propositions we consider if and only if they are true.

EPISTEMIC DUTY AND THE END OF BELIEVING TRULY

Descartes, Locke, and Chisholm, then, would agree with one of the following: (i) As intellectual beings, we adopt what we may call the epistemic end; the end of believing what is true and not believing what is false; the end of believing truly, for short. (ii) The pursuit of this end imposes certain duties on us—epistemic duties. (iii) We may be held accountable for failing to meet these duties because we are endowed with intellectual faculties; we can, as Locke puts it, govern our assent as reason directs us. In this section, we shall discuss precisely which duty the end of believing truly imposes on us.

It is important to see that we shouldn't say our epistemic duty is to believe what is true and to disbelieve what is false, for in cases of misleading evidence, we ought to believe what's false and disbelieve what's true. For example, suppose my watch, which I know to be a reliable one, stopped working at precisely 1:00 P.M. At 1:02, I look at my watch and believe that it's 1:00 o'clock, although (as we have stipulated) it's 1:02. Since I don't yet have a reason for supposing that my watch broke (sooner or later I'll notice, of course), what I believe is what I ought to believe, even though it is in fact false.

Believing what's true and not believing what's false should be viewed, therefore, not as our epistemic duty, but rather as the *end* from which our epistemic duties arise. How should we characterize this end? Let us consider as a proposal what Chisholm says about the requirement we have as intellectual beings: to try our best to believe a proposition we consider if and only if it is true.

E1   For every proposition p I consider, it is my goal to accept p if and only if p is true.

One problem with this proposal is that it applies only to propositions I consider. But we adopt the end of believing truly not only for beliefs that are the result of reflective consideration but also for beliefs that are formed spontaneously. For example, I now believe that it's sunny outside, but this belief is not the result of considering the proposition "It is sunny outside" and deliberating whether I should accept that proposition. This doesn't mean, however, that with regard to this belief I abandon the goal of believing truly. We must, therefore, modify E1 so as to make it applicable to belief formation in general:

E2   For every proposition p, it is my goal to believe p if and only if p is true.

According to E2, as an intellectual being, I aim at believing *only* what is true, and *whatever* is true. The "only" part of this biconditional is certainly plausible, but what about the "whatever" part? Is it really my intellectual goal to believe all the truths there are? Is it my intellectual goal to believe a proposition simply because it is true, no matter how irrelevant and boring this proposition may be? For example, is it an intellectual end of mine to believe all the truths contained in the telephone directory of Hong Kong?

It certainly seems quite odd to maintain it is our end as intellectual beings to believe *every* true proposition. Rather, which of all true propositions a person aims at believing would appear to be an individual matter, dependent on that person's particular interests. For someone who has neither friends nor business contacts in Hong Kong, that city's telephone directory is utterly irrelevant, however many truths it may contain. If, on the other hand, I do know someone in Hong Kong with whom I wish to get in touch, then the truth about that person's telephone number matters to me, and I wish to accept a proposition attributing a telephone number to that person if and only if that proposition is true. These considerations suggest that what we aim at as intellectual beings is not to believe *all* truths, but only those that matter to us. Let us reformulate E2 accordingly.

> E3   For every proposition *p* that matters to me, it is my goal as an intellectual being to believe *p* if and only if *p* is true.

For the sake of simplicity, let us from now on refer to the epistemic end as defined by E3 as the end of *believing truly*.[10] Next, we shall consider the question of how we are to go about achieving this end.

EPISTEMIC DUTY AND EVIDENCE

According to Descartes, the duty that the pursuit of truth imposes on us is to believe only what we perceive clearly and distinctly. According to Locke, it is to "govern our assent as reason directs us." A more recent answer has been proposed by Richard Feldman, who says our epistemic duty is to "believe what is supported or justified by one's evidence and to avoid believing what is not supported by one's evidence."[11]

One problem with these answers is that they don't seem to tell us very much. For unless we are told what it is that reason dictates or what our evidence supports, we still don't know how to go about achieving the epistemic end. To this objection, it can be replied that, as we saw at the end of Chapter 2, there may not be any general principles that tell us what reason dictates or what our evidence supports. Characterizing our epistemic duty as broadly as we did above might, therefore, be the best we can do. But this does not mean that these characterizations are worthless. As Feldman points out, if we know that it is our epistemic duty to believe in accord with our evidence, then we know the fact that believing *p* will make us feel good, or that believing *p* is in our self-interest, is not the kind of thing that epistemically justifies us in believing *p*.[12] Thus, if we answer the question

> What should I do in order to believe truly?

by saying "believe in accord with the evidence," we do not offer a mere truism, but rather make a significant claim. The same can be said for Locke's answer. People who believe and disbelieve propositions as reason directs them do something significant: they form their beliefs without consulting crystal balls, reading tea leaves, or trusting supermarket tabloids.

The deontological concept of epistemic justification, then, involves two key ideas. First, as intellectual beings, we are committed to the end of believing truly. Second, this imposes on us the epistemic duty, as Locke proposes, to believe as reason directs us, or, as Feldman suggests, to believe in accord with the evidence. Let us settle on Feldman's formulation. Let us say that one is epistemically justified in believing *p* if and only if in believing *p*, one meets one's epistemic duty to believe in accord with the evidence. However, there are two different ways in which I can meet that duty. First, believing in accord with the evidence might impose on me the duty to *believe p*; second, it might impose on me the duty to *refrain* from believing *p*.[13] To say that I am *justified* in believing *p* is *not* to say that it is my duty to believe *p* or that I ought to believe *p*. Rather, it is to say something weaker: that it is not my duty to refrain from believing *p* or that it is not the case that I ought not to believe *p*.[14] We shall, therefore, define the deontological concept of epistemic justification thus:

> *The Deontological Concept of Epistemic Justification*
> S is justified in believing *p* if and only if S believes *p* and it is not S's duty to refrain from believing *p*.

Next, we'll turn to a discussion of objections that may be raised against the deontological approach.

EPISTEMIC DUTY AND DOXASTIC INVOLUNTARINESS

Let us distinguish between two kinds of projects: that of deontologically defining the meaning of the concept of epistemic justification, and that of analyzing issues of epistemic justification in terms of epistemic duty. The former project appeals only to the negative duty to refrain from believing *p*, whereas the latter project, which we shall refer to as *epistemic deontologism*, appeals to this duty and the positive duty to believe *p*. In this section, we shall discuss a serious obstacle that stands in the way of both projects.

This obstacle arises from the fact that a wide range of our beliefs are beliefs we can't help having, beliefs that are, so to speak, forced on us. Let us refer to this phenomenon as the apparent *involuntariness* of belief. Critics of epistemic deontologism have argued that because most (if not all) of our beliefs are involuntary, our beliefs can't be subject to epistemic duty.[15] That is, we can't have positive duties to believe, and we can't have negative duties to refrain from believing. If this argument is sound, then epistemic deontologism in general, and in particular the project of explicating the concept of epistemic justification in terms of duty, are misguided.

For the purpose of discussing this objection from doxastic involuntarism (the word "doxastic" means pertaining to belief), let us define involuntary belief thus:

> *Involuntary Belief*
> S believes *p* involuntarily if and only if S believes *p* and S cannot refrain from believing *p*.

Perceptual and introspective beliefs appear to be involuntary. When I believe myself to have a headache, I can't just decide to stop believing this.

Rather, as long as I have the headache, I can't help believing that I have a headache. And when I look out my office window, I see trees, grass, buildings, and people walking across campus. These perceptions trigger beliefs that are forced on me; for example: There are trees outside, there are buildings over there, there are people passing by. These are beliefs that I could not manage to get rid of, no matter how hard I tried.

The apparent involuntariness of introspective and perceptual beliefs poses a problem to epistemic deontologism because, according to the traditional concept of moral responsibility, having *moral* duties requires voluntariness. The following passage by Roderick Chisholm gives a succinct account of this traditional concept of responsibility:

> Let us consider some deed, or misdeed, that may be attributed to a responsible agent: one man, say, shot another. If the man was responsible for what he did, then, I would urge, what was to happen at the time of the shooting was something that was entirely up to the man himself. There was a moment at which it was true, both that he could have fired the shot and also that he could have refrained from firing it. And if this is so, then, even though he did fire it, he could have done something else instead. . . . I think we can say, more generally, then, that if a man is responsible for a certain event or a certain state of affairs (in our example, the shooting of another man), then that event or state of affairs was brought about by some act of his, and the act was something that was in his power either to perform or not to perform.[16]

The same view of responsibility, it might plausibly be claimed, applies to epistemic duties. If I am epistemically responsible for a belief of mine, then it must be within my power either to hold or not to hold that belief. On this view, a belief can be subject to epistemic duty—that is, such that I either ought to have it or ought to refrain from having it—only if it is voluntary. Let us call the principle that epistemic duties are akin to moral duties in requiring voluntariness the *voluntariness principle*, and formulate this principle as follows:

The Voluntariness Principle
　　If my believing p is involuntary, then I can't have an epistemic duty to believe p nor an epistemic duty to refrain from believing p.

From the voluntariness principle, it follows that if introspective and perceptual beliefs are indeed involuntary, they cannot be subject to epistemic duty. It then follows that such beliefs can be neither beliefs we ought to have nor beliefs we ought to refrain from having. If this conclusion is true, then epistemic deontologism would have to be rejected.

The voluntariness principle threatens the deontological concept of epistemic justification as well. It is important, however, to be clear about what an objection to that concept would have to look like. What kind of case constitutes a potential counterexample to our definition of that concept?

Contrary to initial appearance, involuntary introspective and perceptual beliefs do not. Recall our definition of the deontological concept:

D1   S is justified in believing *p* if and only if (i) S believes *p*, and (ii) S does not have an epistemic duty to refrain from believing *p*.

A potential counterexample to D1 is a case in which a subject believes a proposition *p*, does not have an epistemic duty to refrain from believing *p*, but is *not* justified in believing *p*. Involuntary introspective and perceptual beliefs do not fill the bill here, for such beliefs are (typically) justified.[17] What we need is a case of an *unjustified* involuntary belief. And it is not difficult to imagine such a case. Consider an Elvis Presley fan who can't help believing that Elvis is still alive and thus, given the voluntariness principle, cannot have a duty to refrain from believing that Elvis is still alive. Since there is no credible evidence in support of this belief, epistemic deontologists would have to admit that it is unjustified. Thus we have what looks like a decisive counterexample: an unjustified belief that meets the conditions of justification D1 specifies.

FELDMAN'S SOLUTION

Richard Feldman has argued that in order to defend epistemic deontologism against objections from involuntariness, we must reject the voluntariness principle.[18] According to Feldman, it can be my epistemic duty to believe *p*, or to refrain from believing *p*, even if I believe *p* involuntarily. This claim is based on the premise that there are situations in which we have nonmoral duties although we are unable to meet them.

Here is a slightly modified version of one of Feldman's examples. Suppose a student in my logic class has a learning disability: exposure to symbolic notation makes him so nervous that, no matter how well he prepares for the exams, he cannot pass any of them, and thus can't meet the class requirements. Does this mean he is exempt from those requirements and entitled to get credit for the class without passing the required exams? Of course not. If he wishes to get credit for this class, he must pass the exams, just like everybody else. This case shows that a student can be subject to an educational obligation even if he is unable to satisfy it.

A second example that Feldman describes concerns mortgages. Having bought a house, I have a legal obligation to make my monthly mortgage payments. Suppose I have financially overextended myself and am unable to make this month's payment. Clearly, my financial irresponsibility does not excuse me from having to make my payment. I still have a legal obligation to fulfill the terms of my mortgage, despite the fact that I cannot do so.

According to Feldman, epistemic duties are just like educational requirements and legal obligations. The epistemic end of believing truly imposes on me the duty to believe in accord with the evidence, whether or not I am capable of doing so. Consider again our example of an unjustified involuntary belief: an Elvis Presley fan who can't help believing that Elvis is still alive. Feldman would say that the compulsory nature of this belief need not hinder us from saying that, vis-à-vis the goal of believing truly, it is the fan's duty to refrain from believing this. Thus Feldman is in a position to deny that this case is a counterexample to D1. Having rejected the voluntariness principle, he can insist that, in spite of the belief's involuntariness, the Elvis fan has a duty to refrain from believing that Elvis is still alive. Thus his belief turns out to be unjustified, which is the desired result.

Feldman's reply is effective as well as a defense of the claim that we can have positive epistemic duties. If we accept the voluntariness principle, then introspective and perceptual beliefs raise a problem for this claim, for such beliefs appear to be involuntary, and thus beyond the scope of duty. However, if we agree with Feldman in rejecting the voluntariness principle, then we can accept that introspective and perceptual beliefs are involuntary and nevertheless view them as being subject to epistemic duty.

AN ALTERNATIVE SOLUTION

Feldman's solution will be unappealing to those who find the voluntariness principle intuitively plausible. Advocates of the deontological approach might, therefore, search for an alternative solution. Let's see what will be accomplished by making a belief's voluntariness a necessary condition of its justification.

> D2   S is justified in believing p if and only if (i) S voluntarily believes p, and (ii) S does not have an epistemic duty to refrain from believing p.

The motivation for this maneuver arises from the fact that the concept of justification, as it is ordinarily used, undeniably has a deontological meaning.[19] To be justified in doing something is to have permission to do it. If I am justified in performing a certain act, then it is not the case that I have a duty to refrain from performing that act. Consequently, if the voluntariness principle is true, justified acts must be voluntary acts, and justified beliefs must be voluntary beliefs.

D2 is immune to the counterexample we considered above, which was a case of an involuntary unjustified belief. Because of the way we have changed condition (i), we now get the desired result. Since the Elvis fan's belief that Elvis is still alive is the result of psychological compulsion, his belief fails to meet condition (i), and thus is not justified. Indeed, condition (i) has the effect of turning, in one fell swoop, *all* involuntary beliefs into beliefs that fail to be justified.

But now the problem of the involuntariness of perceptual beliefs returns with a vengeance. D2 precludes the existence of involuntary justified beliefs. Perceptual beliefs, however, would appear to be just that: involuntary and justified. According to D2, such beliefs are *not* justified. Surely this is an unacceptable result. In reply to this challenge, deontologists could distinguish between *soft* and *hard* involuntariness. Compare the following two cases:

> *Case 1: Soft Involuntariness*
> Looking out my office window, I see people walking across campus. As long as my evidential situation remains the same, I can't help having this belief. However, nothing is impeding my intellectual faculties, and thus it is within my power to deliberate, to weigh the evidence. If I were to receive further information—if, for example, I were to find out that I'm under the influence of a drug that makes me hallucinate the presence of people outside—then I *could* refrain from believing that there are people walking across campus.

> *Case 2: Hard Involuntariness*
> A mad scientist slips a drug into my coffee. The drug induces in me the belief that there are people walking across campus. Its effects are such that, however my evidential situation were to change, I would be compelled to retain this belief. Thus, even if I didn't see anybody walking across campus, I would still continue believing this. Indeed, no matter how much countervailing evidence were presented to me, I could not refrain from believing that there are people walking across campus.

The difference between the two cases is this: in the second, my belief is beyond my intellectual control. I cannot, therefore, be held accountable for it. Advocates of the voluntariness principle could plausibly argue that it can't be my duty to refrain from holding it. In the first case, however, nothing is impeding my intellectual faculties, which means that my belief is not beyond their reach. Were my evidential situation to change, I could refrain from believing that there are people walking across campus.

Initially, both beliefs appear to be involuntary. However, if we take into account my ability to react to a change in my evidence, a different picture emerges. In the first case, I retain intellectual authority over what I believe, whereas in the second case, this authority is undermined vis-à-vis the belief in question. Thus what the two examples show is this: we must distinguish between involuntary beliefs that are under one's intellectual authority and involuntary beliefs that are not. The former are involuntary in the soft sense, the latter are involuntary in the hard sense.

Let us return to the problem at hand. Deontologists could argue that a person's enjoying intellectual authority over a belief is sufficient to make that belief subject to epistemic duty. On this view, only hard involuntariness precludes a belief from being subject to epistemic duty; soft involuntariness does not, for a belief can be softly involuntary even when one's intellectual authority over that belief is maintained. The involuntariness of perceptual beliefs is of the soft kind, for such beliefs are, neglecting exceptions, under my intellectual authority. Under normal circumstances, they are accessible to an assessment of their epistemic credentials, which means that it is within my power to reject them if I see fit to do so. Consequently, deontologists could conclude that the soft involuntariness of perceptual and introspective beliefs need not prevent us from viewing them as being subject to epistemic duty.[20]

EPISTEMIC DEONTOLOGISM AND TRUTH CONDUCIVENESS

A second objection to epistemic deontologism has to do with the epistemic end of believing truly. Epistemic justification, the kind of justification we seek when we aim at the end of believing truly, must be truth-conducive. In other words, epistemically justified beliefs must be likely to be true. According to William Alston, the most serious defect of the deontological concept of epistemic justification is "that it does not hook up in the right way with an adequate truth-conducive ground."[21] This objection rests on the premise that for a belief to be justified, it must be based on an adequate ground. Let us call this premise the "adequacy principle." We shall now discuss whether the adequacy principle is defensible from the deontological point of view.

Alston thinks that justified beliefs must be based on an adequate ground. A belief's ground, in his theory, consists of either other beliefs or suitable experiences.[22] But how are we to understand the concept of a ground's adequacy? Here is how Alston explicates this concept:

> To get at the appropriate criterion of adequacy, let's note that a belief's *being justified* is a favorable status vis-à-vis the basic aim of believing ... truly rather than falsely. For a ground to be favorable relative to this aim it must be "truth conducive"; it must be sufficiently indicative of the truth of the belief it grounds. In other terms, the ground must be such that the probability of the belief's being true, given that ground, is very high.[23]

According to this passage, adequate grounds must be *truth-conducive*: they must ensure that the beliefs they ground are the kind of beliefs we favor vis-à-vis the end of believing truly, which is to say they must ensure that the beliefs they ground are *likely to be true*, or *probable*. Thus Alston's criticism of the deontological concept of epistemic justification can be reformulated thus: It is possible for a belief to enjoy deontological justification without being based on a truth-conducive ground or on a ground that makes it probable. In short, deontological justification fails to be truth-conducive, and thus is not the right kind of justification vis-à-vis the epistemic end.

Since there are two types of probability—factual and epistemic—in order to evaluate Alston's criticism, we must determine in which of these two senses he is using the concept of probability. First, however, let us briefly review the difference between factual and epistemic probability.[24]

TWO TYPES OF PROBABILITY

Factual probabilities are a function of what the physical world is like. In the factual sense of the term "probable," what is probable is that a thing of one kind is also a thing of another kind. Thus we can attach probabilities to the following items:

(i)   that someone who smokes two packs of cigarettes a day lives to be eighty years old;

(ii)   that a citizen of New York City will get mugged;

(iii) that a tossed coin will come up heads.

The probability of each of these items is determined by what we may call a *relative frequency*: the frequency of one type of occurrence relative to another type of occurrence. Thus the probabilities of the displayed statements depend on the frequency of: (i) those who eventually live to be eighty among people who smoke two packs of cigarettes a day; (ii) mugging victims among citizens of New York City; and (iii) tossed coins coming up heads. Obviously, these probabilities are determined by what the world is like. They are determined by, respectively: (i) the physiological effects of smoking; (ii) the various factors that are responsible for the level of crime in New York City; and (iii) the physical properties of tossed coins. Furthermore, these probabilities are independent of what we *know* about the world. The probability that a heavy smoker will live to be eighty is determined by the impact of smoking on a smoker's health, irrespective of how much we know about the physiological effects of smoking; muggings in New York City occur with the frequency they do no matter how much we know about crime in New York City; and the probability of a coin turning up heads depends on whether the coin toss is fair, regardless of whether or not we know it is.

Epistemic probabilities, on the other hand, are degrees of justification that, *relative to a given body of evidence*, attach to beliefs or propositions. For example, relative to the evidence I have about the effects of smoking, the proposition "I will suffer a significant risk to my health if I smoke two packs of cigarettes a day" has a high degree of epistemic probability for me.

Let us illustrate the difference between factual and epistemic probability with an example. Suppose I draw a ball from an urn that contains nine black balls and one white ball. The factual probability that the ball I'm going to draw will be black is .9. But if I have no information about the colors of the balls in the urn, the proposition "The ball I'm going to draw will be black" does *not* have a .9 epistemic probability relative to the evidence I possess. In fact, in relation to my evidence (or lack of evidence), it is probable that the ball will not be black (for as far as I know it could have any color). However, if the information about the distribution of colors among the balls in the urn is part of my evidence, then the proposition "The ball I'm going to draw will be black" enjoys both a .9 factual probability and, in relation to my evidence, a .9 epistemic probability.

When Alston asserts that justified beliefs must be adequate, and then explicates adequacy in terms of probability, what kind of probability does he have in mind? Although Alston does not address this question directly, he says at least this much:

> Suffice it to say that I am thinking in terms of some kind of "tendency" conception of probability, where the lawful structure of the world is such that one state of affairs renders another more or less probable.[25]

According to this passage, whether a ground G makes a belief P probable depends on whether the world has a lawful structure that makes P relative to G probable. Let's consider Newton's law of universal gravitation as an example of a probability-conferring "lawful structure." This law tells us that physical objects with sufficient mass fall down when released. If we apply this to my pencil, then we may say that, because of the law of universal gravitation, it is highly probable in the factual sense that if I release my pencil it will fall down.[26] Apparently, Alston thinks about the probability of beliefs for which grounds are adequate in the same fashion: what ground makes a belief probable is determined, not by the subject's evidence, but by the laws of nature. For example, in Alston's view, perceptual beliefs are (typically) based on adequate grounds, and thus are probable, because there is a law of nature such that a belief's being based on a perceptual ground makes that belief (more or less) probable. And beliefs based on wishful thinking are not based on adequate grounds because there is no lawlike structure in the world that makes such beliefs probable.

JUSTIFICATION AND FACTUAL PROBABILITY

It would appear, then, that the concept of probability Alston has in mind is *factual* probability.[27] Consequently, we may reformulate his adequacy principle thus: For a belief to be justified, it must be based on a ground that makes it factually probable.

Deontologists would not accept this principle. To see why not, let us consider a situation that involves the concept of moral justification.

Suppose a doctor working with the World Health Organization in a remote African country with poor medical services attends a patient who is suffering from a disease. This disease is fatal unless treated, and adequate treatment calls for either medication A or medication B. The doctor knows that medication A is significantly more effective than medication B: 90

percent of the patients who get medication *A* survive, whereas only 40 percent of the patients who get medication *B* survive. Unfortunately, about 5 percent of patients show a life-threatening allergic reaction to medication *A*. For such patients, medication *B* is the treatment of choice. Under ideal circumstances, tests are done to find out whether the patient is allergic to medication *A* before the medication is administered. However, in the situation we are considering (the location is the remote countryside), there are no means for testing for an allergic reaction. Thus our doctor has to make a decision under uncertainty: she simply does not know how the patient will react to the medication. Finally, let us suppose that, as a matter of fact, the patient belongs to the rare group of people who develop an allergic reaction to medication *A*.

In this situation, what is the doctor justified in doing: to administer medication *A* or medication *B*? If she administers medication *A*, there is a .1 probability that the patient will die of the disease, and a .05 probability that the patient will develop a life-threatening allergic reaction. But if she administers medication *B*, there is a .6 probability that the patient will not survive the disease. Thus, *as far as the doctor can tell at the time she has to make the decision*, choosing medication *B* involves a much greater risk to the patient than choosing medication *A*. Consequently, so it could be argued, what the doctor is justified in doing is to administer medication *A*.

What is crucial in this argument is this: The probabilities appealed to in order to determine whether the doctor's choice of treatment is justified are *epistemic*—that is, they are probabilities depending on the doctor's evidence. These probabilities have to be contrasted with the *factual* probabilities of the case, which are these: If the doctor administers medication *A*, there is a very high probability that the patient will die because of an allergic reaction. But if she administers medication *B*, there is a .4 probability that the patient will be cured. Thus, with regard to the factual probabilities of the case, administering medication *A* presents the greater risk. Consequently, if the doctor's moral justification for her choice of treatment were determined not by *what's probable as far as she can tell*, but by *what's probable given the facts of the case*, then we would have to say that what the doctor is justified in doing is to administer medication *B*.

What, then, *is* the doctor justified in doing? To say that the answer to this question is determined by what's probable *given the facts of the case* would be a significant deviation from how ethicists have traditionally conceived of moral justification. According to this tradition, there is an intimate connection between the concepts of justification, culpability, and blame. To do what one is not justified in doing is to be culpable; it is to have acted in such a way that one can justly be blamed for having acted that way. Obviously, it would not be just to blame the doctor in our example for choosing medication *A*. After all, she has no way of knowing that medication *B* would be the better treatment in this case. Indeed, were she to choose medication *B*, she would be choosing what, given her knowledge at the time, would be the riskier treatment, and that would be a choice for which she could justly be blamed. Thus, from the point of view of those philosophers who accept the traditional concept of justification, the doctor is justified in administering medication *A*, and this verdict is determined by what's probable about the case as far as the doctor can tell—that is, by the epistemic probabilities about the case.

Deontologists tend to think about *epistemic* justification in the same way. What determines one's epistemic justification is not factual, but epistemic probabilities. And the reason for this verdict is the same as that for the parallel verdict about moral justification. What determines whether one is justified in believing a proposition *p* is the probability of *p relative to what one can tell*, or *relative to one's evidence*. Factual probabilities, however, are not always such that one can tell what they are; they are not necessarily part of one's evidence, and thus need not be relevant to a belief's justification.

Suppose, after careful consideration, the doctor comes to believe

(1)   Medication *A* will save the patient's life.

Is she justified in believing (1)? Deontologists would say she is because certainly she can't be blamed for believing (1). Alston, on the other hand, would say that (1), though epistemically blameless, is not really an epistemically justified belief. A belief thus justified would have to have a favorable status vis-à-vis the epistemic end, that is, must be made factually probable by an adequate ground. But the relevant laws of nature—about the chemical properties of medication *A* and the patient's allergy to medication *A*—make (1) factually improbable. Thus (1) isn't based on an adequate ground (for if it was it would have to be factually probable), and hence does not enjoy a favorable status vis-à-vis the epistemic end.

Deontologists would agree with Alston that (1) fails to be factually probable. Contra Alston, however, they would insist that (1) has the required favorable status. For from the doctor's point of view, what epistemic shortcoming can be attributed to (1)? None. Of course we, who are considering this case from a God's eye point of view, know that (1) is factually improbable. What, though, is the significance of its factual improbability? Assume (1) is not only factually improbable, but even outright false. The patient's allergic reaction to medication *A* will be fatal. Note that this is not a reason to say that (1) isn't justified, for a proposition's falsehood is entirely compatible with its having a favorable epistemic status. Surely Alston wouldn't want to defend the dubious position that a belief can't be justified if it is false. However, if a belief's actual falsehood doesn't preclude it from having a favorable epistemic status, then surely the mere factual probability of its falsehood (or the lack of factual probability of its truth) doesn't either. Deontologists would see no reason, therefore, to agree with

Alston that (1) lacks a favorable status vis-à-vis the epistemic end because it isn't factually probable, and hence would reject Alston's principle that a belief is justified only if it is based on an adequate ground.

DEONTOLOGICALLY JUSTIFIED BELIEFS AND TRUTH CONDUCIVENESS

Let us return to Alston's objection that the deontological concept of epistemic justification is flawed because "it does not hook up in the right way with an adequate, truth-conducive ground." Given the way he explicates the notion of adequacy, Alston is saying, in effect, that a belief can be deontologically justified without being factually probable.[28] Deontologists, however, would reject the notion that for a belief to be justified—that is, for it to have a favorable status vis-à-vis the end of believing truly—it must be factually probable. Hence they would be happy to admit that deontologically justified beliefs may fail to be factually probable, for from the deontological point of view, there would be nothing wrong with that. On the other hand, as far as epistemic probability is concerned, deontologists would reject the claim that a belief can be deontologically justified without being epistemically probable. For if, as deontologists would say, it is one's epistemic duty to believe what is supported by one's evidence, then it is logically impossible to meet one's epistemic duty in believing a proposition that fails to be epistemically probable.

What, then, about Alston's criticism that deontological justification fails to be truth-conducive? Deontologists would reply that if the truth conduciveness of justification is to be understood in terms of the probability of justified beliefs, we must distinguish between factual and epistemic truth conduciveness, for what is relevant to justification is not the former but the latter. Deontologically justified beliefs are neither factually truth-conducive nor do they need to be. They are, however, epistemically truth-conducive— likely to be true relative to our evidence—and thus are the kinds of beliefs we favor vis-à-vis the end of believing truly.

INTERNALISM AND EXTERNALISM

In recent epistemology, it has become customary to distinguish between internalist and externalist accounts of justification.[29] Now is a good time to examine this distinction because the controversy we have been discussing in this chapter—that between deontologists on the one hand and Alston on the other—is an instructive example of the debate between internalists and externalists. What makes an account of justification internalist is that it imposes a certain condition on those factors that determine whether a belief is justified. Such factors—let's call them "J-factors"—can be beliefs, experiences, or epistemic standards. The condition in question requires J-factors to be *internal to the subject's mind* or, to put it differently, *accessible on reflection*. What makes an account of justification externalist, in contrast, is that no such condition is imposed. According to externalism, J-factors need not be internal to the subject's mind or accessible on reflection.

The expression "accessible on reflection" may be taken as an elaboration on how the expression "internal to the mind" is to be understood: something is internal to the mind, in the relevant sense of "internal," if and only if it is accessible on reflection. For example, my beliefs are internal to my mind because if I reflect on my beliefs, I can tell what they are. My perceptual experiences are internal to my mind because when I direct my attention accordingly, I can tell what I'm perceptually experiencing. On the other hand, my brain waves are not in the relevant sense internal to my mind because there is very little with regard to my brain waves that I can tell on reflection.

Foundationalism and coherentism are the two prime examples of *internalist* theories.[30] According to foundationalism, there are no other J-factors than these: self-evident epistemic principles, beliefs, and perceptual, introspective, and memorial experiences, all of which are accessible on reflection. And according to coherentism, J-factors are restricted to self-evident epistemic principles, beliefs, and coherence relations among beliefs. Again, all of these are accessible on reflection.

The prime example of *externalist* theories is reliabilism. Reliabilism in its various forms counts the reliability of belief-producing processes as a J-factor. However, the reliability of such processes is not internal to the mind. Suppose you are observing a dog in a park, and the conditions of observation are these: it is getting dark but there is still some light left, the dog is thirty feet away and moving fast, you are nearsighted but wearing eyeglasses, the functioning of your perceptual faculties is somewhat impaired by the consumption of three martinis, and you are preoccupied by thoughts about the unbalanced condition of your checking account. Is the cognitive process that causes you to believe "There's a dog over there" reliable? In other words, would most beliefs caused by this cognitive process be true? Obviously, this isn't something you can tell just by reflecting on it. Rather, an extensive empirical investigation would be required.

From the deontological point of view, no account of justification can be correct unless it includes an internalist condition. The argument for this conclusion begins with a consideration of *moral* duty. What kind of information could at a particular point in time impose on me the duty to do x: information that is accessible to me at that time, or information I could acquire only at a later time? Deontologists would say that if I must act at that time, what my duty is cannot be determined by information I can acquire only later. Rather, my duty can only be determined by information accessible to me at the time I must act.

The same, so the argument would continue, can be said for *epistemic* duty. If the question is whether it is *now* my duty to believe p or to refrain from believing p, evidence I could acquire later through investigation is irrelevant. What determines my epistemic duty can only be evidence I now have. And evidence I now have is something that is accessible to me *on reflection*.[31] So if we think of epistemic justification in terms of duty fulfillment, things not accessible on reflection cannot be a J-factor. Deontological theories, therefore, are necessarily internalist.

In insisting that justifying grounds be adequate, Alston sides with the externalist point of view. As we have seen, for Alston a ground is adequate just in case it is factually probable. But whether a ground is factually probable is not the sort of thing that can be ascertained on reflection. Consequently, Alston's adequacy condition is externalist in character, and his account of justification a version of externalism.[32] Hence when deontologists reject Alston's adequacy condition, what they are rejecting, in effect, is externalism: the introduction of a J-factor that is not internal to the mind or accessible on reflection.

STUDY QUESTIONS

1. What's the difference between the concept of normativity as employed by deontological and as employed by nondeontological theories of justification?
2. Why would it be a mistake to say that it's our epistemic duty to believe what's true and not to believe what's false?
3. What's problematic about saying that for every proposition p, we should believe p if and only if p is true?
4. According to some philosophers, belief is mostly, if not always, an involuntary affair. What's the reason for this view?
5. If it were true that belief is mostly or even always involuntary, why would that be a problem for the deontological approach?
6. How does Richard Feldman solve the problem of doxastic involuntariness?
7. How could advocates of the deontological approach object to the view that belief is mostly or even always involuntary?
8. Why does William Alston think that deontologically justified beliefs are not necessarily truth-conducive beliefs?
9. What does Alston mean by the concept of an adequate ground?
10. How do factual and epistemic probability differ from each other?

EXERCISES

1. Discuss whether getting the truth and avoiding error is a proper epistemic end?
2. Describe a situation in which it would be your epistemic duty to believe what's false.
3. Discuss whether Alston is right in claiming that epistemically justified beliefs cannot be based on adequate grounds.

NOTES

[1] In his paper "Concepts of Epistemic Justification," Alston (1989), pp. 81–114, Alston undertakes the task of analyzing and evaluating various competing concepts of justification. See p. 81, where he explicitly distinguishes between stating *standards* of justification and analyzing the *meaning* of the concept of justification.

[2] There are epistemologists who would disagree. See, e.g., Maffie (1990), p. 285.

[3] See Alston (1981), pp. 83f, and BonJour (1985), pp. 7f.

[4] Alston (1989), p. 97.

[5] Ibid., pp. 105f. Alston adds the qualifier "as *S* did" to indicate that what is evaluated as good is not the fact that *S* believes *p*, but rather the particular *way* in which *S* believes that *p*. See ibid., pp. 97f.

[6] A good account of the historical roots of the deontological concept of justification can be found in Plantinga (1993a), chap. 1.

[7] Locke (1959), pp. 413–414,

[8] The deontological approach is also endorsed by BonJour (1985), Feldman (1988a), and Ginet (1975).

[9] Chisholm (1977), p. 14.

[10] Two questions we can't address here are these: Is it a rational, or perhaps moral, requirement to adopt the end of believing truly? Furthermore, do people have epistemic duties even when they do not adopt the end of believing truly?

[11] See Feldman (1988a), p. 254.

[12] Ibid.

[13] It is plausible to maintain that there are cases where I ought to believe a proposition. For example, when I consider *p* and determine that my evidence supports *p*, it might plausibly be argued that it is my epistemic duty to believe *p*.

[14] See Alston (1989), p. 85.

[15] This objection is discussed in Alston's two papers "Concepts of Epistemic Justification" and "The Deontological Conception of Epistemic Justification." See Alston (1989), pp. 81–115 and 115–153.

[16] Chisholm (1966), p. 12.

[17] Of course there are unjustified perceptual beliefs: beliefs based on perception but defeated by further evidence. However, as far as such beliefs are concerned, it's not at all clear that they are involuntary. For if the subject has defeating evidence, then, unless exceptional circumstances obtain, she can be held responsible for neglecting that evidence. We shall, therefore, stipulate that involuntary perceptual beliefs are justified. What makes them arguably involuntary is precisely the fact that they arise from undefeated, and thus *irresistible*, evidence.

[18] See Feldman (1988a).

[19] Thus Alvin Plantinga writes: "Indeed the whole notion of epistemic justification has its origin and home in this deontological territory of duty and permission, and it is only by way of analogical extension that the term 'epistemic justification' is applied in other ways. Originally and at bottom, epistemic justification *is* deontological justification: deontological justification with respect to the regulation of belief." Plantinga (1993a), p. 14.

[20] To provide further support for this view, deontologists could argue that soft involuntariness can also be attributed to actions that we ordinarily don't hesitate to evaluate deontologically. Consider a situation in which Jane, a woman of sound moral character, answers a question by telling the truth. Suppose that her act of telling the truth is as much compelled by the moral reason in support of it as our perceptual beliefs are compelled by our evidence for them. Wouldn't we, although her act of telling the truth is an example of psychological compulsion, view this act of truth telling as sufficiently voluntary to qualify as an instance of duty fulfillment? The act's voluntariness, so it could be argued, is due to the fact that her intellectual authority over her action is unimpeded. Were the situation different—were the moral reason for telling the truth less stringent—then she *could* refrain from telling the truth.

[21] Alston (1989), p. 95.

[22] A further question that is relevant here is this: What is it for a belief to be *based* on a ground? For elaboration on this point, see Alston (1989), pp. 99f and 229.

[23] Alston (1989), pp. 231f.

[24] For accounts of the difference between factual (or statistical) and epistemic (or normative) probability, see Plantinga (1993a), pp. 115f; Pollock (1986), p. 96; and Skyrms (1986), pp. 15 and 129.

25 Alston (1989), p. 232.

26 Of course, since I know that there is such a thing as gravity, it is also epistemically probable for me that the pencil will fall down.

27 However, as Alston pointed out to me in correspondence, the concept of probability he has in mind is not to be understood in terms of relative frequencies. See Alston (1989), p. 320, where he explains the function reliability plays in his theory. He writes: "I am not thinking of the reliability of a belief-producing mechanism as a function of its actual track record, but rather of its *tendency* to produce true beliefs...." This point does not, however, affect the issue of epistemic and factual probability. There can be no doubt, it seems to me, that the kind of probability Alston has in mind is factual in nature.

28 The phrase "deontologically justified" is to be understood as shorthand for "deontologically justified vis-à-vis the epistemic goal of believing truly."

29 For the internalism externalism distinction, see: Alston (1989), essays 8 and 9, BonJour (1992), and Fumerton (1988).

30 Foundationalism and coherentism will be discussed in Chapters 5–7.

31 If I have an encyclopedia, the information contained in it could reasonably be said to be evidence I now have. But from the internalist point of view, such evidence is not a J-factor because, strictly speaking, the information my encyclopedia provides is only evidence that is easily available to me. In order to *have* that evidence, I must first retrieve and digest the information.

32 Alston explicitly characterizes his theory as a form of externalism, and he identifies his adequacy requirement as the reason for its externalism. See Alston (1989), pp. 239ff. But he also imposes a (watered-down) internalist condition (see p. 233), and thus calls his theory an "internalist externalism."

CHAPTER FIVE

FOUNDATIONALISM

BASIC BELIEFS

Philosophers who advocate foundationalism in one form or another maintain that a person's justified belief system—the totality of her justified beliefs—is structured in the following way.[1] First, there are *basic* beliefs, which make up a belief system's foundation, as opposed to *nonbasic* beliefs, which make up a belief system's superstructure. Second, each belief that belongs to the superstructure owes its justification ultimately to one or several beliefs in the foundation. Although it is agreed that these two claims are essential to any version of foundationalism, there is much disagreement as to what kinds of beliefs are basic and how they are related to nonbasic beliefs. Thus while there is something like *the* foundationalist conception of the structure of epistemic justification—the conjunction of the two claims above—there isn't one particular theory that qualifies as an undisputed representative of foundationalism as such. Rather, there is a multitude of different "foundationalisms," each of which is claimed by its advocates to be superior to the others. Obviously, this raises a difficulty for us: in order to discuss the virtues and vices of foundationalism, which particular version of it should we consider?

When discussing what can be said for and against a certain theory, it would be unfair to consider a version loaded with unnecessary features that are easy targets for criticism. Rather, one should always consider the most plausible construal of the theory in question. Later in the chapter, we shall consider, therefore, three different versions of foundationalism and, for the purpose of subsequent discussion, take as representative that version which asserts no more than what is logically dictated by committing oneself to the two claims mentioned above.

We begin our discussion of foundationalism with an examination of the concept of a basic belief.[2] Basic beliefs have three characteristics. First, they are *noninferential*, which means they are not inferred from other beliefs. Compare, for example, the two beliefs

(1) He's soaked.

(2) It's raining outside.

Suppose you believe that it's raining outside because you see that a man coming in from outside is wet; you infer (2) from (1). (1), in contrast, is not inferred from any other belief. Rather, you simply see, or observe, that the man you're looking at is soaked. In this situation, (2) is an inferential and (1) a noninferential belief.[3]

Here are two more examples of noninferential beliefs that serve as the basis for an inference. You see that your plant's leaves are sadly drooping; you infer you forgot to water it. You hear a certain characteristic sound in the hallway; you infer the mail was just delivered. In each of these cases, you infer one thing from another that is not, in turn, inferred from anything else.

Second, since basic beliefs play the role of justifiers for nonbasic beliefs, they must be *justified* themselves. Thus there can't be such a thing as an unjustified basic belief. Obviously, this is not true for noninferential beliefs in general, which can be justified or unjustified. For example, suppose after many days of rain, wishful thinking induces you to form the noninferential belief

(3) The sun is shining.

You have neither been outside nor looked out the window, nor has anyone told you that the sun is shining. In short, you have no evidence for (3). Thus (3) is not only noninferential but also unjustified, and therefore cannot play the role of a justifier. To see why not, suppose you were to infer

(4) It's warm outside

from (3). Since you are not justified in believing (3) in the first place, you're not justified in believing (4) either. This is so because a belief that doesn't "have" justification can't "give" justification to another. (3), then, is not a basic belief. Unlike (3), basic beliefs must, to repeat the main point, be able to transmit justification onto nonbasic beliefs, and thus must be justified themselves.

The first two characteristics of basic beliefs are closely linked to a third. When beliefs are both noninferential and justified, from where do they receive their justification? Foundationalists would say that they receive their justification from a *nondoxastic* source—that is, not from other beliefs, but from somewhere else: perception or introspection, for example. The third characteristic of basic beliefs, then, is that they are justified *nondoxasti-cally*—that is, *without receiving their justification from other beliefs*. Thus, when foundationalists claim that there are basic beliefs, they are implicitly saying that beliefs can receive justification in two altogether different ways: from other beliefs or from some nondoxastic source. When beliefs are justified in the former way, we shall speak of "doxastic" justification, and when they are justified in the latter way, of "nondoxastic" justification.

Although philosophers often assert that whenever a belief is justified it is justified doxastically, foundationalists insist that there is nondoxastic justification as well. They would say that the kind of justification we have for axiomatic a priori beliefs—which derives from logical or conceptual intuition—is nondoxastic. Furthermore, they would say that perception, introspection, and memory can provide us with nondoxastic justification for our beliefs. Let us consider two examples. Suppose you have formed the noninferential belief

(5)   This book is red.

Foundationalists would say that what justifies you in believing (5) is the perception of redness, or, as it is often put, the experience of *being appeared to redly*.[4] This experience must not be identified with a belief. Though perceptual experiences typically trigger beliefs, perceiving an object is not the same as having a belief about it. It is possible that the book appears redly to you without your believing anything about either it or its color. If you are presently not interested in whether or not there is a book in front of you, then you might not notice its color, even if it is plainly within your view.

Just as perceptual experiences can justify a belief nondoxastically, so can introspective experiences. For example, if you believe

(6)   I have a craving for a piece of chocolate

then that belief is justified, not by any other belief, but by your experience of having a craving for a piece of chocolate. And since this experience is not a further belief, but rather a mental state that is distinct from the belief that you have that craving, (6) is justified without receiving its justification from another belief.[5]

To summarize, basic beliefs are (i) noninferential, (ii) justified, and (iii) nondoxastically justified. Obviously, the third of these characteristics implies the second. Furthermore, if a justified belief is inferred from a second belief, then it receives its justification from this second belief. So, if a belief is justified without owing its justification to any other beliefs, it must be noninferential, which means that the third characteristic implies the first as well. Hence we may define basic beliefs simply by saying that they are justified without receiving their justification from any other beliefs.

FOUNDATIONALISM DEFINED

Having the concept of a basic belief available to us, we can now proceed to define foundationalism as such, or the hard core that is common to all versions of foundationalism.

> *Foundationalism*
> (i)　Many of our beliefs are basic;
> (ii)　Every justified inferential belief ultimately receives its justification from one or more basic beliefs.

Foundationalism, thus understood, is a theory about the *structure of belief systems*. It is not an *analysis* of epistemic justification. Recall what we said about the analysis of epistemic justification in Chapter 2: its objective is to specify what the property of being epistemically justified supervenes on. It should identify a nonevaluative property (or a set of properties) such that, necessarily, any belief instantiating this property (or set of properties) is justified. Obviously, our definition of foundationalism doesn't tell us anything about such a property. There are, however, analyses of epistemic justification that are foundationalist because they imply theses (i) and (ii). The general form of such a foundationalist theory of justification is this:

> S is justified in believing that *p* if and only if either S's belief that *p* has property F or bears relation R to one or more of S's beliefs that has property F.

An analysis of this form turns into a substantive version of foundationalism if F is replaced with a property that is both necessary and sufficient for a belief's being basic. It would then tell us that there are two kinds of justified beliefs: basic beliefs, which are justified by virtue of having property F; and nonbasic beliefs, which are justified by virtue of bearing relation R to one or several basic beliefs. In order to see how such a foundationalist analysis works out in detail, let us consider one particular version.

A SAMPLE FOUNDATIONALIST ANALYSIS

Let property F be the property of being *indubitable*, and relation R that of *entailment*. If a belief B1 entails a belief B2, then it is impossible that B1 is true and B2 is false. And if a belief is indubitable, so let us stipulate, there are no circumstances under which it would be reasonable for the subject who holds that belief to doubt its truth. My belief that I exist, for example, is indubitable in this sense. In contrast, my belief that my car is still in the parking lot where I parked it is not indubitable because there are possible circumstances under which it would be reasonable of me to doubt that belief. For example, if upon returning to the lot I don't find my car where I thought I left it, and I still don't find it after searching for it, then it would be reasonable of me to doubt it's still there.

Let us call our sample analysis "indubitability foundationalism." Indubitability foundationalism tells us the following:

> *S* is justified in believing that *p* if and only if either *S's* belief that *p* is indubitable or entailed by one or more indubitable beliefs.

If this analysis were true, we would have succeeded in specifying the nonevaluative grounds on which the evaluative property of being justified supervenes. However, indubitability foundationalism is unacceptable. There are many justified beliefs that are not indubitable, and there are many justified beliefs that are not entailed by indubitable beliefs. For example, my belief that last night's rainfall hasn't flooded my basement is justified, but it is neither indubitable nor entailed by any indubitable beliefs. A plausible version of foundationalism, then, can't define basic beliefs in terms of indubitability and relation *R* in terms of entailment.

THE REGRESS ARGUMENT

According to foundationalism, many of our beliefs are basic. On what grounds, however, do foundationalists maintain that there are beliefs that are justified without receiving their justification from other beliefs? The classical argument for the existence of basic beliefs is due to Aristotle (although he certainly cannot be called a "foundationalist" in the contemporary sense of the term). In *Posterior Analytics*, Aristotle formulated the following argument for the existence of what he called "nondemonstrative knowledge".[6]

Aristotle's Argument

Whenever you know something, your knowledge is demonstrative (derived from premises) or nondemonstrative (gained without being derived from premises). If what you know is derived from premises, you must know the premises themselves, for it is impossible to derive knowledge from unknown premises. But if your knowledge of these premises is demonstrative again, it must be derived from a further set of premises, which in turn you either known nondemonstratively or on the basis of yet another set of premises, and so forth. Hence whenever you know something, your knowledge is either derived from an infinite set of premises, or ultimately grounded in nondemonstrative knowledge. Knowledge, however, cannot be derived from an infinite set of premises. Hence if you know anything at all, some of your knowledge must be nondemonstrative.

This argument is a special case of what is commonly called a "regress argument." The point of a regress argument is to *support* a proposition by showing that we generate an infinite regress if we deny it, or to *attack* a proposition by showing that we generate an infinite regress if we assert it. In formulating such an argument, it is always presupposed that the infinite regress in question is intellectually unacceptable.[7]

Since knowledge is intimately related to belief and justification, there is a close connection between nondemonstrative knowledge and basic beliefs. If something is known nondemonstratively, the belief in question (i.e., the belief that amounts to an instance of nondemonstrative knowledge) cannot be justified by other beliefs, and thus must be basic. Hence Aristotle's argument can readily be turned into an argument for the existence of basic beliefs.

The Regress Argument for the Existence of Basic Beliefs

Suppose a belief B1 is justified. Either B1 is basic or nonbasic. If B1 is nonbasic, then there must be a belief B2 that justifies B1. But for B2 to justify B1, B2 must be justified itself. If B2 is nonbasic in turn, then there must be a belief B3 that justifies B2. And since B3 must be justified itself, B3 is either basic or there must be a belief B4 justifying B3. This regress either terminates in a basic belief or it continues ad infinitum. However, an infinite regress of justifying beliefs cannot justify anything. Thus, given our assumption that B1 is justified, the regress must terminate in a basic belief.

According to this argument, there cannot be any justified beliefs at all unless there are basic beliefs capable of terminating a regress of justifying reasons. Thus the argument assigns a precise function to basic beliefs: basic beliefs are *regress terminators*. It should be evident, therefore, why we have defined basic beliefs as beliefs that are justified without receiving their justification from any other beliefs: if a basic belief is to play the role of a regress terminator, it must be capable of conferring justification on other beliefs without receiving its own justification from yet another belief in the justificatory chain.

Before we proceed, we should clear up two possible misconceptions. First, foundationalism does not imply that *every* basic belief terminates a regress. After all, you may hold a basic belief without inferring anything from it. Rather, what foundationalism does imply is that whenever a belief derives its justification from a chain of supporting beliefs, there must be a basic belief that terminates this regress. Second, foundationalism does not imply that nonbasic beliefs are always supported by single-string regresses. Rather, a nonbasic belief can lie at the head of a multiple-string regress. The following figure represents a possible foundational structure of justification:

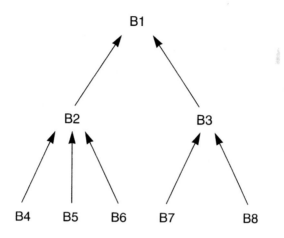

The justificatory regress begins with two nodes connecting B1 with two further nonbasic beliefs, B2 and B3. It ends with the first node branching out into three and the second node branching out into two more beliefs. The epistemic foundation of B1, then, consists in beliefs B4 through B8, while beliefs B2 and B3 function as intermediate justifiers.[8]

THE REGRESS PROBLEM AND SKEPTICISM

It is important to distinguish between the regress *problem* we encounter in the analysis of justification and particular regress *arguments*.[9] The regress problem arises from the threat of infinity in a regress of justifying reasons. Unless a belief B1 is basic, it can be justified only if it is based on a reason— that is, on a belief B2 that justifies B1. But for B2 to justify B1, it must be justified itself. Thus, unless B2 is basic, the necessity of a further reason, B3, arises. Since B3 must be justified in turn, unless B3 is basic, yet another reason is necessary, and so forth. In order to solve the regress problem, it must be shown that it is possible for a belief to be justified without depending for its justification on an infinite regress of reasons.

Particular regress arguments, in contrast, always represent a certain response to the regress problem. The regress argument for *foundationalism*, for example, concludes that there must be basic beliefs, for otherwise the justificatory regress could not be stopped. It would be a mistake, however, to believe that the only cogent response to the regress problem is an argument on behalf of foundationalism. In fact, the regress problem can also give rise to an argument in support of *skepticism*. Notice that the regress argument for the existence of basic beliefs begins with the supposition that B1 is justified. Skeptics about justification could deny this assumption. Since a basic belief is supposed to be a belief that is justified without owing its justification to any other beliefs, skeptics might ask from where its justification comes. Denying that experience by itself can justify, they could argue that either a belief owes its justification to other beliefs or it cannot be justified at all. They could continue the argument by agreeing with foundationalists that if basic beliefs can't exist, regress termination is impossible. And then, pointing out that an infinite regress cannot justify anything, they would conclude that there are no justified beliefs at all. So from the skeptics' point of view, the regress argument as employed by foundationalists shows at best no more than this: *if* there are justified beliefs, then there must be basic beliefs.

However, from the foundationalist point of view, the skeptical employment of the regress argument also yields only a hypothetical result: *if* there are no basic beliefs, then there are no justified beliefs at all. And since foundationalists believe that our beliefs are by and large justified, they ultimately conclude that there must be basic beliefs. Nevertheless, the fact that skeptics can formulate a regress argument for their own purposes shows that if foundationalists wish to derive an advantage from employing a regress argument for the existence of basic beliefs, they must defend the nonskeptical premise that our beliefs are by and large justified.

THE REGRESS PROBLEM AND COHERENTISM

A further premise on which the regress argument rests is the assumption that, should basic beliefs be impossible, the regress of justifying reasons must continue *ad infinitum*. While foundationalists and skeptics both accept this premise, coherentists—who advocate that justification is solely generated through coherence—reject it. Coherentists deny that there is such a thing as nondoxastic justification, and thus deny that there are basic beliefs. On the other hand, taking our beliefs by and large to be justified, they side with foundationalists in rejecting skepticism. Hence in order to avoid skepticism, they must deny what both foundationalists and skeptics accept—to wit, that in the absence of basic beliefs, the regress of justifying reasons will continue forever.

But if the idea of regress termination through basic beliefs is abandoned, how can it be shown that justification is nevertheless possible? For one thing, coherentists might claim that a regress can eventually circle back to its point of origin. Suppose again that B1 is a justified belief, owing its justification to B2, which in turn is justified by B3. Couldn't B3 receive its justification from B1? If it did, then the regress would have come full circle. Foundationalists believe that such circularity is just as unacceptable as skepticism. Thus they typically argue that if we are to avoid the two pitfalls of skepticism and circularity, we must conclude that there are basic beliefs.[10] Coherentists might reply, however, that circularity need not be such a bad thing. They might say that a circular regress can justify the beliefs involved in it if the circle is sufficiently large and rich in content.[11] In the next chapter, we shall return to this argument and examine it in some detail.

Furthermore, coherentists can challenge the *linear* conception of justification that the regress argument presupposes. A conception of justification is linear if it is assumed that whenever a belief B is justified, its justification can be traced back to one or more particular beliefs, and that these beliefs owe their justification in turn to still further particular beliefs. In contrast, according to a *holistic* conception of justification, beliefs are not justified by virtue of bearing such linear relations to other beliefs; rather, they owe their justification to the coherence the subject's belief system enjoys *as a whole*. Now if that is indeed how justification is generated, a justificatory regress doesn't get started in the first place. Suppose once again that B1 is a justified belief. Coherentists could say B1 is justified because it is a member of a system of beliefs that, as a whole, is coherent. Hence there is no need for a belief B2, which justifies B1 and must be justified in turn, thus creating the need for a belief B3. So, according to a holistic conception of justification, a belief's justification involves only a two-place relation—a relation between the belief itself and the subject's belief system as a whole—and thus does not depend on a regress of justifying beliefs.

IS AN INFINITE REGRESS REALLY IMPOSSIBLE?

A third assumption on which the regress argument rests is that if a belief depends for its justification on an infinite regress of beliefs, it couldn't possibly be justified. This assumption can be defended in two ways. First, it could be argued that an infinite regress cannot justify any beliefs because humans, having finite minds, are not capable of forming an infinite number of beliefs. Second, it could be defended on the ground that justification through an infinite regress of reasons is logically impossible. We must, then, examine the following two issues: First, is an infinite regress of beliefs psychologically possible? Second, is it logically possible for a belief to be justified by an infinite regress of reasons?

As to the first question, Ernest Sosa has argued that the possibility of an infinite regress should not be dismissed too easily.[12] Consider the following example:

B1   There is at least one even number.
B2   There are at least two even numbers.
B3   There are at least three even numbers.

Can you add beliefs on to this series ad infinitum? It might be argued that you do in fact hold an infinite number of beliefs, since for any n, you believe this:

Bn   There are at least n even numbers.

However, we must distinguish between your readiness in principle to believe Bn for any n and your actual capacity to form such beliefs for very high numbers. Robert Audi has argued that, beyond a certain point, the requisite beliefs could not be formed by finite minds. According to Audi,

> for a finite mind there will be some point or other at which the relevant proposition cannot be grasped. The required formulation (or entertaining of the proposition) would, at some point on the way "toward" infinity, become too lengthy to permit understanding it. Thus, even if we could read or entertain it part by part, when we got to the end we would be unable to remember enough of the first part to grasp and thereby believe what the formulation expresses.[13]

Audi's argument provides us with a strong reason against the psychological possibility of an infinite regress of reasons in the form of an actual infinite series of beliefs in a person's mind. Thus as far as the first question is concerned, our verdict should be a negative.

Let us now turn to the second question. For the sake of argument, let us grant the psychological possibility of an infinite regress of reasons—that is, let us suppose we can in fact form beliefs of the form Bn for any n. Could the belief at the head of the regress, B1, be justified by the infinity of the beliefs succeeding it? The argument to the effect that it could not runs as follows: B1 is justified only if B2 is justified. So B1 depends for its justification on B2. Likewise, B2 depends for its justification on B3, and so forth. To generalize: Each member of the series depends for its justification on the immediately succeeding member. But this means that B1 remains unjustified unless the regress terminates in a belief that does not depend for its justification on yet another belief in the series.

Consider an analogy. Suppose I wish to borrow five dollars from you and you tell me: "I don't have five dollars right now, but over there is Jack, who owes me five dollars. If I get five dollars from him, then I'll give them to you." Now when you ask Jack, he tells you what you told me: "I don't have five dollars right now, but over there is Jim, who owes me five dollars. If I get five dollars from him, then I'll give them to you." Clearly, if the search for someone to borrow five dollars from continues ad infinitum, I'll never get the five dollars I need. *Someone* in the chain of potential lenders actually has to have the five dollars without in turn depending on someone else from whom to get five dollars. Likewise, if the regress of beliefs of the form Bn continues ad infinitum, B1 will never get justified. At some point in the regress, a belief must be justified without depending for its justification on yet another belief, or else there will never be any justification generated that can be transmitted all the way up to B1.

It is safe to say, then, that at least one of the premises of the regress argument for basic beliefs is beyond reproach: for a regress of justifying reasons that doesn't terminate, it is impossible to justify the belief at its beginning. However, foundationalists must admit that the regress argument does not straightforwardly establish the existence of basic beliefs. It is an effective defense of foundationalism only if accompanied by further argumentation against coherentism and skepticism.

SELF-JUSTIFICATION

We have defined basic beliefs as beliefs that are justified without owing their justification to other beliefs. However, both advocates and critics of foundationalism have typically assumed that for a belief to be basic, it must enjoy what is called an "epistemic privilege." For a belief to be epistemically privileged, it must have a feature that the ordinary mass of beliefs lacks. Standard examples of an epistemically privileged status are that of being self-justified, certain, indubitable, or infallible. In this section, we shall examine whether for a belief to be basic, it must really enjoy any of these epistemic privileges.

According to Keith Lehrer, a leading coherentist and critic of foundationalism, a belief cannot be basic unless it is *self-justified*. He writes that foundationalism can be characterized

> by specifying the conditions that must be met for a belief to be basic. The first is that a basic belief must be self-justified rather than being justified entirely by relations to other beliefs.[14]

This claim raises two issues. First, is it possible for a belief to be self-justified? Second, is Lehrer right in claiming that for a belief to be basic, it must be self-justified?

The first question must be answered negatively.[15] The relation "*x* justifies *y*" is *irreflexive*, which means that just as one can't be one's own father, a belief can't be its own justifier.[16] Compare self-justification with the idea that God created himself. When God created himself, either he existed already or he did not. If he did, then he existed in the first place, and thus could not have created himself. And if he did not, then he *could* not have created himself. In the first case, self-creation could not have taken place because what exists already cannot be created again, just as a child that is already born cannot be born again, or a cup of coffee that is already brewed cannot be brewed again. In the second case, God could not have created himself, for in order for him to create anything, he must exist already. The idea of self-creation, then, is an idea of something that is impossible; nothing can create itself.[17]

A parallel argument applies to self-justification. Any allegedly self-justified belief is either justified in the first place or it is not. If it is, then it can't justify itself because it is *already* justified, just as one can't bake a loaf of bread that is already baked, write a letter that is already written, or melt an ice cube that is already melted. And if the belief is not already justified, then it can't justify itself because a belief that doesn't have justification can't transmit justification on to any other beliefs or itself, just as somebody who doesn't have any money can't give money to anyone, including himself.[18] We are to conclude, therefore, that self-justification is impossible.

Let us now turn to the second issue Lehrer raises. Is he right in claiming that basic beliefs must be self-justified? Suppose he is. Since self-justification is impossible, in that case there couldn't be any basic beliefs, and foundationalism would certainly be a mistaken view. However, foundationalists need not agree with Lehrer that basic beliefs must be self-justified. In the passage cited above, it is clear that Lehrer makes this assumption: either a belief is justified by relations to other beliefs or it is self-justified. From the foundationalist point of view, however, this is a false dichotomy, for Lehrer's assumption leaves out the possibility of justification arising from nondoxastic sources. Recall what it takes for a belief to be basic—that is, to play the role of a regress terminator: it must be justified without owing its justification to another belief. Surely this doesn't imply that it must receive its justification from itself. Rather, as pointed out above, foundationalists can maintain that basic beliefs are justified by perceptual, introspective, and memorial experiences. According to this view, basic beliefs, unlike self-justified beliefs, do have an external source of justification—a source, however, that does not include any beliefs. They are neither justified by other beliefs nor self-justified.

INDUBITABILITY, INFALLIBILITY, AND CERTAINTY

In this section, we shall examine why basic beliefs, if defined as beliefs that are nondoxastically justified, need be neither indubitable nor infallible nor certain. Let us begin with *indubitability*, and let us define indubitable beliefs as a beliefs that it would, under any circumstances whatever, be unreasonable to doubt. Descartes's first Meditation provides us with the standard example of such a belief: I exist. Since the activity of doubting would always be evidence for one's existence, there cannot be any circumstances under which it would be reasonable to doubt that one exists.

Now, what is constitutive of basic beliefs is this: they are justified without owing their justification to any other beliefs. Foundationalists would say that if, for example, the belief

(1)   This object is red

is justified through a perceptual experience, without receiving any of its justification from other beliefs, then it is basic. But (1) is not an indubitable belief, for certainly there are situations in which it would be reasonable to doubt that (1) is true. For example, if I am wearing red sunglasses, then I might have reason to doubt that the object before me is really red. Thus, according to our definition of basic beliefs, a belief's being basic does not require indubitability.[19]

A parallel argument will show that basic beliefs need not be *infallible*. A belief is infallible if there are no circumstances under which the subject could form a belief of that type and be mistaken. The belief "I exist" may serve us again as an example. Since believing anything presupposes the believer's existence, one couldn't possibly believe oneself to exist and be mistaken in this belief.

To see that a belief can be basic without being infallible, consider again belief (1), which we are assuming to be basic—that is, to be justified by a nondoxastic source. However, (1) is not an infallible belief. For example, if I am looking at a white object and unbeknownst to me it is illuminated by red light, then I might mistakenly believe the object to be red. Nondoxastic justification, therefore, does not require infallibility, which means that being infallible is not a condition basic beliefs must meet.

Finally, let's turn to *certainty*. Let us say that a belief B is certain if and only if it enjoys the highest possible epistemic status. This means that if B is certain, there couldn't be another belief B^* such that B^* is justified to a higher degree than B.[20] Now consider again our example of a basic belief:

(1) This object is red.

This belief is not certain, even if it is justified by an undefeated experience of being appeared to redly, for there are other beliefs—for example, the belief that two plus two equals four and the belief "I exist"—that are justified to a higher degree than (1). Hence certainty is not a necessary condition of basic beliefs.

None of these arguments establishes that it really is possible for a belief to be basic in the sense in which we defined basic beliefs. They merely demonstrate that *if* we define basic beliefs in the way we have, then they need not be indubitable, nor infallible, nor certain. Having established that much, we shall next examine the question of *how* it is possible for beliefs to be basic.

BASIC BELIEFS AND EXPERIENCE

As members of complex belief systems, basic beliefs function as regress terminators. In order to perform this function, they must be justified without receiving their justification from other beliefs. One way in which beliefs can be thus justified is through perceptual *experience*. For example, my belief "There is a red object before me" is basic if it is justified by the experience of being appeared to redly. And my belief "There is a triangular object before me" is basic if it is justified by the experience of being appeared to triangularly. The general idea is that the experience of *being appeared to F-ly* can, without the help of any further beliefs, justify my belief "There is an *F* before me." However, we shall now see that it is not easy to turn this idea into an account of justification that is immune to objections.

To begin with, let us ask whether *being appeared to F-ly* is sufficient for *being justified in believing that there is an F before one*. Suppose I know that I am not reliable in discerning whether an object is an *F* or not: I know that most of the time when I try to decide whether what I am looking at is an *F* or not, I get things wrong. Under such conditions, I am *not* justified in believing an object before me to be an *F* even if it looks like an *F* to me. Hence, *being appeared to F-ly* is not sufficient for *being justified in believing there is an F before me*.

Consider an example. I know that I am reliable in recognizing, without counting sides, triangles, but not dodecagons (polygons with twelve angles).[21] If I look at a triangle, I am appeared to triangularly, which justifies me in believing that the object before me has a triangular shape. In contrast, if I look at a dodecagon, then I am appeared to dodecagonally, but I am *not* justified in believing that the object before me is shaped dodecagonally. The difference between the two cases is that the experience of *being appeared to triangularly* is evidence for me to believe that the object before me is triangular, while the experience of *being appeared to dodecagonally* is not evidence for me to believe that the object before me is a dodecagon, simply because I lack the ability to recognize twelve angles without counting.[22] Consequently, the former experience can justify me in believing that there is a triangular-shaped object before me, but the latter experience cannot justify me in believing that there is a dodecagonal object before me. We must conclude, therefore, that it is possible to be appeared to *F*-ly without being justified in believing that there is an *F* before one, which is to say that being appeared to *F*-ly is not sufficient for being justified in believing that there is an *F* before me.

We are now in a position to see clearly what problem foundationalists face when they try to explain how basic beliefs are justified. According to foundationalists, a belief such as "This is an *F*" can be basic. When such a belief is basic, they would claim, then it is justified by the experience of *being appeared to F-ly*. But as we just saw, it is possible for me to be appeared to *F*-ly without being justified in believing that there is an *F* before me. This means foundationalists can't explain how a basic belief such as "This is an *F*" is justified simply by saying that it is justified by the experience of being appeared to *F*-ly. Rather, in addition to the condition of being appeared to *F*-ly, some further condition must be satisfied in order for me to be justified in believing "There is an *F* before me." We shall now examine three candidates for the missing condition.

BASIC BELIEFS AND RELIABILITY

One prominent approach to explaining how basic beliefs are justified appeals to the concept of reliability.[23] Let us consider, then, the idea that the needed condition is that *S* be reliable in discerning *F*-things. According to this proposal, my belief "This is an F" is basic if the following three conditions are satisfied: (i) I am appeared to F-ly; (ii) there are no other beliefs of mine justifying my belief "This is an F"; (iii) I am reliable in discerning F-things.

This proposal is open to an objection we will discuss again in the chapter on reliabilism: the objection that in an evil-demon world one's beliefs are justified even though one's cognitive faculties are unreliable. Suppose the totality of your perceptual experiences is caused by an evil demon. You are an immaterial spirit deceived into believing that there is a world of physical objects when in fact there is none, but you don't have any reason to suppose that you are the victim of such a deception. Under such conditions, condition (ii) of our proposal is not satisfied, yet your beliefs about the actually nonexisting physical world are by and large justified, just as they are in the actual world.

This verdict is based on the premise that if an experience E1 in a world W1, and a further experience E2 in a world W2, are phenomenally indistinguishable, then either both E1 and E2 are justifying experience or neither is. Suppose you are having an experience E1 in the actual world that justifies you in believing that there is a cat before you. Suppose further that in the evil-demon world we are considering you have an experience E2 that is, from your subjective point of view, indistinguishable in its qualities from E1. According to the objection, given that E1 justifies you in believing that there is a cat before you, E2 in the evil-demon world justifies you in believing the same. However, while in the actual world you are reliable at discerning cats, in the evil-demon world you are not. (If you were, then you would notice that there aren't any cats in that world.) It is possible, therefore, to be justified in believing that there is a cat in front of one even if one is not reliable at discerning cats.

Foundationalists who take this objection to be decisive must conclude that it is possible to be justified in believing "This is an F" without being reliable in discerning F-things, and thus that condition (i) must be abandoned.

BASIC BELIEFS AND PRESUMPTIVE RELIABILITY

Yet it is difficult to brush away the idea that reliability is important. Neglecting bizarre scenarios such as being deceived by an evil demon, a lack of reliability *does* typically mean a lack of justification. If you are unreliable in discerning cats—that is, if you really can't successfully identify cats—then you cannot be justified in believing an animal to be a cat (unless someone else whom you can trust on this matter tells you so). Let us consider, therefore, a condition that demands, not that I *am* reliable in discerning F-things, but rather that I *have good evidence* for believing myself to be reliable in discerning F-things. According to this proposal, my belief "There is an F before me" is basic if the following three conditions are satisfied: (i) I am appeared to *F*-ly; (ii) there are no other beliefs of mine justifying my belief "There is an *F* before me"; (iii) I have good evidence for taking myself to be reliable in discerning *F*-things.

Condition (iii) in this proposal may be regarded as an *internalist* reliability condition, as opposed to condition (iii) in the previous proposal, which is an *externalist* reliability condition.[24] According to the latter, justification requires *de facto* reliability. According to the former, justification requires only *presumptive* reliability: reliability one would, on the basis of good evidence, be justified in attributing to oneself. Let us, therefore, call condition (iii) in our second proposal the "presumptive reliability condition." Whether I am, as a matter of fact, reliable in discerning *F*-things is, in relation to my subjective point of view, an external affair in the sense that I might be unable to tell whether I am. In contrast, whether I have good evidence for taking myself to be reliable in discerning *F*-things is a question that is internal to my subjective perspective: as long as I am capable of evaluating the evidence, I can tell whether I have good evidence for taking myself to be reliable in discerning *F*-things.

Condition (iii), then, requires that reliability be discernible on the basis of "internal" evidence. What, however, does it take to satisfy this condition? Under which conditions do you have good evidence for believing yourself to be reliable in discerning a certain thing? Let's consider an example. Do you have good evidence for believing yourself to be reliable in discerning kiwi fruit? Well, if you know what a kiwi looks like, then your evidence would be a piece of self-knowledge: your knowing that you know what a kiwi looks like. You can picture a kiwi in your mind, and you know that if you were to go to the produce section of a supermarket, you could pick out kiwis without any trouble. Here is another example. I can't tell a raven from a crow, and I know I can't. Hence I do *not* have good evidence for believing myself to be reliable in recognizing crows and ravens. To the contrary, I have good evidence for believing myself to be unreliable in recognizing crows and ravens. If I were to see a raven and thus be appeared to raven-like, I would not (without further evidence) be justified in believing that I am seeing a raven. If, however, I were appeared to kiwi-like, then I would be justified in believing that there is a kiwi before me, for knowing myself to know what kiwis look like, I have good evidence for taking myself to be reliable in discerning kiwis.

Is the second proposal superior to the first? The second proposal acknowledges the intuitive plausibility of a reliability condition but, unlike the first, avoids the problems of externalist reliabilism by internalizing it. The externalist reliability condition runs into the problem of an evil-demon world, as explained in the previous section. The presumed reliability condition, however, does not: though the victim of an evil demon's deception lacks, ex hypothesi, de facto reliability, she need not lack presumptive reliability. Hence the third proposal, unlike the second one, does not imply that the empirical beliefs of an evil-demon victim are unjustified.

Next, let's see how the presumed reliability condition solves the problem foundationalists face when they attempt to explain how basic beliefs such as "The object before me is red" are justified. As explained at the beginning of this section, this problem arises when we consider the experience of being appeared to dodecagonally. Since this experience is no evidence at all for me to believe "The object before me is a dodecagon," *being appeared to dodecagonally* does not justify me in believing "This object is a dodecagon." How can foundationalists maintain that, on the other hand, the experience of *being appeared to redly* can justify me in believing "The object before me is red"? Precisely what is the difference between the two experiences? According to the second proposal, the difference is that I have evidence for taking myself to be reliable in discerning the color red, whereas I do not have evidence for taking myself to be reliable in discerning dodecagons.[25] Hence the experience of being appeared to redly can justify me in believing that there is a red object before me, whereas the experience of being appeared to dodecagonally cannot justify me in believing that there is a dodecagonal object before me.

According to our second proposal, then, the question of how basic beliefs are justified can be answered thus: Basic beliefs are justified by appropriate experiences of being appeared to in certain ways and, in addition, by the fact that the subject may presume the relevant experiences to be a reliable source of information.

CLASSICAL FOUNDATIONALISM

A foundationalist account of justification must, as we have seen, provide an answer to two questions: (i) What makes a belief basic? (ii) How is justification transmitted from basic to nonbasic beliefs? Different versions of foundationalism answer these questions differently. In this section of the chapter we shall study three such versions: classical, strong, and minimal foundationalism.

According to classical foundationalism, a belief cannot be justified unless what justifies it provides the subject with a guarantee of its truth. Now in order for us to get a guarantee of truth extending to both basic and nonbasic beliefs, two conditions would have to be met: basic beliefs would have to be *infallible*, and nonbasic beliefs would have to follow *deductively* from basic beliefs. According to classical foundationalism, then, basic beliefs cannot be false, and nonbasic beliefs receive their justification from basic beliefs via deduction. An example of classical foundationalism is Descartes's epistemology. In his *Meditations on First Philosophy*, Descartes attempted to prove the existence of an external world from such infallible certainties as "I exist" and "I am thinking."

Among contemporary philosophers, it would be quite difficult to find advocates of classical foundationalism. In fact, today there is widespread agreement that classical foundationalism is a philosophical dead end. To appreciate the reasons for this verdict, we must distinguish between *appearance* beliefs (a subspecies of introspective beliefs) and *physical object* beliefs. The former are beliefs about how the physical world appears to me. Thus beliefs such as "I am appeared to redly" or "There appears to be a triangular object before me" are appearance beliefs. In contrast, physical object beliefs are about the physical world itself; examples are "This object is red" and "There is a triangular object before me." Now, what matters about physical object beliefs is that they are fallible. When we form beliefs about the world around us, there is always some risk of error involved.

What, then, is so objectionable about classical foundationalism? To begin with, since physical object beliefs are fallible, classical foundationalists must exclude them from the foundation. Rather, the foundation must consist of beliefs that, unlike physical object beliefs, are infallible. Appearance beliefs are supposed to fill the bill: according to foundationalists, they are infallible. But are they really infallible? Critics of foundationalism would say that the number of infallible beliefs is extremely limited, even among appearance beliefs.[26] If they are right, then classical foundationalism would imply that the number of basic beliefs is extremely small, restricted to beliefs such as "I exist" and "I am thinking right now." Certainly that would be a serious problem for classical foundationalism, for we may wonder how the entire range of our physical object beliefs could be justified by such a thin foundation.

For the sake of argument, though, let us suppose that there are indeed many introspective beliefs about one's perceptual experiences that are infallible. We are assuming, then, that when you believe yourself to be appeared to in a certain way, you couldn't be mistaken about the way you are appeared to. Nevertheless, the number of justified nonbasic beliefs will remain unimpressive. In fact, it's hard to see how, if classical foundationalism were true, there could be *any* justified nonbasic beliefs, because physical object beliefs don't follow deductively from beliefs about perceptual experiences. There is a logical gap between propositions describing perceptual experiences and propositions describing external physical objects. A proposition of the latter kind can't follow deductively from a set of propositions of the former kind. Suppose I believe

B1   I'm appeared to redly

from which I infer the belief

B2   There is a red object before me.

According to classical foundationalism, if B2 is a justified nonbasic belief, then it must receive its justification from B1 via a deductive support relation. This means that B2 is justified only if the argument "B1, therefore B2" is deductively valid, which, of course, it is not. If, for example, I am under the influence of a drug that makes me hallucinate the presence of a red object when in fact there is nothing red before me, the argument's premise is true and its conclusion false. In general, since it is possible to be appeared to F-ly when there is no object that is an F in front of one, no argument of the form

> I'm appeared to F-ly
>
> Therefore:
>
> There is an object before me that is F

can be valid.[27] Thus it follows that appearance beliefs can't justify physical object beliefs via deductive support relations. Hence, if classical foundationalism were true, it would be a version of skepticism, for then our beliefs about the physical objects surrounding us would all be unjustified.

MODERN FOUNDATIONALISM

Modern foundationalism is akin to classical foundationalism in demanding that basic beliefs enjoy an epistemic privilege, but differs from it in allowing for *nondeductive* transmission of justification from basic to nonbasic beliefs. Thus while modern foundationalism is not vulnerable to the objection that the evidential gap between the foundation and the superstructure cannot be bridged deductively, it is still vulnerable to the criticism that appearance beliefs are not capable of enjoying an epistemic privilege such as certainty, indubitability, or even infallibility. However, advocates of modern foundationalism need not agree with this criticism. Indeed, it is far from obvious that there couldn't be a wide range of appearance beliefs about one's own perceptual experiences that are either certain, indubitable, or infallible.[28]

However, even if advocates of modern foundationalism could make a good case for the claim that, in typical cases, introspective beliefs about one's own perceptual states are infallible, there would still be a formidable problem, for normally we just don't form introspective beliefs about the ways in which we are appeared to. When you see a cat, you believe "There is a cat there," but you don't believe "I am appeared to cat-like."[29] In fact, with the exception of those who have studied the epistemology of perception, most people would not even know how to form such beliefs. It takes training to distinguish between the actual cat that is being perceived and the corresponding cat-like visual experience (the state of being appeared to cat-like). Finally, it is only natural to ignore the phenomenology of one's perception and instead to focus directly on the objects one perceives. For example, if the cat is hungry and must be fed, what matters is not the cat-like visual experience, but the cat itself. And when you cross a street and a truck is approaching, it would be a big mistake to focus your attention on the quality of your present perceptual experiences instead of on the truck.

This is not to say that we never pay attention to the phenomenal quality of our experiences. We do, for example, when we suspect that our senses might be deceiving us. The point, however, is that such situations do not occur very often. *Normally*, we just don't form beliefs about how we are appeared to. Consequently, if basic beliefs must indeed be infallible, then under ordinary circumstances (i.e., those in which we don't form beliefs about the phenomenal qualities of our perceptual experiences), there simply wouldn't be any foundation for physical object beliefs to rest on.[30]

A parallel argument can be formulated for other kinds of epistemic privilege. The gist of any such argument is the same: Physical object beliefs don't enjoy any epistemic privilege, only appearance beliefs do. So if basic beliefs must enjoy an epistemic privilege, only appearance beliefs can be basic. However, typically we don't form any appearance beliefs. Thus the requirement that basic beliefs enjoy an epistemic privilege leads to the consequence that our physical object beliefs are not normally justified, and hence turns foundationalism into a version of skepticism.

MINIMAL FOUNDATIONALISM

Minimal foundationalism marks a significant departure from the foundationalist tradition. Typically, foundationalists have held an elitist conception of basic beliefs: for beliefs to be eligible for membership in the foundational club, they had to have an epistemic privilege of one form or another. Thus the typical foundationalist picture of the structure of belief systems has been this: the superstructure comprises physical object beliefs, the foundation comprises introspective beliefs about one's own perceptual experiences. Minimal foundationalism revises this picture. Basic beliefs need not be epistemically privileged, so nothing bars them from being about physical objects. According to minimal foundationalism, then, the difference between beliefs in the superstructure and those in the foundation is not a function of belief content; rather, whether a belief belongs to the foundation or the superstructure is solely a function of how it received its justification. If it received its justification through an experience and not from any other beliefs, then it is foundational. If, however, it received its justification from one or more other beliefs, then it belongs to the superstructure.

Here is an example to illustrate how minimal foundationalism is supposed to work. Suppose that, coming home from work, I see my wife's coat in the closet, which surprises me, for normally she comes home after me. I also see a bag of groceries on the counter in the kitchen, I smell coffee, and I hear footsteps upstairs. I form these four beliefs:

> Her coat in the closet. There's a bag of groceries in the kitchen. I smell coffee. I hear footsteps upstairs.

An advocate of minimal foundationalism would say that each of these beliefs is justified by a perceptual experience, without owing any of its justification to any other beliefs. Hence, each of these beliefs is basic—that is, a member of the foundation of my belief system at the time in question. From these beliefs, I infer about my wife:

> She came home early. She went grocery shopping. She made coffee. She is upstairs.

Since these beliefs owe their justification to the beliefs in the first set, and to certain other beliefs of mine (e.g., that my wife normally comes home after me, that there is no one else living in my house who could have bought groceries and made coffee, etc.), they are nonbasic, and thus members of the superstructure. Now, what divides the two sets of beliefs is not that the members of the first set enjoy a certain epistemic privilege that the members of the second set do not. Rather, what divides the two sets is how their members are justified. The members of the first set are justified nondoxastically, the members of the second set doxastically—that is, by other beliefs. Notice that both sets contain beliefs about objects external to the world of my perceptual experiences. The first set contains beliefs about a coat and a bag of groceries, and the second set beliefs about my wife.

Unlike its classical and modern counterparts, minimal foundationalism is not vulnerable to criticisms according to which the vast majority of our beliefs fall short of enjoying any epistemic privileges, for it doesn't make having any such privilege a necessary condition for basic beliefs. To the contrary, minimal foundationalism makes it quite easy for a belief to be basic: if it's justified by reason, perception, introspection, or memory, and does not receive any of its justification from other beliefs, then it is basic. On this view, basic beliefs are not a select few, but instead make up a rather large proportion of a person's doxastic system. Thus, in judging the viability of minimal foundationalism, the chief question we have to discuss is this: Is it really possible for a belief to be justified without receiving its justification from other beliefs? In Chapter 7, we shall examine, among other related issues, arguments for and against answering this question with "yes."

FOUNDATIONALISM AND COHERENCE

Before we move on to examine coherentism and then discuss the pros and cons of foundationalism and coherentism, respectively, one last thing needs to be emphasized. Whereas coherentists assert that foundationalism is false because there can't be basic beliefs, foundationalists do not assert that coherentism is false because coherence is not a source of justification. To the contrary, foundationalists fully acknowledge that a belief system's coherence contributes to the justification of its members.

They do so in two ways. First, they make coherence a necessary condition for justification by viewing coherence as resulting from the absence of defeating background beliefs. Consider again the example from the previous section. Hold everything constant except for one change: as soon as I come home, my wife calls me on the phone and tells me that she will be late tonight. In that case, the evidence I have for believing that she's at home is defeated. Foundationalists hold, therefore, that a belief is justified only if it coheres with—in the sense that it is not defeated by—the subject's relevant background beliefs.[31]

Second, there is no reason foundationalists should not acknowledge that if a belief coheres with other beliefs, it is more justified than it would be if it did not. For an illustration of this point, the same example will serve us again. Suppose the only evidence I have for believing my wife to be already at home is the fact that her coat, which she usually wears when she goes to work, is in the closet. However, couldn't it be that today she decided to wear her leather jacket? Or couldn't it be that she came home, put her coat in the closet, and then left to go to the gym? Because of these possibilities, if the presence of my wife's coat in the closet were the only evidence of my wife's early arrival, then I would have some justification for assuming she's at home, but certainly not very much. However, if I also smell coffee, see new groceries on the kitchen counter, and hear footsteps upstairs, then my justification is much stronger, for then I am forming a group of beliefs that compose a coherent whole, and under these circumstances my belief that my wife is at home is supported very well. In this first situation, I not only have more evidence, I have evidence that is qualitatively better than the evidence I have in the first situation. In that situation, I have just one bit of evidence that stands on its own; whereas in the second situation, I have several pieces of evidence that support one another.[32]

It would be a mistake, then, to think that foundationalists must deny that the concept of coherence has an important role to play in the account of the structure of epistemic justification. In fact, recent advocates of foundationalism have explicitly acknowledged coherence as a source of justification.[33] They are not at all opposed to appreciating the epistemic virtues of coherence, only to the view that, in addition to coherence, there are no other sources of justification. Nevertheless, many philosophers think that the foundationalist approach to the analysis of epistemic justification is mistaken. In the next chapter, we will examine the views of two philosophers who reject foundationalism and defend coherentism instead.

STUDY QUESTIONS

1. Can basic beliefs, as defined in this chapter, be unjustified?
2. What are the two defining tenets of foundationalism?

3. What kind of a regress problem arises when we ask the question of how it is possible for a belief to be justified?
4. How do (i) foundationalists, (ii) coherentists, and (iii) skeptics respond to this problem?
5. Which reasons support the claim that an infinite regress of reasons can't justify a belief?
6. Need basic beliefs, as defined in this chapter, be (i) self-justifying, (ii) indubitable, (iii) infallible, or (iv) certain?
7. Which problem arises in the attempt to explain how basic beliefs are justified?
8. What objection is there to a reliabilist solution to this problem?
9. How could this problem be solved in terms of presumptive reliability?
10. How do (i) classical, (ii) modern, and (iii) minimal foundationalism differ from one another?

EXERCISES

1. Here is an argument against foundationalism based on an objection formulated by Keith Lehrer:[34]

   > Basic beliefs are beliefs that don't depend for their justification on any further information. But every perceptual belief depends for its justification on information about oneself and the conditions of observation. Hence perceptual beliefs cannot be basic.

   Consulting Lehrer's text, examine how he develops the details of this argument, and discuss whether you agree or disagree with him.
2. Do you agree with the foundationalist tenet that there is such a thing as nondoxastic justification, or do you side with coherentists in believing that a belief always derives at least some of its justification from other beliefs? Defend your answer with one or two arguments.
3. Do you think that perceptual beliefs can be certain? Begin your discussion of this issue by explaining in which sense you use the term "certainty."[35] If you think there are perceptual beliefs that are certain, give some examples and explain them in detail. And if you think perceptual beliefs cannot be certain, explain why they can't.

NOTES

1 Descartes, Bertrand Russell, Moritz Schlick, and A. J. Ayer may be viewed as foundationalists. C. I. Lewis developed an articulate defense of foundationalism in 1929 and 1946. Among contemporary philosophers, foundationalism is defended by Audi (1988), (1993a), and (1993b); Chisholm (1982) and (1989); Foley (1987); and Moser (1985) and (1989). For a brief characterization and discussion of foundationalism, see Alston (1992).
2 In the relevant literature, we can't find a definition of basic beliefs that is universally agreed on, and consequently lends itself to a textbook exposition. Thus our discussion of basic beliefs will follow the same guiding principle as our discussion of foundationalism: we shall consider what seems to me the most plausible conception of basic beliefs.

3 Of course, under different circumstances, (1) might be inferential and (2) noninferential. For example, you might infer that he's soaked from puddles on the floor, and know noninferentially that it's raining because you see that it's raining.

4 If I am looking at a red object under ordinary circumstances, that object "looks red" to me. Thus when we are using the phrase "*x* looks red to *S*," we are assuming the existence of two things: the perceiving subject, *S*, and the perceived object, *x*. There are, however, situations in which one has an experience as though there were an object of a certain kind when in fact there is no such object. In order to have a way of describing experience that leaves open whether there actually is a perceived object, epistemologists use the phrase "being appeared to F-ly." Thus when we say that *S* is appeared to redly, we leave open the question whether there is an object that looks red to *S*. We merely assert that *S* has an experience as though there were a red-looking object in front of *S*. See Chisholm (1977), pp. 26ff.

5 It's difficult to imagine how one can have a craving for chocolate without believing oneself to crave chocolate, but that doesn't mean that the craving and the belief are one and the same.

6 *Analytica Posteriora*, Book 1, chap. 1 and 2. The argument displayed in the text is a reconstruction from the relevant passages in the text.

7 For an instructive brief account of regress arguments, see Post (1992).

8 See Sosa (1991), pp. 167f.

9 For an illuminating account of the regress problem, see Armstrong (1973), chap. 11, and Audi (1988), pp. 83–86.

10 An example of such argumentation can be found in Chisholm (1977), p. 19. Once the regress is started, Chisholm writes, we "might try to continue *ad infinitum* . . . Or we might be tempted to complete a vicious circle. . . . But if we are rational beings, we will do neither of these things. For we will find that our Socratic questions lead us to a proper stopping place."

11 See Plantinga (1993a), p. 69.

12 See Sosa (1991), pp. 149f and 173ff.

13 Audi (1993a), p. 209; see also (1988), p. 83.

14 Lehrer (1990), p. 41.

15 This should not come as a surprise. For when critics of foundationalism claim that basic beliefs must have a feature *F*, the very idea of attributing feature *F* to basic beliefs is to conclude that since it is impossible for beliefs to have feature *F*, there can't be any basic beliefs.

16 A *reflexive* relation is a relation such that, if there are two things *x* and *y*, and *x* bears that relation to *y*, then *x* bears that relation to itself. For example, "has the same weight as" and "has the same color as" are reflexive relations. In contrast, an *irreflexive* relation is a relation that nothing has to itself. For example, "is married to" and "is parent of" are irreflexive relations.

17 The idea of self-creation must be distinguished from the idea of necessary existence. To deny that God created himself is not to deny that he exists necessarily.

18 This point can also be stated by pointing out that transmission is an event that involves three entities: *x* transmits *y* onto *z*. That is, for a transmission to take place, there must be a transmitter, something that is transmitted, and a recipient for the transmission. In the event that any of these three elements is missing, there can be no transmission. See Van Cleve (1985), p. 100; see also Plantinga (1993a), p. 76.

19 An argument along the same lines can be formulated to make the same point for alternative definitions of indubitability.

20 This definition of certainty is based on Chisholm's concept of certainty in [1977], p. 10. For alternative definitions, parallel arguments can be formulated.

21 See Sosa (1991), Introduction.

22 I lack this ability, presumably like most people. However, that doesn't mean there couldn't be people who can recognize a dodecagon without counting angles. Oliver Sacks (1987) reports a case of two twins who can, he suspects, "see" numbers. He relates the following episode: "A box of matches on their table fell, and discharged its contents on the floor: '111,' they both cried simultaneously.' . . . I counted the matches—it took me some time—and there were 111. 'How could you count the matches so quickly?' I asked. 'We didn't count,' they said. 'We *saw* the 111' " (p. 199).

23 See Armstrong (1973), chap. 12 and 13.

24 For an explanation of the internalism-externalism distinction, see Chapter 4, p. 84.

25 What is my evidence for taking myself to be reliable in discerning the color red? Well, there is something like a common framework of reference involving red objects—e.g., tomatoes, Coke cans, Ferraris. My own identifications of red objects cohere with this framework. What

other people identify as red, I identify as red, and vice versa. This provides me with a good reason for taking myself to be a reliable discerner of redness.

26 See Pollock (1986), pp. 59f.

27 Deductive validity could be achieved by adding a further premise: If I'm appeared to F-ly, then there is an object before me that is F. However, any such argument would contain a false premise, which means that no such argument could be sound.

28 See Chisholm's account of self-presentation in Chisholm (1989), Alston's account of self-warrant in Alston (1989), and Moser's defense of the given in Moser (1989).

29 The expression "being appeared to cat-like" is a special case of the phrase "being appeared to F-ly." See footnote 4.

30 For an argument along these lines, see Pollock (1986), pp. 61f.

31 For the concept of evidential defeat, see Chapter 1, pp. 12ff.

32 For a coherentist ingredient in an overall foundationalist theory, see Chisholm (1989), pp. 69f, and (1977), pp. 82f.

33 Chisholm and Audi are representatives of this approach. See Audi (1988) and (1993b).

34 See Lehrer (1990), p. 64.

35 Here you might want to consult Firth (1967) and Klein (1992a).

CHAPTER SIX

COHERENTISM

NEURATH'S METAPHOR

The supporting rationale of coherentism, the theoretical alternative to foundationalism, derives from rejecting the view that knowledge and justification rest on a foundation of basic beliefs. According to that view, justification can arise from neither an infinite regress nor a circular chain of justifying reasons. Foundationalists believe, therefore, that if there are justified beliefs at all, there must be basic beliefs. Coherentists, however, maintain that it is impossible for a belief to be basic on the ground that what justifies a belief must always be one or more other beliefs. Since they agree with foundationalists that an infinite regress of reasons can't justify, they must somehow make sense of the idea of circular justification: of beliefs justifying each other without there being any foundation or bedrock in which the process of justification can be grounded. Otto Neurath, one of the first philosophers to advocate coherentism, formulated the situation thus: "We are like sailors who must rebuild their ship upon the open sea."[1]

In order to make sense of Neurath's metaphor, we must recall that there are two different epistemological projects: one theoretical, the other practical. Epistemologists are interested in theoretical questions concerning the concepts of knowledge and justification, questions such as, What are the meanings of these concepts? What are the criteria for their application? and What is the range of their extension? But they are also interested in evaluating their own belief systems and revising them if necessary.[2] Neurath's metaphor is best interpreted as applying to this second project.

When we, as epistemologists, evaluate our beliefs in terms of what we take to be appropriate standards of justification, then we might find reasons to make changes in what we believe: to reject some of our beliefs and to adopt certain others. In terms of Neurath's metaphor, this means we might find out that our ship contains some rotten planks that need to be replaced

114

with new and sound ones. If foundationalism were true, then we could simply remove our ship from the open sea, lay it up in a dock and inspect it from the outside, all the while resting firmly on solid ground. But since foundationalism is false, we can't do that. We can't leave the open sea, which is to say we can't go outside of the system of our beliefs. If we want to decide which beliefs—planks of our ship—we want to reject and which to retain, we can't assume an external point of view—enter a dock on firm ground—from which to inspect our entire belief system all at once. Rather, all we can do is inspect our belief system from within—remaining afloat on the open sea, as it were—with no choice but to evaluate particular beliefs that strike us as questionable in terms of what else we believe.

The point of Neurath's metaphor can be summed up by saying that when we evaluate our beliefs and attempt to make appropriate changes, there is no exit from the circle of our beliefs. But this, so coherentists would argue, affects not only the practical project of making changes to our belief system but also the theoretical project of identifying what it is that makes justified beliefs justified. For if we are like sailors on the open sea of our beliefs, then a belief's justification can be derived from nothing but other beliefs. Hence coherentists hold that epistemic circularity—the idea of beliefs justifying each other—is not such a bad idea after all. As Laurence BonJour aptly puts it: "Having rejected both foundationalism and the actual-infinite-regress position [according to which an actual infinite regress can generate justification], coherentists must hold . . . that the regress of empirical justification moves in a circle."[3]

COHERENTISM AND CIRCULARITY

It is sometimes said that, according to coherentism, circular justification is just fine provided the circle of justifying beliefs is sufficiently large.[4] But it is quite mysterious how a circle's size could have any effect on its justificatory capacity. If we agree that a small circle can't justify, why should we assume that a large one can?

Before concerning ourselves with large-scale circularity, let's consider what reason there is in the first place for viewing the idea of circular justification as objectionable. The argument against circularity rests on two premises. First, self-justification is impossible; a belief can't be its own justifier or contribute to its own justification.[5] Second, the relation "x is a justifier for y" is transitive: for any three beliefs, B1, B2, and B3, if B1 is a justifier for B2 and B2 is a justifier for B3, then B1 is a justifier for B3.[6] To see how the argument goes, consider three beliefs, B1, B2, and B3, and assume they form a small circular justificatory chain:

B1 justifies B2, B2 justifies B3, and B3 justifies B1.

If we now take into account the second premise asserting the transitivity of "x is a justifier for y," we get

B1 is a justifier for B1.[7]

But the first premise tells us that a belief can't contribute to its own justification. Thus it's impossible for B1 to be a justifier for itself. Hence either there is, in addition to B2 and B3, a further belief that justifies B1, or the justification of B1 remains mysterious.

This argument applies to any circle, however large it may be. We must conclude, therefore, that simply increasing the number of beliefs a justificatory circle contains does not avoid the main problem of circularity—that circular reasoning collapses into self-justification. Hence there can be no such thing as a belief that is justified through a circular chain of reasons.[8]

How can this result be reconciled with BonJour's statement that coherentists are committed to circularity? As BonJour points out, to give coherentism a fair hearing, we must replace the *linear* conceptual framework within which the regress problem arises with a *holistic* conception of justification. In reply to the argument we just considered, BonJour writes:

> The crucial, though tacit, assumption which underlies this seemingly devastating line of argument is the idea that inferential justification is essentially *linear* in character, that it involves a one-dimensional sequence of beliefs, ordered by the relation of epistemic priority, along which epistemic justification is passed from the earlier to the later beliefs in the sequence via connections of inference. It is just this linear conception of justification which generates the regress problem in the first place. [Hence coherentists must] repudiate the linear conception of justification in its entirety.[9]

What coherentists must put in the place of the linear conception is, in the words of Laurence BonJour, the view that justification is

> essentially systematic or holistic in character: beliefs are justified by being inferentially related to other beliefs in the overall context of a coherent system.[10]

As we pointed out in the previous chapter, if a particular belief's justification is viewed as a relation between it and the doxastic system of which it is a member, we need no longer search for a solution to the regress problem because this problem doesn't arise in the first place. Consider a particular belief B. Coherentists would say that whether it is justified depends on whether it enjoys membership in a coherent belief system. Suppose B does not. In this case, no regress problem arises. Now suppose it does. In that case, it isn't particular beliefs—say, B^*, B^{**}, and so on—that are candidates for conferring justification on B, but rather the entire doxastic system of which *B* is a member, whose justification in turn is generated by coherence. So in that case, a regress problem doesn't arise either.[11]

Of course, if we explain a particular belief's justification by saying that it is a member of a coherent system of beliefs, we may wonder precisely which conditions a belief system must meet in order to enjoy coherence. This brings us to our next topic: What are the elements of coherence?

PUTATIVE ELEMENTS OF COHERENCE

In this section, we shall discuss three potential contributors to a belief system's coherence: (i) entailment relations, (ii) logical consistency, and (iii) explanatory relations.

A belief B1 entails a belief B2 if and only if it is impossible that B1 is true and B2 false. Does a belief system's coherence increase to the extent its members entail one another? At first sight, an affirmative answer to this question seems plausible. After all, the more entailment relations obtain among my beliefs, the more tightly they would appear to be interwoven.[12] The following consideration, however, strongly suggests a negative answer. If entailment relations could generate coherence, then deductive logic could be used to generate coherence in any belief system whatever. Suppose you hold two beliefs:

(1) *A*
(2) *B*

Since it is a law of logic that *Q* entails *If P then Q*, deductive logic tells us that you are entitled to believe

(3)   If *A*, then *B*.
(4)   If *B*, then *A*.

If entailment relations can generate coherence, we are now looking at a small belief system that enjoys a high degree of coherence by virtue of the following entailments:

(i)   (1) entails (4).
(ii)   (2) entails (3).
(iii)   (1) and (3) entail (2).
(iv)   (2) and (4) entail (1).

Since such a maneuver can be repeated over and over again, you can add on to your initial stock of beliefs whatever further beliefs strike your fancy, thus creating a tightly interwoven doxastic system of whatever size and richness you desire. Deductive logic can thus be used to make *any* belief system coherent, no matter how absurd and therefore unjustifiable it is. This strongly suggests that a belief system's internal entailment relations don't contribute to its coherence.[13]

Let us continue with *consistency*. A system of beliefs {B1, B2, . . . B*n*} is consistent if and only if it is possible for all members of that system to be true. Our question is whether consistency contributes to coherence in the sense that it is necessary for coherence, and thus, according to coherentism, necessary for justification. That is, we are to ask whether a belief system lacking consistency is necessarily a belief system lacking justification. If it isn't, then coherentists would have to conclude that even an inconsistent belief system can enjoy coherence.

Now, it is not difficult to imagine a belief system that lacks consistency, yet is justified. Consider the following two propositions:

P1   If two collections of grains of sand differ in number by just one grain, then either both collections are heaps of sand or neither is.

P2   If a collection of grains of sand contains one grain only, then it is not a heap of sand.

P1 and P2 are inconsistent with each other. If P1 is true, then P2 is false.[14] However, we can imagine situations in which you would be justified in believing both P1 and P2, for the inconsistency in question is not immediately obvious; it takes some thinking and ingenuity to discover it. Someone who is unaware of it might very well be justified in believing both propositions.

A famous example of a set of inconsistent, yet justified, beliefs is that of Frege's basic laws of arithmetic. Frege proposed these laws as the result of a long and careful study. Nevertheless, he failed to see the inconsistency they involved until Bertrand Russell sent him a letter demonstrating that inconsistency. What matters about this example is this: We can't say that Frege's belief in the laws he proposed was unjustified simply because they were inconsistent with one another. Had Frege overlooked the inconsistency as a result of carelessness or hastiness, then we would have a reason for denying that he was justified in believing them. However, in the absence of such a reason, we must grant that Frege's belief in these laws was justified.[15] Hence we must conclude that if a belief's justification is a function of its coherence with other beliefs, consistency is not a necessary condition of coherence.[16]

Finally, let us turn to the question of how a belief system is related to explanatory relations among its members.[17] Coherentists such as Keith Lehrer and Laurence BonJour maintain that a belief system's members are the better justified the more the belief system exhibits what they call "explanatory coherence." A belief can enjoy explanatory coherence either by explaining other beliefs or by being explained by other beliefs. Consider the following three beliefs:

(5) He missed the nail and hit his thumb;

(6) He cursed and kicked a chair;

(7) He was drunk.

(5) explains (6): he cursed and kicked a chair because he missed the nail and hit his thumb. Furthermore, (5) is explained by (7): the reason he missed the nail and hit his thumb was that he was drunk.[18] Coherentists would say that the epistemic status of (5) is increased by the fact that it both explains and is explained by other beliefs.

In order for a belief to be justified, *must* it bear explanatory relations to other beliefs? It would seem the answer is "no." For example, let us imagine a situation with the following features: First, you believe.

(8) I am nervous.

Second, you are justified in believing (8). Third, you believe nothing that explains, or is explained by, (8). About this situation, we are not assuming that there is no explanation of your nervousness. We are only imagining that you have no idea of what the explanation is. Unless coherentists can convince us that such a situation is impossible, we are to conclude that explanatory coherence is not a necessary condition of justification.

On the other hand, even though explanatory coherence might not be necessary for coherence, it could nevertheless be claimed to be such that it adds to, or increases, a belief's justification. Though there is no obvious reason to reject this suggestion, a problem arises from the fact that there are good and bad explanations. How are we to distinguish between them? Compare the following beliefs:

(9) I believe my cat is meowing;

(10) My cat is meowing;

(11) An evil demon makes me believe that my cat is meowing.

(10) strikes us as a better explanation of (9) than does (11), but why? On what grounds can we prefer (10) to (11)? Because of the absurdity of (11), the problem would not appear to be serious. After all, if we compare how (10) and (11) in turn can be explained, it would seem that preference should be given to a scientific explanation in terms of digestive processes over an explanation in terms of demonology.

Yet the problem of distinguishing between good and bad explanations should not be underestimated, for alternative explanations need not be as far-fetched as (11). Thus Richard Fumerton writes: "If you want an example of an intuitively implausible system of beliefs with maximum explanatory power and simplicity, look at Berkeley's theory of perception."[19] Fumerton's point is this. Whereas our ordinary, commonsense view of the world as a collection of physical objects is justified (assuming a nonskeptical, science-oriented point of view), a Berkeleyan view of the world as a collection of immaterial ideas is not. Yet our scientific worldview fails to beat Berkeley's immaterialism as far as explanatory coherence is concerned.

The force of this objection should not, however, be overstated. The objection makes it clear that it is not easy to explain what makes one explanation better than another. It also shows that there must be more to coherence than explanatory relations. It does not, however, provide us with a compelling reason to dismiss the idea that explanatory relations between beliefs can contribute to a belief system's coherence.

Keith Lehrer and Laurence BonJour both take explanatory relations to be an ingredient of coherence.[20] Alas, when they actually begin to spell out how a coherence theory of justification is supposed to work in detail, explanatory coherence drops out of the picture. Instead, they give an account of what coherence amounts to in terms of defeasibility and level ascent, or metajustification. Let us, then, proceed to examine what shape and form a belief system's coherence assumes in the theories of Lehrer and BonJour.

LEHRER ON ACCEPTANCE

To develop an appreciation of Lehrer's theory, we must begin with his notion of acceptance. Unlike other epistemologists, Lehrer does not take as the object of his analysis the notion "S is justified in *believing* that p," but rather the notion "S is justified in *accepting* that p." According to Lehrer, not all beliefs are acceptances, but all acceptances are beliefs. Lehrer, then, views acceptances as a subclass of beliefs.[21]

What distinguishes acceptance from belief is this: Whereas acceptance is always formed in the "interest of obtaining a truth and avoiding an error in what one accepts," belief is not always formed in the interest of obtaining a truth and avoiding error.[22] The objective in believing a proposition might not be the attainment of truth, but rather usefulness, happiness, or the fulfillment of a moral duty. Whenever that is the case, a belief falls short of being an acceptance.

Furthermore, Lehrer conceives of acceptances as functional states. He writes:

> Acceptance is the sort of mental state that has a specific sort of role, a functional role, in thought, inference, and action. When a person accepts that p, he or she will draw certain inferences and perform certain actions assuming the truth of p. Thus, if a person accepts that p, then the person will be ready to affirm that p or to concede that p in the appropriate circumstances.[23]

In order to appreciate what Lehrer wants to convey in this passage, let us conceive of *pain* as a functional state. A functional state is defined in terms of its causal relation to input and output. For example, the *input* that causes you to be in pain might be a hammer blow to your thumb (you missed the nail you were aiming at), and the *output* of your being in pain might be cursing and kicking a chair. Someone who is a functionalist about pain would say that any state resulting from input such as physical damage or trauma and output consisting in what we consider pain behavior (screaming, cursing, wincing, etc.) is a state of being in pain.

Likewise, someone who is a functionalist about acceptances would say that any mental state resulting from a certain type of input and resulting in output manifesting itself in inferences and actions is a state of accepting something. Suppose you hear the doorbell ring. This auditory experience is the input into the resulting state of accepting that the doorbell is ringing. You then infer that someone is outside, and you go and open the door. This inference and this action are the output of your accepting that the doorbell is ringing.

Lehrer's functionalist analysis of acceptance faces the following problem: What is essential to the functionalist approach is that the content of an acceptance is solely a result of its *relations* to those things that function as its input and output. The problem is whether input and output relations completely determine the content of an acceptance.[24] Suppose you are buying apples at your local grocery store, and you are now putting them in a produce bag. The input here comes in the form of tactile and visual stimulations and background beliefs about apples, whereas the output consists in a certain type of behavior: walking over to the apples, ripping off a produce bag, filling it with apples, and putting the bag in your cart. The acceptance in question is "These are apples," and this acceptance plays the functional role of being (i) triggered by your present sensory experience and background beliefs and (ii) inducing the behavior just described. However, is this functional role sufficient for determining the specific content of what you accept?

It would seem it is not. Rather, it would appear that the same functional role allows for a wide range of different acceptances: "These are green apples," "These are beautiful green apples," "These are beautiful, large apples," or perhaps "These are Granny Smith apples." Thus the problem Lehrer's functionalism raises is this: By making the content of an acceptance solely a function of its *relations* to other mental and nonmental things, his account of acceptance ignores the inner, qualitative or nonrelational character that determines its specific *content*.

This objection calls into doubt what Lehrer said about the relation between acceptance and belief. According to Lehrer, acceptances are a *subclass* of beliefs. But if it is true that input and output relations underdetermine the content of an acceptance, then it follows that some acceptances are not beliefs. Consider the following two situations. In the first, you believe

(1)   These are beautiful *green* apples

but you do not believe

(2)   These are beautiful *large* apples.

In the second situation, you believe (2) but not (1). Is it plausible to assume that in both situations the input and output conditions are identical? That is, can we imagine two situations that differ as indicated, but otherwise are such that the perceptual experiences you undergo, the inferences you draw, your background assumptions about apples, and your behavior are the same in both situations? There is at least no obvious reason for denying that there could be such a pair of situations.[25] The first of these situations would be such that you *accept but do not believe (2)*, and the second such that you *accept but do not believe (1)*. In either situation, there would be an acceptance that is not a belief. Thus if we believe that such a pair of situations is possible, we must conclude that acceptances are not, as Lehrer has suggested, a subclass of beliefs. Later on we shall see that there is a further reason for concluding that not all acceptances are beliefs.

COHERENCE AS THE BEATING OF COMPETITORS

Having examined what Lehrer means by acceptance, we must next focus on how he construes the inner mechanics of coherence. According to Lehrer, a belief of mine is justified if and only if it coheres with what he would call my "acceptance system": the set of all the propositions I accept. In general terms, the acceptance system of a person S at a time t is the set of all true propositions of the form "S accepts that p at t."[26] Lehrer conceives of coherence, then, as a relation between a particular proposition and the relevant acceptance system.

Lehrer's analysis of this relation involves two key ingredients in the form of necessary conditions. According to the first, my acceptance of p coheres with my acceptance system only if p wins out over all the propositions that compete with it. According to the second, for my acceptance of p to cohere with my acceptance system, I must accept that my acceptance of p is based on a trustworthy source. We shall consider the first condition in this section, and the second in the next.

According to Lehrer, when a proposition wins the competition with its competitors, it *beats* its competitors. In which sense, however, can one proposition be said to "compete" with another one? When you deliberate on which propositions to accept, propositions present themselves to you as competing contenders for the status of being accepted. The question you must ask yourself is which of them are worthy of your acceptance and which are not. For example, suppose you have a cat, and having noticed her right in front of you, you ask yourself whether you should accept

(1)   I see a cat before me

or instead

(2)   I hallucinate that there is a cat before me.

(2) is a competitor for (1), and vice versa. (For if you do see a cat before you, you do not hallucinate that there is one before you; and if you hallucinate a cat before you, then you do not see one before you.) The question before you is whether it is more reasonable to accept (1) or to accept (2). The answer to this question, Lehrer would say, depends on your acceptance system. Suppose you also accept

(3)   I have not ingested any hallucinogenic substances;
(4)   There is no indication of hallucination in my present experi-ence.[27]

Given that you accept (3) and (4), it is more reasonable of you to accept (1) than to accept (2). If, however, your acceptance system were to include

(5)   I took LSD an hour ago;
(6)   LSD induces in me a propensity to hallucinate the presence of cats;
(7)   I am in my own living room, and I don't have any cats;

then it would be more reasonable of you to accept (2) than to accept (1). According to Lehrer, which of two competing propositions coheres with your acceptance system is determined by which of the two propositions it is more reasonable for you to accept vis-à-vis your acceptance system. Hence he would say that (1) coheres with your acceptance system if it includes (3) and (4), and (2) coheres with your acceptance system if it includes (5), (6), and (7). Let us call the acceptance system including (3) and (4) *System A*, and the one including (5) through (7) *System B*. Lehrer would say that vis-à-vis *System A*, (1) beats (2), whereas vis-à-vis *System B*, (2) beats (1).

Lehrer, then, views "beating the competitors" as an essential ingre-dient of coherence. In his account, for a proposition *p* to cohere with your acceptance system, it must beat every proposition you accept that competes with it.[28]

TRUSTWORTHINESS

The second key ingredient of Lehrer's coherentism comes into play when we consider what it actually takes for a proposition to beat all of its competitors. Consider again the proposition

(1)   I see a cat before me

and its competitor

(2)   I am hallucinating that there is a cat before me.

For (1) to beat (2), your acceptance system must include propositions such as

(3)   I have not ingested any hallucinogenic substances;
(4)   There is no indication of hallucination in my present experience.

Why, however, do (3) and (4) give (1) the epistemic strength to beat (2)? Why is it that, vis-à-vis (3) and (4), it is more reasonable of you to accept (1) than to accept (2)? Lehrer would say that when you accept (3) and (4), you are, in effect, accepting that under the present circumstances you can trust perception as a source of information. That is, there is a further relevant proposition in your acceptance system, to wit:

(5)   Under the present circumstances I can trust my perceptions.

The value of having (3) and (4) as members of your belief system, then, is that under the present circumstances you can trust that acceptances based on perception are true, which you could not if (2) were true. Hence, in relation to your acceptance system, it is more reasonable for you to accept (1) than to accept (2).

According to Lehrer, assumptions about one's own trustworthiness are an essential ingredient of coherence. For me to be justified in accepting *p* under conditions *C*, my acceptance system must include propositions to the effect that under conditions *C* I can trust the source of information on which my acceptance of *p* is based. Such propositions are not about the objects of perception, introspection, or memory, but rather about the conditions under which I accept propositions on the basis of perception, introspection, and memory. In accepting such propositions, I am ascending, so to speak, to a higher level: a level from which I evaluate the trustworthiness of sources of information under certain conditions. We shall, therefore, call the second ingredient of Lehrer's coherentism the *requirement of level ascent*.

Lehrer's commitment to the requirement of level ascent is explicitly stated in his response to a certain objection to coherentism. According to this objection, it is possible for perception alone to justify a belief. Put differently, in order for perception to justify a belief, so the objection goes, it isn't necessary that the proposition accepted receive support from the perceiver's acceptance system. In reply to this objection, Lehrer insists on the necessity of level ascent.

> Any claim that we see, remember, or introspect that something is the case immediately confronts the . . . objection that the belief does not emanate from a trustworthy source but arises in some untrustworthy manner. To be . . . justified in accepting that one sees, remembers, or introspects something, one must, therefore, accept that these are trustworthy sources of information.[29]

According to Lehrer, then, you can't have justified beliefs that stem from sources such as perception, memory, and introspection unless your acceptance system includes higher-level propositions asserting that these sources are trustworthy.

Let us summarize what, from Lehrer's point of view, it takes for an acceptance of yours to be justified. To begin with, Lehrer would say you are justified in accepting that p if and only if p coheres with your acceptance system. And in order for your acceptance of p to cohere with your acceptance system, p must beat all of its competitors. Finally, your acceptance system must include one or several propositions to the effect that, under the present circumstances, the source from which your acceptance arises is trustworthy.

LEVEL ASCENT, ACCEPTANCE, AND BELIEF

In Chapter 5, we encountered a forceful objection to modern foundationalism: people typically don't form the kind of beliefs strong foundationalism would countenance as basic.[30] The point of this objection is that modern foundationalism must be considered a version of skepticism. A similar objection can be formulated against coherentism if level ascent is taken to be an essential ingredient of coherence. Level ascent is a sophisticated intellectual procedure, so it could be objected, a procedure familiar to philosophers, but alien to people who have never studied philosophy. Under ordinary circumstances, people instinctively presume the trustworthiness of their perceptions, without forming actual beliefs about this matter.[31] Consider the proposition

(1)   I see a cat before me

and assume that nothing is evident to me that would undermine my justification for believing (1). According to Lehrer, (1) coheres with my acceptance system only if I accept some proposition to the effect that

(2)   Under the present circumstances, my perceptions are trustworthy.

But what if, though I don't disbelieve (2), I don't actually believe it either? Perhaps I did not reflect on the question of whether my perceptions are trustworthy under the present circumstances, and thus didn't form any belief about that matter. If so, am I really unjustified in believing (1)? It seems reasonable to say that I would not be unjustified. It would appear, therefore, that Lehrer's theory amounts into a version of skepticism because it demands too much of justification. Under ordinary circumstances, empirical beliefs are simply not accompanied by beliefs such as (2). Hence, so the objection against coherentism concludes, the requirement of level ascent Lehrer imposes implies that ordinary empirical beliefs are not justified.

In reply to this objection, Lehrer could argue that, according to him, coherence does not require *beliefs*, but only *acceptances* about level ascent. And when we consider, he might say, how people typically form beliefs, draw inferences, and act upon their beliefs, quite clearly our verdict ought to be that people do accept, unless they have evidence to the contrary, that perception is a trustworthy source of information.

In fact, Lehrer makes a parallel move concerning competition. Recall that, according to Lehrer's coherentism, for me to be justified in believing

(1)   I see a cat before me

(1) must beat any competitor—for example, the competitor

(3)   I am hallucinating that there is a cat before me.

Suppose I haven't considered the matter of hallucination at all, and thus don't believe such things as

(4)   I have not ingested any hallucinogenic substances;
(5)   There is no indication of hallucination in my present experience.

Does this mean I am not justified in believing (1)? Lehrer handles this difficulty by saying the following:

> It is not necessary that a person have reflected on the competitor for the competitor to be beaten, but it is necessary that the acceptance system of the person imply that it is more reasonable to accept the claim than the competitor. If the acceptance system of a person implies that it is more reasonable to accept that *p* than to accept that *c*, then the person must be in a state to think and reason as though this were true.[32]

Clearly, I can be in a state to think and reason as though (4) and (5) were true—that is, be in a state of *accepting* (4) and (5)—even if, because I have not reflected on the possibility of hallucination, I fail to believe (4) and (5).[33]

Hence I can be justified in believing (1) even if (4) and (5) are not propositions I believe.

The same reasoning can be applied to trustworthiness. I can be in a state to think and reason as though

(2)   Under the present circumstances, my perceptions are trustworthy

were true—that is, be in a state of accepting (2)—even if I have not reflected on the trustworthiness of my perceptions, and thus have formed no belief about this matter. Hence Lehrer could reply to our objection that my being justified in believing (1) does not require that I actually believe (2). It only requires that I accept (2).

In the earlier section on acceptance, we discussed Lehrer's claim that acceptances are a subclass of beliefs and found reasons to suspect that this claim is false. This suspicion is now reinforced. For in order to defend his version of coherentism against the objection that ordinarily the required acceptances about competition and trustworthiness don't take the form of actual beliefs, Lehrer would have to say that these acceptances need not be beliefs.[34]

LEHRER'S COHERENTISM AND FOUNDATIONALISM COMPARED

We may now, however, wonder whether Lehrer's coherentism and foundationalism are really competing and mutually inconsistent theories. Putting the two key ingredients of Lehrer's coherentism together, we may sum up his theory thus:

(JL) $S's$ acceptance A is justified if and only if (i) in $S's$ acceptance system all of $A's$ competitors are beaten; (ii) S accepts that she is a trustworthy source of information under the circumstances under which A was produced.

Does (JL) imply that it is impossible for beliefs to be basic? Recall how we have defined basic beliefs: they are beliefs that are justified without owing their justification to any other beliefs. Now take yourself to hold a putatively basic belief:

(1)   There is a red object before me.

Condition (i) of (JL) demands that in your acceptance system all competitors of (1) be beaten. So according to Lehrer, for (1) to be justified, you must accept, though you need not believe, those propositions that are necessary for beating all of the competitors of (1). Consequently, condition (i) does not imply that for (1) to be justified, there must be further *beliefs* from which (1) receives its justification. Nor does condition (ii) imply any such thing, for condition (ii) demands acceptances, not beliefs, about your own trustworthiness. Thus if it is true that acceptances need not be beliefs, then (JL) is entirely compatible with the foundationalist assertion that beliefs can be justified without help from any other beliefs. And as we saw above, there is an excellent reason for Lehrer to concede that, indeed, acceptances need not be beliefs: the fact that under ordinary circumstances people just don't form beliefs about whether or not they are trustworthy sources of information under the circumstances under which they form beliefs.

In fact, Lehrer's coherentism seems not only compatible with, but indeed akin to, foundationalism as construed in Chapter 5. Recall that we construed foundationalism as a theory according to which *S's* belief *B* is basic, and thus justified, only if

(i)   *S* does not have any evidence that defeats *S's* justification for *B*;

(ii) *S* has evidence for believing that *B* was formed in a reliable manner.

These conditions roughly correspond to the two conditions of Lehrer's theory. Like Lehrer's theory, foundationalism (as developed in Chapter 5) makes justification negatively dependent upon the believer's entire belief system: for a belief to be justified, there must not be any further beliefs that would defeat it. Second, it makes justification dependent upon level ascent. This second condition, however, is spelled out in terms of evidence for appropriate metabeliefs, and not, like Lehrer's, in terms of meta-acceptances. Thus the dispute between Lehrer and foundationalists may be viewed as one about how the intuitions underlying the two conditions are best captured, rather than one reflecting a conflict between irreconcilable intuitions about the structure of justification.

LAURENCE BONJOUR: COHERENCE AS METAJUSTIFICATION

Like Lehrer, BonJour conceives of justification in terms of coherence. Unlike Lehrer, however, he insists that coherence must be understood in terms of relations between actual *beliefs*. BonJour's reason for holding this view has to do with the idea of epistemic responsibility. Before we can examine BonJour's thoughts on this topic, however, we must first discuss how he conceives of coherence.

According to BonJour, for an empirical belief of mine, *B*, to enjoy coherence, I must have two further beliefs that, taken together, make it likely that *B* is true.[35] Put differently, *B* coheres with my background beliefs if and only if I have a reason, or a justificatory argument, for the truth of *B*. The form of such an argument is the following:

(1)   *B* has feature *F*.

(2)   Beliefs having feature *F* are very likely to be true.

Therefore:

(3)   *B* is very likely to be true.[36]

It is impossible to formulate such an argument without engaging in what we have called "level ascent."[37] If you believe the first premise, then you have formed a higher-level belief: a belief about a belief of yours. The same holds for the second premise and the conclusion. If you believe (2), then you hold a belief about beliefs of a certain type, and if you believe the conclusion, then you believe that a belief of yours is likely to be true. Now, the point that matters most in this context is this: According to BonJour, my belief *B* can be justified only if I actually *believe* premises (1) and (2). He writes: "In order for *B* to be justified for a particular person A (at a particular time), it is necessary, not merely that justification along the above lines exist in the abstract, but also that A himself be in cognitive possession of that justification, that is, that he *believe* the appropriate premises of form (1) and (2). . . ."[38]

Lehrer and BonJour, then, agree that coherence is, at least in part, a function of level ascent. Unlike Lehrer, however, BonJour insists that level ascent must take the form of actual beliefs. Next, we shall examine BonJour's reasons for this view.

BONJOUREAN JUSTIFICATION AND EPISTEMIC RESPONSIBILITY

According to BonJour, the requirement that premises (1) and (2) be actually believed is imposed by considerations of epistemic responsibility.[39] For a subject *S* to be epistemically responsible in holding belief *B*, *S* must "be in cognitive possession" or "have access to" the justification for *B*. BonJour writes that if *S* does not have access to the justification, then *S* "has no reason for thinking that the belief is at all likely to be true."[40]

In order to evaluate this argument, we must determine how we are to interpret phrases like "being in cognitive possession of a justification" and "having access to a justification." And here we can distinguish between a strict and a liberal interpretation. According to the latter, I have access to the justification for a belief of mine if, in order for me to recognize my belief's justification, I need to do no more than reflect on the belief's epistemic credentials. According to the strict interpretation, justification of which I am in cognitive possession, or to which I have access, must come in the form of beliefs. As we have seen, BonJour prefers the strict interpretation, for he demands that the premises of the argument displayed above take the form of actual beliefs.

But a problem arises for BonJour's argument. Unless he justifies his preference for the strict interpretation of the phrase "having access to a justification," it remains unclear why considerations of epistemic responsibility necessitate the truth of the argument's conclusion. There is no doubt that BonJour's perspective on justification is decidedly *internalist*, which is why he insists that a belief's justification must be cognitively accessible to the subject.[41] Internalists, however, need not agree with BonJour that justification is accessible only if it comes in the form of further beliefs. They might hold that justification is also accessible if it comes in the form of evidence, where it doesn't matter whether this evidence manifests itself in further beliefs or not.[42] It must be said, therefore, that the underpinnings of BonJour's strictly doxastic perspective on the nature of justification display a conspicuous weakness, one that assumes special importance when we consider, as we shall do next, what consequences BonJour's doxasticism incurs.

BONJOUREAN LEVEL ASCENT

As we have seen, the basic idea of BonJourean coherentism is that for an empirical belief B to be justified, the subject must have a further justified belief to the effect that beliefs like B are likely to be true. In order to examine how this works out in detail, let us consider one of BonJour's own examples. Suppose I see a red book on my desk and accordingly believe

(1) There is a red book on the desk.

What justification might I have for believing this proposition?

According to BonJour, my justification for (1) comes in the form of two propositions. The first of these is about what kind of a belief (1) is. BonJour points out that (1) is noninferential: it is not inferred from any other belief; it simply occurs to me. In BonJour's terminology, such beliefs are *cognitively spontaneous*. Second, he refers to (1) as a belief of kind K: a belief about the color and general classification of a medium-sized object. Third, he points out that (1) is formed under what we consider standard conditions of observation: I am neither too close to nor too far away from the book, my eyes are functioning well, and the lighting is good. Putting these three points together, we shall express the first proposition thus: I have a cognitively spontaneous belief of kind K under conditions C that there is a red book on the desk.

The second proposition that, according to BonJour, justifies me in believing (1) is this: Cognitively spontaneous beliefs of kind K under conditions C are very likely to be true. Now, if I conjoin both of these propositions, BonJour's says, I am in a position to offer a justificatory argument for believing (1):

P1   I have a cognitively spontaneous belief of kind K under conditions C that there is a red book on the desk.

P2   Cognitively spontaneous beliefs of kind K under conditions C are very likely to be true.

Therefore:

(C)   My belief that there is a red book on the desk is very likely to be true.

The formulation of such an argument necessarily involves level ascent. The first premise and the conclusion are about the "red book" belief, and the second premise is a generalization about a certain kind of belief held under certain conditions. It is impossible, therefore, to believe the premises and the conclusion of this argument without forming beliefs about beliefs. Unfortunately, this means, as we shall see next, that BonJourean standards of justification are very difficult to satisfy.

LEVEL ASCENT AND SKEPTICISM

One serious issue raised by BonJour's justificatory argument is whether it is psychologically realistic to view justification as resulting from arguments of that type. Referring to his own belief that there is a red book on the desk, BonJour says that *he* believes the premises of his argument.[43] What, however, about ordinary people with no schooling in philosophy? When they form cognitively spontaneous beliefs about medium-sized objects, do they believe the premises of a justificatory argument like the one BonJour has proposed? It seems quite doubtful that they would. As pointed out earlier in the discussion of Lehrer's coherentism, epistemic level ascent is a sophisticated epistemological procedure. Ordinarily, people don't perform cognitive operations of such complexity.[44]

This objection can be further advanced by bringing the concept of coherence into the discussion. The point of BonJour's justificatory argument is to show that his belief "There is a red book on the desk" coheres with his other beliefs. So, according to BonJour, a belief of mine is justified only if I *believe it to cohere* with my other beliefs. However, ordinary people don't have a grasp of the concept of coherence, and hence can't form higher-level beliefs according to which their beliefs enjoy coherence.[45] In reply to this argument, BonJour points out that he disagrees with the claim that

> philosophically uneducated adults . . . have no grasp at all of this concept. On the contrary, I think that such persons frequently find failures of coherence intuitively objectionable (even though they of course wouldn't formulate the point in that way).[46]

Now, the extent to which philosophically uneducated people do or do not grasp the concept of coherence is an empirical question that cannot be settled from the philosopher's armchair. What can be settled, however, is this: Even if it were right that ordinary people find a lack of coherence objectionable, it would not follow that when their beliefs do enjoy coherence, their doxastic systems include the kind of beliefs that are suitable as premises for justificatory arguments à la BonJour. Just reflect on the complexity of the premises in BonJour's argument. In order to hold higher-level beliefs that can play the role of these premises, people would constantly have to consider what kind of lower-level beliefs they are forming, under which conditions they are forming these beliefs, and whether beliefs of so-and-so kind held under such-and-such conditions are very likely to be true. It seems doubtful that ordinary people would bother considering such matters, and even more unlikely that they would know how to carry out the discriminations level ascent demands.

In fact, BonJour admits that coherence as a standard of justification is so difficult to meet that "even we philosophically sophisticated ones fail to have a fully explicit and adequate grasp of this concept." Then he goes on to conclude:

> To the extent that this is so, I hold . . . that even we fall short of and hence only approximate ideal epistemic justification.[47]

In response to this verdict, BonJour distinguishes between *approximate* and *ideal* justification. As far as the latter is concerned, BonJour passes an explicit verdict in favor of skepticism. Concerning the former, he does not.[48] Indeed, he should not, for the coherence theory of justification he advocates is supposed to provide a rebutting response to skepticism. Thus he writes:

> It is . . . worth emphasizing at the outset that I am concerned here only with coherence theories which purport to provide a response to skepticism.[49]

However, if ordinary people don't form the kind of beliefs necessary for BonJour's justificatory argument—and it seems very likely that they don't—then the empirical beliefs of ordinary people don't even approximate justification. It is hard to see, therefore, how we can escape the conclusion that BonJour's coherentism must be considered a version of full-fledged skepticism about the extent to which ordinary empirical beliefs are justified.

THE ISOLATION OBJECTION

We shall conclude this chapter by considering how coherentists would reply to a standard objection to coherentism, according to which coherentism isolates belief systems from the world.[50] Coherentism asserts that beliefs are justified by virtue of relations between, not beliefs and the world, but beliefs only. Why, then, should it matter, as far as a belief system's justification is concerned, what the world is like? Coherentism, so the objection goes, implies that it does not matter—or, to be more precise, that it does not matter enough.

The isolation objection can be formulated in two different ways. In the words of Ernest Sosa,

> the view that justification is a matter of relations among beliefs is open to an objection from *alternative coherent systems* or *detachment from reality*, depending on one's perspective. From the latter perspective the body of beliefs is held constant and the surrounding world is allowed to vary; from the former it is the surrounding world that is held constant while the body of beliefs is allowed to vary. In either case, according to the coherentists, there could be no effect on the justification for any belief.[51]

In order to discuss both forms of the isolation objection, we must consider an example. Let's introduce a world W in which you are visiting a zoo and are looking at an enclosure with two aardvarks that are clearly within your view. You form the cognitively spontaneous belief

(1)   There are two aardvarks in this enclosure,

and this belief, so let us assume, coheres with your overall belief system M. We also assume that, besides what you observe, you don't have any other information about the number of aardvarks before you. Furthermore, let's introduce a world W^* that differs from W in this respect: in W^*, you clearly see *three* instead of two aardvarks.

In order to illustrate the *detachment objection*, we must hold M constant in both worlds: M is coherent in W, and equally coherent in W^*. According to the detachment objection, since coherentism makes justification solely a function of coherence, coherentism implies that you are equally justified in believing (1) in both W and W^*. But this is utterly implausible because when you clearly see three aardvarks in the enclosure, as you do in W^*, you can't be justified in believing that there are only two aardvarks in the enclosure (supposing, as we are, that you don't have any additional relevant information).

Let's consider how coherentists could reply to this objection. Suppose the transition from W to W^* takes place as you are observing the aardvarks: the two aardvarks that were there to begin with are joined by a third, which emerges from an opening in an adjacent building. Yet, so we are imagining, you continue believing

(1)   There are two aardvarks in this enclosure.

Coherentists would reply that if you continue believing (1), the immediate result will be a lack of coherence, for as soon as the third aardvark enters the scene, your visual perceptions will induce you to believe things that are incompatible with (1); for example:

(2)   The two aardvarks in this enclosure are joined by another one.

Thus the change from *W* to *W** is unlikely to leave your belief system's coherence intact (unless you make appropriate changes to your belief system). Coherentism does not, therefore, imply that your belief system is disconnected from the world. Rather, coherentism can easily maintain that your belief system's coherence is, via perception, responsive to how the world changes.

In response to this move, critics of coherentism could concede that coherentism does indeed allow for a perceptual connection between our beliefs and the world. But they could insist that this connection is not tight enough. True, it is *unlikely* that once the change we are imagining has taken place, your belief system's coherence remains preserved. What, however, if it *does* remain preserved? In that case, coherentism implies—absurdly—that you are justified in believing in the presence of *two* aardvarks when you are clearly seeing *three* of them.

In order to appreciate the force of the detachment objection, suppose that, unbeknownst to you, a mad scientist has decided to make you a guinea pig for his cognitive ray gun. The rays his gun emits are perceptual neutralizers. They partially eliminate the doxastic effects your perceptual experiences tend to have. Because you are exposed to these rays, all those beliefs are eliminated from your belief system that, if induced by perceiving the third aardvark, would fail to cohere with (1). Thus, when you believe that there are two aardvarks in the enclosure although you are perceiving three, you don't believe anything that would contradict, or somehow undermine (i.e., fail to cohere with), this belief.

The significance of the case we are presently considering is this: Your belief that there are two aardvarks in the enclosure conflicts with your perceptual evidence, and thus is a prime example of an unjustified belief. Yet coherentism, since it makes justification solely a function of coherence relations among beliefs, implies that your belief is justified. Hence coherentism must be rejected.

Next, let us reformulate our example so as to illustrate the *alternative systems* objection. Again, let's suppose that, observing the aardvarks, you believe

(1)   There are two aardvarks in this enclosure,

and your belief coheres with everything else you believe. However, the person next to you (let's call him "Next") believes

(3)   There are three aardvarks in this enclosure.

Next is epistemically situated just as you are. He perceives what you perceive, and he lacks any additional information about the aardvarks just as you do. Furthermore, Next's belief system is, so we must of course assume, perfectly coherent. True, just as you are, Next is perceiving *two* aardvarks. Coherentists would point out, therefore, that Next's belief system is bound to fall into incoherence: his perceptions will trigger beliefs that conflict with (3). Critics of coherentism could reply, however, that Next's perceptions do not *necessarily* generate incoherence in his belief system. We need only assume again that a mad scientist eliminates with his cognitive ray gun from Next's belief system all those perceptually induced beliefs that conflict with (3). Coherentism implies that, under such circumstances, Next is as justified in believing (3) as you are in believing (1). But this is absurd. Since both you and Next are perceiving two aardvarks, and since neither of you has any further information about the number of aardvarks in the enclosure, you are justified in believing (1), while Next is not in believing (3).

The detachment and the alternative systems objections raise the same difficulty for coherentism. Coherentism is sensitive to epistemic conflict between different beliefs, but not to epistemic conflict between beliefs and perceptual *experiences* that do not manifest themselves in *beliefs*. According to foundationalist critics of coherentism, nondoxastic perceptual experience can be relevant in two ways: they can justify other beliefs, and they can prevent other beliefs from being justified. Coherentism is vulnerable to the two counterexamples we developed above precisely because it acknowledges the relevance of perception only in the form of perceptual beliefs, not in the form of perceptual experience itself.

How do BonJour and Lehrer respond to the isolation objection? According to BonJour, the isolation objection shows that coherentism must be supplemented with what he calls the "observation requirement": for a belief system M to be a justified belief system about world W, M must receive observational input about W. If thus supplemented, coherentism, so BonJour argues, "can allow for, indeed insist upon, the possibility that a cognitive system which is coherent at one time may be rendered incoherent . . . by subsequent observational input."[52]

In light of our two thought experiments, it is clear that this reply, as it stands, is insufficient. BonJour's point is that coherentists can appreciate the importance of perception and observation as the connecting link between our beliefs and the world. But such appreciation does not preclude counterexamples. The problem is that coherentism acknowledges the relevance of perception only in the form of perceptual beliefs, not in the form of nondoxastic perceptual experiences. Consequently, foundationalist critics of coherentism can construe cases in which a belief's justification is undermined, not by other beliefs, but only by a perceptual experience, and then reject coherentism on the ground that it doesn't give us the right results for such cases.

On the other hand, BonJour could reject such counterexamples on the ground of his strict doxasticism: his view that beliefs can be justified—and undermined in their justification—only by other beliefs. Denying that perceptual experience by itself can undermine a belief's justification, he could rebut the detachment objection by saying that *if* a mad scientist ensures that your belief system stays coherent after the third aardvark emerges, then you *are* justified in believing that there are two aardvarks in the enclosure although you are perceiving three. And concerning the alternative systems objection, he could say that *if* Next's belief system is rendered coherent because a mad scientist eliminates all those beliefs that would give rise to incoherence, then he *is* justified in believing that there are three aardvarks in the enclosure although he is perceiving only two.[53]

Whether these maneuvers enjoy plausibility, however, is a further question. In any case, what the isolation objection brings clearly into focus is what the foundationalism-coherentism controversy is ultimately about: the legitimacy of nondoxastic justification. If foundationalists are right in claiming that nondoxastic perceptual experiences are epistemically relevant, then the two cases we considered must be deemed compelling counterexamples to coherentism. If, on the other hand, coherentists are right in denying the relevance of nondoxastic perceptual experiences, then they are also right in asserting the plausibility of the very implications foundationalists claim to be absurd.

Lehrer's reply to the isolation objection is similar to BonJour's. Since we are connected with the world through perception, changes in the world are reflected in our perceptual beliefs. Consequently, Lehrer would argue, if you believe in the presence of three aardvarks when you clearly see only two, your belief will have plenty of competitors in those things you accept on the basis of what you perceive, and it will not beat all of these competitors.[54]

The foundationalist rebuttal to Lehrer's reply is the same as that to BonJour's. Lehrer's reply is that because of the condition that for a belief to be justified all of its competitors must be beaten, coherentism does assign an important role to perception. What this reply achieves is this: Lehrer's coherentism implies that the cases we considered above are *unlikely*, but it does not demonstrate that they are *impossible*. In order to establish that they could not possibly arise, Lehrer would have to formulate an additional reply: one that demonstrated that perceptual experiences, if they do not take the form of either beliefs or acceptances, are epistemically irrelevant.

We must turn, therefore, to precisely this question: Do nondoxastic experiential states have epistemic significance? Can they justify beliefs, and can they prevent beliefs from being justified? In the next chapter, we will examine what both foundationalists and coherentists have to say on this matter.[55]

STUDY QUESTIONS

1. Why do coherentists accept the idea that there is such a thing as circular justification?
2. How does Laurence BonJour conceive of circular justification?
3. What objections are there to viewing coherence as a function of entailment relations, consistency, and explanatory relations?
4. How does Lehrer conceive of acceptance, and how is acceptance different from belief?
5. What, according to Lehrer, is the relation between coherence and competition?
6. What role does trustworthiness play in Lehrer's theory?
7. How does Lehrer's theory generate level ascent?
8. In BonJour's theory, what is the connection between coherence and metajustification?
9. What role does the concept of epistemic responsibility play in Lehrer's theory?
10. How does BonJour's theory generate level ascent?
11. Why does BonJour's version of coherentism have skeptical implications, and what is BonJour's response to these implications?
12. What are the two forms the isolation objection can take?

EXERCISES

1. Is justification through a circular chain of reasoning possible? Discuss the reasons for both an affirmative and a negative answer to this question.
2. Construct two cases illustrating how Lehrer's version of coherentism works. First, construct a case in which a belief is justified because it coheres with *S's* acceptance system—that is, beats all of its competitors. Second, construct a case in which a belief is unjustified because there is one competitor it fails to beat.
3. Construct a case illustrating the detachment objection, and another one illustrating the alternative systems objection.
4. Describe a concrete example that illustrates BonJour's conception of coherence through metajustification.

NOTES

1 Neurath (1932).
2 See Chapter 1, pp. 0f.
3 BonJour (1985), p. 89
4 See Plantinga (1993a), p. 69.
5 For a discussion of the possibility of self-justification, see Chapter 5, pp. 99ff.
6 We must be careful here to distinguish between "*x* is a justifier for *y*" and "*x* completely justifies *y*," which are two different relations. A belief B3 can receive all of its justification from two further beliefs, B1 and B2, in such a way that B1 and B2 each functions as a justifier for B3, but neither B1 by itself nor B2 by itself completely justifies B3. A belief, then, can be a justifier for another one without completely justifying it. Now, the relation "*x* is a justifier for *y*" is clearly

transitive. Consider three beliefs, B1, B2, and B3, such that B1 justifies B2 and B2 justifies B3. Since B1 contributes to the justification of B3 via B2, B1 is a justifier for B3. However, the relation "x completely justifies y" is not transitive. For what *completely* justifies B3 is not B1 by itself, but the conjunction of B1 and B2.

7 The phrase "x justifes y" is ambiguous; it may mean either that x contributes to y's justification or that x completely justifies y. However, when a belief B1 justifies a belief B2, minimally it would have to be true that B1 is a justifier for B2. Consequently, however we interpret our circular chain—as one of justification contributors or as one of complete justifiers—the transitivity of "x is a justifier for y" gives us the result that B1 is a justifier for B1.

8 See Plantinga (1993a), pp. 74ff.

9 BonJour (1985), p. 90.

10 Ibid.

11 Or so it would seem. In Chapter 7, however, we shall see that, according to BonJour, a belief system's justification actually is not generated by its coherence, but rather by *beliefs* about coherence. Thus construed, coherentism can't avoid an infinite regress after all.

12 Consider, for example, the following statement by Brand Blanshard: "Fully coherent knowledge would be knowledge in which every judgment entailed, and was entailed by, the rest of the system." Blanshard (1939), p. 264.

13 See Sosa (1991), p. 114, and Fumerton (1993), p. 243.

14 Thus P1 and P2 present us with a paradox: each of these propositions appears to be obviously true, yet they cannot both be true. For an explanation of why this is so, see Chapter 3, footnote 9.

15 For a discussion of this example, see Kornblith (1989), p. 208.

16 For further discussions of coherence and consistency, see Fumerton (1993) and Klein (1985).

17 For accounts of the concept of explanatory coherence, see BonJour (1985), p. 99, and Lehrer (1990), chap. 5. For critical discussion, see Fumerton (1980) and (1993).

18 Of course there can be other explanations of why my cat is meowing. But let's simply assume that in the situation we are imagining, she is meowing because she is hungry and wants me to get her food.

19 Fumerton (1993), p. 244.

20 BonJour (1985), p. 99 and Lehrer (1990), chap. 5.

21 Lehrer (1990), p. 11.

22 Ibid., p. 4.

23 Ibid., p. 35.

24 See Churchland (1984), p. 38.

25 In order to make this counterexample stick, we would have to explain why the two situations differ with regard to beliefs (1) and (2) without, however, differing in input conditions. It would not appear that such an explanation is difficult to find. For example, we could say that the difference between the two beliefs is caused by a drug. You took this drug in the first situation, but not in the second. Are the chemical effects of the drug on your brain to be counted as input conditions? Certainly they are not to be so counted in a traditional view of cognitive input, according to which input is produced by such things as perception, memory, and introspection.

26 See Lehrer (1990), p. 117.

27 See ibid., p. 116.

28 For a complete account of these matters, see Lehrer (1990), chap. 6. Actually, Lehrer defines coherence not only in terms of beating but also in terms of what he calls "neutralizing." For our purposes in this chapter, however, we need not concern ourselves with this second concept.

29 Lehrer (1990), p. 145.

30 See Chapter 5, pp. 107f.

31 Of course, when there are specific reasons for doubt, second thoughts about one's perceptions come naturally. When wearing blue glasses, few people believe that things are really as bluish as they appear to be.

32 Lehrer (1990), p. 119.

33 The assumption here is not, of course, that I disbelieve (4) and (5), but only that (4) and (5) are not among the propositions I believe.

34 From Lehrer's remarks on the nature of acceptance, it is not ideally clear how he conceives of the relation between acceptance and belief. On the one hand, he claims that acceptances are a subclass of beliefs. On the other hand, he says that "most of what we accept, for example, that

57 is an odd number, we accept without ever having considered it." Lehrer (1989), p. 270. Certainly, prior to reading this sentence, I had not held the belief that 57 is an odd number, for I had indeed never considered this matter. Yet Lehrer seems to be suggesting that it had been an acceptance of mine. But if it had been, then that acceptance was not a belief of mine. See Greco (1993), in which Greco takes Lehrer to be claiming that "acceptances need not be explicit believings" (p. 112).

35 The restriction to empirical beliefs here is important: as far as a priori justification is concerned, BonJour holds a foundationalist view. See BonJour (1985), app. A.

36 See ibid., pp. 30f.

37 BonJour cites Wilfrid Sellars as an influential advocate of the necessity of level ascent. BonJour sums up Sellars's view as follows: According to Sellars, "the justification of an observational belief always depends on the general knowledge that beliefs of that specific kind are nomologically reliable indicators of the actual presence of the sort of factual situation whose existence they assert." BonJour (1985), p. 116; cf. Sellars (1963).

38 BonJour (1985), p. 31 (my italics). See also pp. 122f.

39 See ibid., p. 31.

40 Ibid.

41 See the last section in Chapter 2.

42 Rather, what does matter is that it's possible for the subject to reflect on her evidence and thus to form appropriate beliefs about her evidence.

43 BonJour (1985), p. 117.

44 See Greco (1993), Goldman (1989), and Kornblith (1989).

45 See Goldman (1989).

46 BonJour (1989b), p. 284.

47 BonJour (1989b), p. 284. Cf. BonJour (1985), p. 152, where the same point is made.

48 See BonJour (1989b), p. 285.

49 BonJour (1985), p. 88.

50 This objection is discussed in BonJour (1985), pp. 106ff and 139ff; Lehrer (1990) pp. 143f; Pollock (1986), pp. 76f; and Sosa (1991), pp. 157 and 184. The term "isolation objection" comes from Pollock.

51 Sosa (1991), p. 184.

52 BonJour (1985), p. 144.

53 See ibid., p. 150.

54See Lehrer (1990), pp. 143f.

55 According to John Pollock, the isolation objection is inconclusive because coherentism can easily acknowledge that our beliefs are connected with the world through perception. Pollock (1986), pp. 76f. But as we have seen, this reply misses the point. It only establishes that coherentism makes the kind of counterexamples we have considered unlikely, not that it makes them impossible. Furthermore, Pollock claims that foundationalism does not differ from coherentism "with respect to the relationship between our beliefs and the world. The only way the world can influence our beliefs on either a foundations theory or a coherence theory is causally" (p. 76). However, given the way we have construed foundationalism, there is indeed a crucial difference between how coherentism and foundationalism view perception as the epistemic link between beliefs and the world. According to foundationalism, perceptual states have epistemic significance even when they do not manifest themselves in beliefs. According to coherentism, perception matters only in the form of perceptual beliefs.

CHAPTER SEVEN

THE DEBATE OVER FOUNDATIONALISM AND COHERENTISM

DAVIDSON'S "CIRCLE OF BELIEF" ARGUMENT

In his paper "The Coherence Theory of Truth and Knowledge," Donald Davidson has formulated an important objection to foundationalism. According to Davidson, advocates of coherentism maintain

> that nothing can count as a reason for holding a belief except another belief. Its partisan rejects as unintelligible the request for a ground or source of justification of another ilk.[1]

This passage raises the issue that lies at the heart of the debate over foundationalism and coherentism. According to foundationalists, there is such a thing as nondoxastic justification: justification that has its ground or source in something other than beliefs. Coherentists assert, however, that the source of a belief's justification must always be one or more other beliefs. Davidson sides with the coherentists, on the basis of the following argument:

> We have been trying to see it this way: a person has all his beliefs about the world—that is, all his beliefs. How can he tell if they are true, or apt to be true? Only, we have been assuming, by connecting his beliefs to the world, confronting certain of his beliefs with the deliverances of the senses one by one, or perhaps confronting the totality of his beliefs with the tribunal of experience. No such confrontation makes sense, for of course we can't get outside our skins to find out what is causing the internal happening of which we are aware.[2]

Let us briefly review Davidson's line of argument. What he wants to establish is that a belief's justification must always have its source in other beliefs: the circle-of-belief thesis. This thesis implies, of course, that there is no such thing as nondoxastic justification. Davidson's reason for this thesis is that a confrontation of our beliefs with experience is impossible, for such a confrontation would amount to "getting outside our skins." Consequently, we cannot tell whether a given belief is true by confronting it with an experience, but only by confronting it with other beliefs.

In reply to Davidson's argument, foundationalists could employ a distinction that was introduced above—that between a belief's property of being justified and a person's act of justifying a belief—and interpret Davidson's argument as being concerned, not with the former, but with the latter.[3] Note that Davidson's argument is about how we can *tell* whether a belief is true (or false). But if we want to tell whether a belief is true (or false), then we must engage in the activity of justification. For what is involved in telling a particular belief's truth value is asking oneself whether the belief in question is true, and then *showing* or *arguing* that it is true (or false).

Now as far as the activity of justifying one's beliefs is concerned, Davidson is certainly right. When we engage in that activity, whatever we say in defense of something we believe would always have to be something else we believe. For example, if I tried to show that my belief "The book in front of me is red" is justified by saying "It looks red to me," then I would be stating just another belief of mine. And if I were to justify my belief that it looks red to me by saying that introspection into one's own perceptual states is a reliable source of information, I would again be stating just another belief. It must be conceded, therefore, that when we engage in *argumentation* to justify our beliefs and convictions, there is nothing other than our beliefs to go on. Foundationalists should admit, therefore, that as far as the act of justifying one's beliefs is concerned, the circle-of-belief thesis is true.

When foundationalists claim that there is such a thing as nondoxastic justification, however, what they are concerned with is not the act of justifying, but rather the *property* of being justified and how beliefs acquire that property. Thus they would reply to Davidson's argument that premises that are true about the act of justifying a belief prove nothing regarding a belief's property of being justified. It is one thing for a belief to *be* justified through a perceptual experience and without the aid of any other beliefs, and quite another to *tell* whether, or to *argue* that, a particular belief is thus justified. If one were to do the latter, one would say that the belief in question is justified through a perceptual experience. Alas, saying that is just stating another belief, and thus one would remain confined within the circle of beliefs. But that doesn't mean that the belief in question enjoys the property of being justified by virtue of that further belief rather than the perceptual experience itself.

Let us consider an analogy. In ethics, many philosophers endorse a view called "consequentialism": the view that an act's moral status (its property of being right or wrong) is determined by its consequences. Suppose somebody performs an act that is morally wrong because it has bad consequences. Consequentialists would say that the act is wrong whether or not the agent formed any beliefs about the consequences. They would insist that it is the consequences themselves that make the act wrong.

An objection to consequentialism tailored after Davidson's argument against foundationalism would go like this: When judging the moral status of an act in light of its consequences, we've got nothing to go on except our beliefs about consequences, for we can't "get out of our skins" and ascertain an act's consequences directly. Thus it's unintelligible that an act's moral status can be determined by its consequences, and hence consequentialism is false.

Consequentialists would not be impressed by this argument. Their reply would be parallel to the foundationalist rebuttal to Davidson. They would say that we must distinguish between the act of evaluating an act's moral status and how an act acquires its moral status. When we wish to *judge* whether an act is right or wrong, they would say, we will indeed always be confined within our beliefs about the act's consequences. But this doesn't mean that it's our beliefs about the act's consequences that makes the act right or wrong. Rather, the act is right or wrong depending on its actual consequences, irrespective of what we believe about them.[4]

The foundationalist reply to Davidson's argument runs parallel. Foundationalists claim that there is nondoxastic justification: that beliefs can be justified solely through experience. Now when we endeavor to show that a particular belief is justified by a particular experience, then of course whatever we say will represent not the experience itself but a belief about it. But this doesn't mean that it isn't the experience itself that makes the belief justified.

Before moving on, we should take note of the fact that the foundationalist reply to Davidson's argument should not be construed as an argument supposed to show that there is such a thing as nondoxastic justification. It does no such thing. Rather, its point is merely to show that Davidson's argument does not succeed in establishing that nondoxastic justification is impossible.

BONJOUR'S ARGUMENT AGAINST NONDOXASTIC JUSTIFICATION

Next we shall consider an argument of Laurence BonJour's that, unlike Davidson's, is aimed directly at the viability of basic beliefs.[5] The conclusion of this argument is that a nondoxastic experiential state can't confer on a belief the property of being justified. Thus the maneuver that allows foundationalists to rebut Davidson's argument—that of distinguishing between the act of justifying a belief and the process by which a belief acquires the property of being justified—won't be applicable here. BonJour's argument must be viewed, therefore, as a serious challenge to the foundationalist claim that there is such a thing as nondoxastic justification. How, then, does BonJour arrive at the conclusion that there is no such thing?

According to BonJour, the idea of nondoxastic justification—of justification that is conferred on a belief by an experiential state that is not a state of believing—involves the following dilemma:

> *The Dilemma of Nondoxastic Justification*
>
> Nondoxastic experiences are either states of awareness or they are not. If they are states of awareness, then they can justify only if they are justified themselves. If they are not states of awareness, then they can't be justified themselves and thus can't justify any beliefs.[6]

Suppose the first horn of the dilemma is true: nondoxastic experiences are states of awareness. If so, they can't confer justification on beliefs unless they are justified themselves. But this means that they themselves are in need of justification, and thus can't function as regress terminators. So if the first horn of the dilemma is true, beliefs justified through experiences are just as much in need of justification as beliefs justified by other beliefs, and thus cannot be basic.

Suppose the second horn of the dilemma is true: nondoxastic experiences are not states of awareness. In that case, they are not the kind of thing that can enjoy justification, just as tables and chairs are not the sort of thing that can. But if nondoxastic experiences can't "have" justification, then they can't "give" justification. Thus if the second horn of the dilemma is true, we get again the consequence that there can't be basic beliefs.

In a nutshell, BonJour's argument asserts this: The idea of nondoxastic justification poses the problem of having to choose between two alternatives. Whatever alternative is chosen, it follows that there can't be basic beliefs. Hence it is impossible for basic beliefs to exist.

How would foundationalists reply to this argument? To begin with, it is clear they do have to choose between the two horns of the dilemma, for nondoxastic experiences indeed are either states of awareness or they are not. Second, it is also clear that foundationalists cannot choose the first alternative, for if they did, they could not maintain that basic beliefs can function as regress terminators. Hence, in order to rebut BonJour's argument, foundationalists must show that the second alternative is acceptable: that nondoxastic states actually can confer on beliefs the property of being justified although they are not themselves the sort of thing that can have that property. In short, they must maintain that nondoxastic states can "give" justification although they can't "have" justification.

This seems, at least initially, to be a hopeless task. Recall our earlier argument against the possibility of self-justification. We argued that a belief is either justified to begin with or it is not. If it is, it can't justify itself because it is already justified. And if it isn't, then it can't justify itself because a belief that doesn't "have" justification can't "give" justification to any other belief. BonJour's verdict about the second horn of the dilemma seems to rest on the same intuition: if nondoxastic states are not capable of "having" justification, they are not capable of "giving" justification. Foundationalists, then, face the task of having to defend the view that a nondoxastic state can manage to justify a belief although it isn't the sort of thing that is capable of being justified itself. In the next section, we shall consider how foundationalists might go about accomplishing this feat.

A FOUNDATIONALIST REPLY TO BONJOUR'S ARGUMENT

The issue BonJour's dilemma argument raises is whether a belief's justification can have its source in something that is not itself capable of being justified. BonJour claims that a belief's justification can't have its source in any such thing. Yet, and this is what foundationalists should say in reply to BonJour's argument, his own coherentist position appears to presuppose that it can. The central thesis of coherentism, after all, is that beliefs are justified by coherence. As BonJour puts it: "the justification of a particular empirical belief finally depends . . . on the overall system and its coherence."[7] A belief system's coherence, however, is not itself something capable of justification. A belief system's coherence can be neither justified nor unjustified; yet, according to BonJour, it is the very source from which all justified beliefs receive their justification.

Thus it would appear that coherentists themselves countenance a nondoxastic source of justification, to wit, coherence. But then they are in no position to reject foundationalism on the ground that nondoxastic justification through experiential states is impossible because there is no such thing as nondoxastic justification. Indeed, to deny the possibility of such justification with regard to basic beliefs, but to affirm it with regard to coherence, is arbitrary, if not wholly incoherent.[8]

Although BonJour's dilemma argument seemed initially quite forceful, it must now be said that the foundationalist countermove is at least equally forceful. It derives its strength from pointing out that the coherentist attack on the possibility of nondoxastic justification runs the risk of undermining not only its intended target, foundationalism, but also the coherentist position itself. There is, however, one reply coherentists can resort to in order to recover from this setback. They could say that justified beliefs are justified, not by virtue of coherence relations themselves, but rather by virtue of the subject's *beliefs* about her belief system's coherence. And, in fact, BonJour seems to conceive of coherentism in precisely that way, as borne out by his thorough doxasticism, which manifests itself in the way he conceives of the necessity of level ascent.[9]

This coherentist rejoinder—let's call it the "doxastic move"—does not, however, achieve a complete recovery from the foundationalist counterattack, for it invites two rather serious objections. According to the first, a thoroughly doxastic conception of coherentism generates an *infinite regress* that makes justification impossible. According to the second, the doxastic move is at odds with a thesis that enjoys a high degree of plausibility: the thesis that an evaluative property such as a belief's status of being justified must *supervene* on, or be anchored in, a set of nonevaluative properties.

Before moving on to discuss these two objections, let's summarize the foundationalist countermove to BonJour's dilemma argument. Note that the point of this countermove is that coherentists face a dilemma themselves.

> *The Dilemma of Coherentism*
> According to coherentism, justification is conferred on beliefs either by coherence itself or by beliefs about coherence. If justification is conferred by coherence itself, nondoxastic justification is admitted in principle, for a belief system's coherence is nondoxastic in nature. If, on the other hand, justification is conferred by beliefs about coherence, then the resulting conception of justification suffers from two flaws: first, it generates an unpalatable infinite regress; and second, it is at odds with the thesis that the property of being justified, as an evaluative property, supervenes on nonevaluative properties.

However coherentists try to get around this dilemma, the problems they encounter are formidable. If they accept that coherence itself is a source of justification, then they are forced to admit in principle that there is such a thing as nondoxastic justification—which makes it rather tenuous to maintain that nondoxastic justification through coherence is possible, while nondoxastic justification through experience is not.[10] On the other hand, if coherentists make the doxastic move—if they argue that justification is generated not through coherence itself but only beliefs about coherence— then they face two problems that are just as serious as the one they encounter if they don't make the doxastic move. These problems will be the subject of the next three sections.

COHERENTISM AND THE REGRESS OF LEVELS

According to the doxastic move, the source from which a justified belief receives its justification consists in beliefs about coherence. Coherentism, if it involves the doxastic move, can therefore be represented thus:

(J)   For every belief B that S holds, B is justified if and only if S believes that B coheres with the other beliefs of S's belief system.

Coherentism, thus understood, implies that for every justified belief B, there must be a metabelief B^* to the effect that B coheres with the other beliefs of the subject's belief system. So if *B* is a justified belief of mine and its justification is derived from beliefs about coherence, then I must hold at least one belief *B** to the effect that *B* coheres with my belief system. What, however, about the justification of *B** itself? According to (J), the justification of *B** has its source in a belief *B*** to the effect that *B** coheres with my belief system. The same is true, of course, of *B***, *B****, and so on. (J) generates, therefore, an infinite regress of the following kind:

> *B**   My belief *B* coheres with my other beliefs.
>
> *B***   Belief *B** coheres with the rest of my beliefs.
>
> *B**** Belief *B*** coheres with the rest of my beliefs.

About this regress, it is important to notice that it isn't simply an ordinary regress of justifying beliefs; rather, it is a regress that traverses through an infinite series of doxastic levels. *B** is a belief about a belief, and thus a metabelief; *B*** is a belief about a metabelief, and thus a meta-metabelief, and so forth. In this way, the doxastic move generates an infinite hierarchy of doxastic levels.[11]

Such an infinite hierarchy is problematic for two reasons. First, quite early in the regress, such beliefs become too complicated to be comprehended. Just consider what *B*** amounts to when we let *B* stand for the belief that there is a book on the desk:

> My belief that my belief "There is a book on the desk" coheres with my other beliefs coheres with my other beliefs.

Second, it is impossible for finite minds to hold an infinite series of such beliefs. The doxastic move must be considered, therefore, a prescription for skepticism. Let us see why.

According to the doxastic move, the source from which every justified belief receives its justification consists in beliefs about coherence. In other words, it is a necessary condition of justification that every justified belief *B* be accompanied by a belief *B**, which attributes to *B* the property of being a member of a coherent system of beliefs. Since each belief attributing this property must itself be accompanied by a belief attributing this property, the doxastic move in effect implies that every justified belief be accompanied by an infinite series of metabeliefs. Since it is impossible for finite minds to form such an infinite series of metabeliefs, the doxastic move imposes a condition on justification finite minds cannot satisfy. Hence humans, falling short of having infinite minds, cannot have justified beliefs.

Could coherentists reply that the formation of a metabelief of the form "*B* coheres with my other beliefs" is not really a necessary condition? Of course they could do so, but not without implicitly admitting the possibility of nondoxastic justification. For the point of the doxastic move is to maintain the coherentist position—according to which nondoxastic justification is impossible—without admitting coherence itself as a source of nondoxastic justification. Hence the result the doxastic move is supposed to ensure is this: *Every* justified belief owes its justification, at least in part, to beliefs about coherence. But as we have seen, this result comes with the price tag of an infinite regress. It is true that this regress can be avoided by abandoning the idea that justification through beliefs about coherence is a *necessary* ingredient of all justification. However, as soon as that idea is abandoned, the door is opened to let nondoxastic justification in and let it play its proper part within a foundationalist theory.

THE BONJOUREAN LEVEL REGRESS

It is worthwhile to examine precisely how BonJour's conception of level ascent, which is based on what we have called the "doxastic move," generates an infinite regress. According to BonJour, basic beliefs are impossible because every justified empirical belief owes its justification to at least two premises, as exhibited in the following schema:

(1)   *B* has feature *F*.

(2)   Beliefs having feature *F* are very likely to be true.

Therefore:

(3)   *B* is very likely to be true.[12]

This schema is an account of how beliefs receive their justification: a belief is justified if and only if it is supported by premises (1) and (2). While the schema itself is silent as to whether premises (1) and (2) must simply be true or must take the form of actual beliefs, BonJour is explicit about his view on this matter. He demands that (1) and (2) take the form of actual beliefs. What justifies our beliefs, according to BonJour, isn't the *fact* of coherence, but rather our *beliefs* about coherence.[13]

BonJour's schema does not impose as a necessary condition that each justified belief *B* must be accompanied by an explicit belief to the effect that *B coheres* with the subject's other beliefs. After all, a subject who does not have the concept of coherence and so could not ask herself whether her belief system enjoys coherence could still believe (1) and (2), and thus believe what in effect amounts to the requisite beliefs about coherence. Nevertheless, BonJour's schema does generate a regress just as serious as the one we considered above. The point of the displayed schema is this: No belief can be justified unless it is accompanied by further beliefs that are reasons for its truth, such as (1) and (2). And clearly these reasons themselves must be justified. Hence (1) and (2) in turn must satisfy BonJour's schema—which is what generates a level regress.

To see how this goes, let's focus on (1). For the original belief, *B*, to be justified, (1) must be justified. Consequently, it is a necessary condition of *B's* justification that the subject form the metabelief

B^* (1) has feature *F*.

This metabelief, too, must satisfy BonJour's schema. Thus we are led to a meta-metabelief:

B^{**} My belief "(1) has feature *F*" has feature *F*.

And since this belief as well must satisfy the schema, we get a meta-meta-metabelief B^{***}:

B^{***} My belief "My belief that (1) has feature *F* has feature *F*" has feature *F*.

Each further metabelief in the series must be justified in the same way, and thus an infinite regress of doxastic levels is generated, a regress that is just as pernicious as the one we considered above. Consider the complexity of the metabelief at the third level, and let the belief to be justified be "There is a book on the table":

My belief that my belief that there is a book on the table has feature *F* has feature *F* has feature *F*.

To impose the formation of an infinite series of such metabeliefs as a necessary condition on justification is to make justification impossible. We are led to conclude, therefore, that BonJour's doxasticism—his insistence that a belief's justifying grounds must consist in further beliefs—leads straight into the abyss of skepticism about the possibility of justified belief.

In response to this argument, BonJour has argued that although a justified belief is always justified through further beliefs that are reasons for its truth, *these further beliefs need not be metabeliefs*.[14] This claim, however, is at odds with BonJour's own general justificatory schema, which makes the formation of metabeliefs a necessary condition of justification. Now, BonJour tries to get around this difficulty by conceding that the formation of actual beliefs in the form of premises (1) and (2) is a necessary condition of justification—but not for just any belief, merely for beliefs of a certain kind. Thus, in the following passage, he points out that his schema is intended to require metajustification only for "putatively foundational" beliefs:

It needs to be stressed, however, that the schema was formulated with puta- tively foundational beliefs, those for which no ordinary inferential justification is offered, in mind and was not necessarily intended to generalize to all cases in which one belief provides a reason for thinking another to be true.[15]

BonJour proposes, then, that the schema in question is applicable only to those beliefs foundationalists would take to be basic: beliefs for which an "ordinary inferential justification" cannot be offered. Concerning those beliefs for which an ordinary inferential justification *can* be offered, the beliefs justifying them need not be metabeliefs. Rather, such beliefs can be justified by ordinary reasons that are located at the first level. Thus BonJour writes:

> But what is essential, on my view, is simply that the believer possess such a cogent reason, whatever form it may take. . . . It is not necessary that a reason for thinking that a belief is likely to be true take the form of a metabelief.[16]

BonJour, then, distinguishes between two kinds of beliefs: (i) beliefs for which an ordinary inferential justification *cannot* be offered (the kind of beliefs that foundationalists take to be basic); and (ii) beliefs for which an ordinary inferential justification *can* be offered. Let's refer to the former as *noninferential* and the latter as *inferential* beliefs. BonJour maintains that both types of beliefs cannot be justified unless supported by justifying reasons in the form of further beliefs. For noninferential beliefs, these reasons must take the form of metabeliefs, because, as BonJour concedes, such beliefs must satisfy the schema displayed above. For inferential beliefs, however, justifying reasons need not take the form of metabeliefs. And therefore, according to BonJour, the problem of the infinite level regress is avoided.

It is not difficult to see why this reply enjoys only limited success. BonJour states explicitly that his schema was formulated with those beliefs in mind that foundationalists take to be basic: cognitively spontaneous beliefs for which an ordinary inferential justification is difficult to come by. His own example of such a belief is "There is a red book on the desk."[17] Now, our beliefs about our physical surroundings are to a very large extent beliefs of this type. If beliefs of this type must satisfy BonJour's schema, then it follows, because of the infinite regress BonJour's schema generates, that it is impossible for beliefs of this type to be justified. Thus BonJour's theory leads to a strange consequence: whereas inferential beliefs can be justified, noninferential beliefs such as "There is a red book on the desk" cannot. This is a reversal of what epistemologists have typically thought: that the potential strength of an empirical belief's justifiation is a function of its proximity to perceptual experience. The closer a belief is connected to perceptual experience, the better its potential for justification, and the further inference removes a belief from justification, the worse its potential for justification. Be this as it may, the implication that cognitively spontaneous beliefs about ordinary physical objects can't be justified should be unacceptable to anyone opposed to skepticism about the possibility of justified belief.

Suppose BonJour were to say that even as far as noninferential beliefs are concerned, the necessary justifying reasons need not be metabeliefs. In that case, we would have to ask what types of justifying reasons we could possibly find for such beliefs except for reasons such as premises (1) and (2) in BonJour's schema. After all, BonJour himself describes the beliefs in question—putatively foundational beliefs—as those for which no ordinary inferential justification can be offered. Hence if BonJour were to abandon his justificatory schema even for noninferential beliefs, it would remain entirely mysterious how, according to his theory, such beliefs could be justified at all.[18]

Thus the objection that BonJour's doxastic conception of coherentist justification generates an infinite level regress remains in full force at least as far as noninferential beliefs are concerned. The moral of this objection would seem to be this: Either coherentism turns into a version of skepticism with regard to noninferential beliefs, or it is construed as a theory that views coherence itself as a source of justification, and thus allows for nondoxastic justification in principle. This, of course, is a bitter pill for coherentists to swallow, for once the possibility of nondoxastic justification is conceded, it becomes unclear how they could justify their principled opposition to the foundationalist claim that there are basic beliefs.

SUPERVENIENCE: THE CASE FOR NONDOXASTIC JUSTIFICATION

In Chapter 2, we studied what reasons there are for claiming that a belief's justification—a special kind of evaluative status—must supervene on a set of nonevaluative properties. Let's briefly restate the main two points. First, we argued that two beliefs that share their nonnormative properties must share their epistemic properties. This is the view that a belief's epistemic status weakly supervenes on the belief's descriptive nature. Second, we argued that if a belief has the nonnormative properties that make it justified in *one* possible world, then it is justified in *all* possible worlds in which it has these nonnormative properties. This is the thesis that a belief's epistemic status *strongly* supervenes on its descriptive nature.[19]

Now, when coherentists make the doxastic move—when they claim that the source of justification is to be found, not in coherence itself, but in beliefs about coherence—then it becomes mysterious how coherentism can be reconciled with the supervenience of epistemic status on nonnormative properties. The reason is as follows.

Suppose that, as the doxastic move asserts, the source from which a belief receives its justification lies in beliefs about coherence. Clearly, though, it cannot lie in *unjustified* beliefs about coherence. Rather, if a belief receives its justification from beliefs about coherence, then these further beliefs must be justified in turn. So what coherentism, if it incorporates the doxastic move, tells us, in effect, is that the source of a belief's justification always lies in further *justified* beliefs about coherence. Consider a particular belief B and assume B is justified. Now, if foundationalists ask a coherentist (who endorses the doxastic move) to say what it is that justifies B, the coherentist would have to answer: B derives its justification from at least one further justified belief about coherence that functions as B's justifying reason. But if the coherentist answers the foundationalists' question in this way, she is explaining one belief's justification in terms of another belief's justification—which is to say, she is failing to make the analytic step from the evaluative level of justification to the domain of those nonevaluative properties that generate justification.[20]

At this juncture, foundationalists will press their point. They will ask the coherentist: "Does epistemic justification ultimately arise from a nonnormative source, or does it not?" If the coherentist remains faithful to the doxastic move, she will say: "No, it does not." In light of our discussion of supervenience in Chapter 2, we must say that this would not be a plausible answer. If, however, the coherentist answers the foundationalists' question by saying "Yes, it does," then, in effect, she abandons the doxastic move and identifies coherence itself, understood as a nonepistemic relation between beliefs, as the ultimate source of justification. And in doing so, she admits in principle that there is such a thing as nondoxastic justification.[21]

At the end of the section on BonJour's argument against nondoxastic justification, we noted that our argument against the possibility of self-justification presupposes a principle that relies on the very intuition that drives BonJour's argument. That principle is that if a belief doesn't already "have" justification, it can't "give" justification to itself. The underlying intuition, it appears, is that something can justify only if it has justification itself. However, if we accept that a belief's property of being justified supervenes on nonevaluative properties, then we must resist this intuition. And doing so poses no insurmountable obstacle, for we must distinguish between the following two principles:

(A) For any two beliefs B1 and B2, if B1 justifies B2, then B1 must be justified itself.

(B) For any two things x and y, if x is the source of y's justification, then x must be something that has justification itself.

(A), which is the principle we appealed to in our argument against the possibility of self-justification, does not imply principle (B). Principle (A) is about *beliefs*, which are capable of being justified or unjustified. And the intuition behind (A) is that whatever is *capable of being justified* must be justified itself in order to justify something else. Principle (B), in contrast, is about anything whatever; it is a principle that includes within its scope things that are *incapable of being justified*. Clearly, we may maintain that what is capable of being justified must be justified itself in order to justify without also having to maintain that what is incapable of being justified must be justified itself in order to justify. Indeed, if we accept the supervenience thesis about justification, we must view such things as a belief system's coherence and a belief's perceptual ground as sources of justification: as things that can justify but which are not themselves capable of being justified. Hence there is no inconsistency involved, in asserting (A) and rejecting (B).

It would appear, then, that the foundationalist commitment to nondoxastic justification is in good shape after all. It should be seen, however, that the reasoning in support of nondoxastic justification does not, ipso facto, amount to an argument for foundationalism and against coherentism. For coherentists can admit that there is nondoxastic justification and still maintain that foundationalism and coherentism are mutually incompatible theories. If they were to do so, they would have to claim that there is one, and only one, nondoxastic source of justification: coherence relations among beliefs. In this view, justification is generated through certain nonevaluative relations beliefs bear to other beliefs, and never through relations beliefs bear to things other than beliefs. Now, while there is nothing obviously incoherent about this view, it is unclear what argument can be made in its support. For once it is granted in principle that nondoxastic justification is possible, and indeed necessary if there is justification at all, then it is difficult to see what reason there might be to exclude perceptual, introspective, and memorial states from the club of nondoxastic justifiers.

Let us briefly sum up where the debate over foundationalism and coherentism has led us. The debate's starting point is BonJour's dilemma argument against the possibility of nondoxastic justification: Nondoxastic justifiers are either states of awareness, and therefore need to be justified themselves; or they are not states of awareness, and thus, not being capable of being justified themselves, cannot justify anything. The foundationalist reply to this argument is that the second horn of the dilemma is false: nondoxastic states can justify even though they are not states of awareness and thus are not capable of being justified themselves. In support of this claim, foundationalists confront the coherentists with a dilemma objection of their own: Either coherentists admit coherence as a nondoxastic source of justification or they don't. If they do, then it remains mysterious on what grounds they can maintain that there are no sources of justification other than coherence relations among beliefs. If they don't, then they initiate an unacceptable level regress, and furthermore fail to identify the nonevaluative grounds on which justification supervenes.

LEHRER'S COHERENTISM RECONSIDERED

In light of the regress problems BonJour's version of coherentism generates, how does Lehrer's theory fare? As we saw in our examination of the theory in Chapter 5, Lehrer's notion of coherence involves two ingredients: (i) competitors must be beaten; (ii) the subject must take herself to be a trustworthy source of information under the relevant circumstances. Let's summarize Lehrer's coherentism as follows:

(JL) *S's* acceptance *A* is justified if and only if (i) in *S's* acceptance system, all of *A's* competitors are beaten; (ii) *S* accepts that she is a trustworthy source of information under the circumstances under which *A* was produced.

Does (JL) generate an infinite level regress? To find that out, we must focus on condition (ii). If condition (ii) is satisfied, then *S's* belief system contains the meta-acceptance

A* I am a trustworthy source of information under the circumstances under which *A* was produced.

How is this meta-acceptance justified in turn? Here is Lehrer's answer to this question:

The claim that I am trustworthy in any particular matter under any special set of circumstances may be justified on the basis of the other things that I accept; I accept that I have had success in reaching the truth about similar matters in similar circumstances in the past and that the present circumstances do not differ in any relevant way from past circumstances when I was correct.[22]

This sounds plausible enough, but it does not address the issue that is crucial: in order for *A** to be justified, must *A** itself meet condition (ii) of (JL)? If it must, then we do get an infinite regress, for then *A** must be accompanied by the meta-meta-acceptance

A** I am a trustworthy source of information under the circumstances under which *A** was produced.

which in turn must be accompanied by a meta-meta-meta-acceptance *A****, and so forth.

Of course, the infinite regress thus generated is one of *acceptances*, not of beliefs. We might wonder, therefore, whether an infinite regress of acceptances, unlike one of beliefs, might not be innocuous. Now, according to Lehrer, "the mental state of acceptance is a functional state, one that plays a role in thought, inference, and action."[23] Consequently, if *A** must be justified itself, then (JL) implies that every justified acceptance comes accompanied by an infinite series of mental states, each of which plays a role in thought, inference, and action. But it is doubtful, to say the least, that finite minds are capable of having an infinite series of such mental states.[24] We are to conclude, therefore, that an infinite regress of acceptances is just as pernicious as one of beliefs. Hence, if (JL) generates an infinite regress of meta-acceptances, then it must be viewed as a prescription for skepticism.

Lehrer, however, seems to be claiming that A^* need not be justified by a meta-acceptance such as A^{**}. Unfortunately, his reasoning behind this claim is not ideally clear. Right after the passage quoted above, he says this:

> There is, however, more to the issue. I may accept that my faculties, perception, memory, reasoning, and so forth are trustworthy guides to truth in circumstances of the sort that I find myself in when I accept some claim of those faculties. I must accept, however, that I am trustworthy as well: that when I accept something, that is a good enough reason for thinking it to be true, so that it is at least more reasonable for me to accept it than to accept its denial.[25]

Now, if someone takes herself to be trustworthy in the way suggested in this passage, so Lehrer continues to argue, she accepts the following principle:

(T)   Whatever I accept with the objective of accepting something just in case it is true, I accept in a trustworthy manner.[26]

Suppose, then, you take yourself to be a trustworthy source of information, and thus accept (T). How do we get from here to the result that A^* need not be justified by a meta-acceptance such as A^{**}? As mentioned above, Lehrer's exposition of this issue fails to make the desired connection ideally clear, but perhaps the following attempt at getting at the gist of his argument is a fair try.

To begin with, let us refer to (T) as the *global trustworthiness principle*, for if you accept (T), then you take yourself to be a trustworthy source of information with respect to all of your cognitive faculties: perception, memory, introspection, and reasoning. The global trustworthiness principle must be distinguished from *local trustworthiness claims* of the form A^*, which are demanded by condition (ii) of (JL). Our problem is to find out precisely how the global trustworthiness principle is supposed to exempt local trustworthiness claims of the form A^* from having to meet condition (ii)—that is, from the need to be justified by meta-meta-acceptances of the form A^{**}.

Lehrer's proposal seems to be this: The desired connection is that if you accept the global trustworthiness principle, then *whatever* you accept is more reasonable than its denial. So if you accept the global trustworthiness principle, then all your local trustworthiness claims of the form A^* are more reasonable than their denial. In this way, your local trustworthiness claims acquire a positive epistemic status without owing anything to higher-order acceptances of the form A^{**}.

How does this connection make local trustworthiness claims *completely* justified? After all, the epistemic status they receive from principle (T) is rather modest: (T) makes them merely more reasonable than their denial. Lehrer himself points out that this falls short of full-fledged justification.[27] Recall, however, what Lehrer says in the first passage we quoted above about how

> A^* I am a trustworthy source of information under the circumstances under which A was produced

can be justified. According to Lehrer, it can be justified by acceptances such as these:

> A1   In the past, I had success in reaching the truth about similar matter A is about under circumstances similar to those under which A was produced;
>
> A2   The circumstances under which I was right about these matters in the past don't differ in any relevant way from the circumstances under which A was produced.[28]

Now, the solution to our problem suggests itself. Acceptances such as A1 and A2 lift the epistemic status of A^* from that of merely being more reasonable than its denial to that of full-fledged justification. Moreover, *the meta-meta-acceptance A^{**} plays no part in how A^* acquires this status.* We can see, then, how Lehrer manages to produce the rabbit—full-fledged justification for A^*—out of the top hat. First, principle (T) endows A^* with the status of being more reasonable than its denial. Second, acceptances such as A1 and A2 elevate A^*'s status of being more reasonable than its denial all the way up to complete justification. Thus it would appear that Lehrer's theory accomplishes what BonJour's does not: it makes metajustification a necessary condition of justification without, however, generating an infinite level regress.

Reviewing this line of argument, we might wonder whether its result isn't too good to be true. Let's reconsider Lehrer's theory:

> (JL) S's acceptance A is justified if and only if (i) in S's acceptance system, all of A's competitors are beaten; (ii) S accepts that she is a trustworthy source of information under the circumstances under which A was produced.

According to (JL), for an acceptance to be justified, it must meet condition (ii). As we have seen, if this is upheld for acceptances and meta-acceptances alike, then a pernicious infinite level regress is inevitable. Consequently, the upshot of Lehrer's story about principle (T) must be that the *meta-acceptances condition (ii) generates can be justified without having to meet condition (ii)*. But this means that in order to avoid the regress problem, Lehrer's theory of justification splits into two separate accounts: one of first-order acceptances and another of meta-acceptances. Condition (i) is an ingredient of both theories: both acceptances and meta-acceptances are justified only if all of their competitors are beaten. Condition (ii), however, if a level regress is to be avoided, must not be imposed on the justification of meta-acceptances. But now we may wonder why it is that the standard of justification meta-acceptances of the form

> A^* I am a trustworthy source of information under the circumstances under which A was produced

must meet is less stringent than the standard of justification first-order acceptances must meet. Why is it that an acceptance such as

> (1)   There is a book on the desk

must be accompanied by the meta-acceptance

> (1*)   I am a trustworthy source of information under the circumstances under which (1) was produced

whereas this meta-acceptance *need not* be accompanied by a meta-acceptance about my trustworthiness under the conditions under which *it* was produced? Why is it that (1) must, whereas (1*) need not, meet condition (ii) in (JL)? Surely we need to know what rationale there is for this difference in treatment of first-order and second-order acceptances.

It is in response to this challenge that Lehrer's principle of global trustworthiness is supposed to kick in. (T), making all of my acceptances such that they are more reasonable than their denials, so Lehrer's account would appear to go, exempts (1*) from having to meet condition (ii). But the following question immediately presents itself: Why is it that (T)'s benefits are restricted to meta-acceptances only? Why doesn't (T) exempt (1) as well from metajustification? According to Lehrer, (T) makes *all* acceptances of the acceptance system of which it is a member more reasonable than their denials. It stands to reason, therefore, that if (T) does have the epistemic effect Lehrer attributes to it, this effect should be the same for first-order and higher-order acceptances alike.

Thus Lehrer's different treatment of first-order and second-order acceptances remains unjustified, which means that Lehrer's discrimination in favor of meta-acceptances—their exemption from having to meet condition (ii)—is arbitrary. Lehrer, then, faces an unfortunate dilemma. Either he exempts meta-acceptances from having to meet condition (ii) of (JL) or he does not. If he exempts them, then it becomes unclear why metajustification is necessary for first-order acceptances although it is not for higher-order acceptances. And if he does not exempt them, then a pernicious level regress is inevitable. Therefore it would seem that, in the final analysis, Lehrer's approach to level ascent is no more successful than BonJour's.

A FINAL VERDICT

Coherentism, as a view about the structure of empirical justification, is essentially antifoundationalist. According to BonJour, foundationalism is false because no belief can be justified without receiving its justification from other beliefs. According to Lehrer, foundationalism is false because no acceptance can be justified without receiving its justification from other acceptances.[29] In addition to its antifoundationalism, coherentism—at least as represented by BonJour and Lehrer—involves a commitment to level ascent or metajustification. Both BonJour and Lehrer insist that a belief cannot be justified without an accompanying metajustification: an epistemic evaluation of the conditions under which the belief was formed. BonJour demands that this evaluation take the form of beliefs, Lehrer that it take the form of acceptances.

In this chapter, we have seen that these two ingredients of coherentism—antifoundationalism and the commitment to level ascent—are at variance with each other. BonJour's and Lehrer's antifoundationalism manifests itself in, and is dependent upon, the conditions they impose on justification. BonJour demands metabeliefs, Lehrer meta-acceptances, that evaluate the circumstances under which beliefs are formed. It is precisely this demand that makes coherentism antifoundationalist in nature, for if every belief's justification depends on another one that provides metajustification for it, then there can't be any basic beliefs. But these metabeliefs and meta-acceptances must themselves meet the conditions BonJour and Lehrer impose, which is what generates an infinite regress of doxastic levels. The chief problem coherentists face is how to avoid this type of regress.

Since it is Lehrer's and BonJour's antifoundationalism that is responsible for the regress problems to which their theories succumb, the question we must ask is obvious: Why not retain the second ingredient of coherentism—its commitment to level ascent—but discard the first—its antifoundationalism? Why not demand metajustification without demanding that it take the form of beliefs or acceptances? Indeed, given the seriousness of the regress problems BonJour and Lehrer face, it would seem reasonable to combine the virtues of both coherentism and foundationalism into a single theory of justification.

How could a theory of justification handle the problem of demanding metajustification without generating a level regress? In Chapter 5, we outlined an evidentialist answer to this question. If we want to insist on the importance of metajustification without generating an infinite regress, then we ought to demand no more than this: that for a belief *B* to be justified, the subject have *evidence* for taking herself to be reliable under the conditions under which *B* was formed. But if our view of justification exhibits such modesty—if the demand for metajustification is construed as a demand, not for the formation of metabeliefs, but for the presence of evidence that would justify appropriate metabeliefs if they were formed—the door is opened for what we have called "nondoxastic justification." For then there are no grounds left for opposing the view that if an empirical belief is supported by appropriate perceptual, introspective, or memorial evidence, it can be justified without receiving its justification from any other beliefs or acceptances.

Our final verdict, then, is that foundationalists and coherentists can mutually benefit from the respective virtues their theories have to offer. Foundationalists, as we saw in Chapter 5, need to appeal to level ascent in order to explain how basic beliefs are justified. And coherentists, as we have seen in this chapter, need to come to terms with nondoxastic justification if they are to tame the regress spirits their antifoundationalism is bound to call up.

STUDY QUESTIONS

1. How does Davidson argue in support of coherentism?
2. Which distinction would foundationalists employ in order to reply to his argument, and how would they try to take advantage of that distinction?
3. According to BonJour, what dilemma do advocates of nondoxastic justification face?
4. According to foundationalists, what dilemma do advocates of coherentism face?
5. When coherentists try to resolve this dilemma by making the doxastic move, exactly what do they assert?
6. Why does the doxastic move generate a level regress?
7. What form does this level regress take in BonJour's theory?
8. How does BonJour reply to the charge that his theory generates a level regress?
9. How could foundationalists rebut BonJour's reply?
10. Why does the supervenience thesis pose a problem for coherentists?
11. Why does Lehrer's theory face the threat of a level regress?
12. What role does the "global trustworthiness" principle play in Lehrer's theory?

EXERCISES

1. Make what you take to be the strongest possible case for coherentism.
2. Make what you take to be the strongest possible case for foundationalism.
3. Discuss how coherentism could avoid the problem of the level regress.
4. Discuss whether Lehrer's theory ultimately does, or does not, avoid the problem of a level regress.
5. State and defend your own verdict on the foundationalism-coherentism controversy.

NOTES

1 Davidson (1983), p. 426.

2 Ibid., p. 431.

3 An argument along these lines can be found in Sosa (1991), pp. 109f. For the act/property distinction, see Chapter 1, p. 10.

4 This is not intended as a defense of consequentialism. Rather, the point is that a Davidson-type objection to consequentialism is not conclusive.

5 See BonJour (1985), p. 75, and BonJour (1989b), p. 281.

6 In BonJour (1989b), the argument is spelled out in terms of experiences that are states of awareness and those that are not; in BonJour (1985), it is formulated in terms of judgmental or cognitive states versus nonjudgmental or noncognitive states.

7 BonJour (1985) p. 92. Cf. the following passage on p. 101: "According to a coherence theory of empirical justification, as so far characterized, the epistemic justification of an empirical belief derives entirely from its coherence with the believer's overall system of empirical beliefs. . . ."

8 This problem is made worse by the fact that BonJour endorses foundationalism for beliefs that are justified a priori. See BonJour (1985), app. A, pp. 191–211. The grounds of the justification for such beliefs must lie either in the nature of the propositions that are believed (their necessity or their axiomatic nature, for example) or in psychological states such as intuitive apprehension or grasp of necessity. What all of these grounds have in common is that they are nondoxastic sources of justification.

9 See our account of BonJourean coherentism in Chapter 6.

10 Note that BonJour's dilemma argument makes no such discrimination between possible and impossible types of nondoxastic justification. Instead, its point is that nondoxastic justification as such is impossible because what can't be justified itself cannot confer justification.

11 See Fumerton (1993), p. 242.

12 See BonJour (1985), p. 31. For a discussion of this issue, see Steup (1989).

13 See BonJour (1985), pp. 31 and 101f.

14 See BonJour (1989a).

15 See ibid., p. 58.

16 Ibid.

17 BonJour (1985), pp. 116f.

18 Notice the sample justifications of observational beliefs in BonJour (1985), chap. 6: all of them contain metabeliefs for their premises.

19 See Chapter 2, pp. 30–34.

20 See Sosa (1991), pp. 110f.

21 One way in which the supervenience thesis is significant then, is that the argument for it is an argument for the existence of nondoxastic justification. See Sosa (1991), pp. 149–164, and Van Cleve (1985).

22 Lehrer (1990), p. 122.

23 Ibid., p. 174.

24 Is it reasonable to assume that there could be an actual mental state that plays the functional role of a meta-acceptance at the 5873rd level?

25 Ibid., p. 122.

26 Ibid.

27 See ibid., pp. 123f.

28 We might ask how A1 and A2 are justified themselves. The answer is that they are justified if they satisfy the two conditions of (JL): they must beat all of their competitors, and S must accept a meta-acceptance to the effect that she is trustworthy under the circumstances under which she is accepting A1 and A2.

29 However, as we saw in Chapter 6, this argument poses no threat to foundationalism as defined in Chapter 5. A basic belief is one that is justified without owing its justification to any other beliefs. Thus a belief can be basic even if it owes its justifiation to further acceptances—provided these acceptances are not in turn beliefs.

CHAPTER EIGHT

RELIABILISM

PROCESS RELIABILISM

Among those who are proponents of reliabilism, Alvin Goldman may be considered the most influential contributor. Let us, therefore, focus on various versions of reliabilism Goldman has proposed in a series of important papers. We shall begin with the account he developed in his 1979 paper "What Is Justified Belief?" in which he introduces the concept of *belief-producing* or *belief-causing processes*. As examples of such processes, Goldman mentions the following:

> confused reasoning, wishful thinking, reliance on emotional attachment, mere hunch or guesswork, and hasty generalization

which he compares with

> perceptual processes, remembering, good reasoning, and introspection.[1]

These two sets of processes differ in the following respect: those in the first group produce beliefs that are mostly false, whereas those in the second group produce beliefs that are mostly true. In short, those in the second group are *reliable*, while those in the first are not. Goldman's proposal is that

> the justification status of a belief is a function of the reliability of the process or processes that cause it, where (as a first approximation) reliability consists in the tendency of a process to produce beliefs that are true rather than false.[2]

In order to examine the implications of this proposal, let us formulate it in the form of a biconditional. Since the items that are supposed to be reliable are belief-producing processes, we shall refer to this particular version of reliabilism as *process* reliabilism. And for the sake of simplicity, we shall call belief-producing processes *cognitive* processes.

Process Reliabilism (Initial Version)
>   *S's* belief *B* is justified if and only if *B* is produced by a reliable cognitive process.[3]

As Goldman himself points out, reliabilism thus understood is vulnerable to objections from evidential defeat. Such objections describe beliefs that, although reliably produced, fail to be justified because the subject has evidence for taking them to be caused by an *unreliable* process.[4] Suppose Spencer suffers from an apparent memory loss and decides to consult a neurophysiologist about his problem. This neurophysiologist, an eminent authority in his field, tells Spencer that his childhood memories are extremely unreliable.[5] Suppose further that although Spencer's childhood memories are in fact very reliable, Spencer is fully justified in believing the neurophysiologist's assertion to the contrary. The neurophysiologist's verdict defeats the reliability of Spencer's memories as a source of justification, and thus, if Spencer were to retain his beliefs about what happened during his childhood, these beliefs would be unjustified. According to our initial version of process reliabilism, however, they would be justified because they are reliably produced.

To handle cases of this kind, Goldman introduces a further condition, which is motivated by the idea that "the justificational status of a belief is not only a function of the cognitive processes actually employed in producing it; it is also a function of processes that could and should be employed."[6] Let us amend our initial version of process reliabilism with this condition:

Process Reliabilism (Final Version)
>   *S's* belief *B* is justified if and only if (i) *B* is produced by a reliable cognitive process; (ii) there is no alternative reliable process available to *S* that, had it been used by *S* in addition to the process actually used, would have resulted in *S's* not forming *B*.[7]

Let's apply this improved version of process reliabilism to the case involving the neurophysiologist. Suppose Spencer, ignoring the neurophysiologist's verdict, retains his memory beliefs about his childhood. In so doing, he ignores evidence that undermines his beliefs about his childhood. We may say, therefore, that Spencer uses the evidence available to him improperly. As Goldman points out, "the proper use of evidence would be an instance of a reliable process."[8] This process was available to Spencer, but he did not use it, although he could and should have. And had Spencer used this process, he would not have retained his memory beliefs about his childhood. Thus condition (ii) is not satisfied, and we get the correct result: Spencer's memory beliefs about his childhood are unjustified.

There are three main objections to process reliabilism. According to the first, there is the possibility of an evil-demon world in which perceptual beliefs are justified although they are unreliably produced. This objection raises the issue of whether reliability is necessary for justification. The second objection presents the challenge of a reliably clairvoyant subject who does not know that he is reliably clairvoyant; his beliefs are supposed to be unjustified even though they are reliably produced. This objection raises the issue of whether reliability is sufficient for justification. And according to the third objection, when we apply process reliabilism to particular cases, it is not possible to specify the relevant cognitive process in a way that is neither too broad nor too narrow. This objection raises what is commonly referred to as the "generality problem."

RELIABILISM AND NATURALISTIC EPISTEMOLOGY

Ever since the work of W. V. Quine gained prominence, the program of naturalizing epistemology—of replacing old-fashioned a priori armchair philosophizing with a new, thoroughly scientific approach—has enjoyed increasing support. In the next chapter, we shall discuss the merits of this project. For our present purposes, what matters is that in proposing his 1979 version of process reliabilism, Goldman intended to advance naturalized epistemology. Process reliabilism is supposed to be a naturalistic theory, one that differs in significant respects from theories advanced within nonnaturalized, traditional theories.[9] What is typical of such theories is that they analyze the nature of justification by employing evidential considerations— that is, by using conditions that are formulated in epistemic terms. Hence Goldman attempts to analyze the concept of epistemic justification without engaging in evidentialist language—that is, without using any epistemic terms such as "reasonable," "certain," or "evident."[10]

Process reliabilism also differs from traditional theories in being an *externalist* theory. Recall that according to externalist theories, factors that determine a belief's justificatory status need not be accessible on reflection.[11] From the naturalistic point of view, a theory of justification *ought* to be externalist, for whether a belief is justified is not, according to naturalized epistemology, a matter the subject can determine on reflection. Rather, it is a scientific matter that must be settled by cognitive scientists and neurophysiologists.

Why is process reliabilism an externalist theory? It is an externalist theory because whether a given belief is produced by a reliable process is something that can—at least in principle—be found out, given enough time and scientific resources. But it certainly cannot be found out on *reflection*. Even if on reflection the subject could pin down the cognitive process that produced the belief in question—which is by no means something that should be taken for granted—she would then have to determine whether that process produces mostly true beliefs. This could not be done merely by reflecting on the matter. Rather, an extensive empirical study would be necessary.

By being a version of externalism, process reliabilism satisfies the demand for naturalization. It is less clear, however, that it satisfies this demand also by avoiding evidentialist language. Indeed, we have already seen that Goldman solves the problem of evidential defeat by appealing to cognitive processes such as properly and improperly using one's evidence. If this difference is not in turn analyzed in nonepistemic terms, it would appear that the intended departure from traditional epistemology was not entirely successful.

THE EVIL-DEMON PROBLEM

Perhaps the most formidable difficulty process reliabilism faces comes in the form of cases that challenge the claim that reliability is *necessary* for justification. The most prominent such case is that of an evil-demon world. Suppose you are the victim of an evil demon: all of your perceptual beliefs are false because the evil demon manipulates your perceptual experiences in such a way that the existence of a physical world appears obvious to you when in fact there is no such world. All that exists are nonphysical minds without bodies, and you are one of them. Your perceptual beliefs are false because the objects your beliefs are about don't exist. For example, when you believe that there is a dog in front of you, your belief is false since, under the circumstances we are imagining, there is no dog before you simply because there are no dogs to begin with.

One crucial assumption we must make here is that the experiences the evil demon induces in you are phenomenally indistinguishable from the experiences you actually have. They are exactly the same type of experiences you would have if you were not deceived by an evil demon, but rather lived a normal life in an ordinary physical world. This assumption is crucial because it provides us with a strong reason for saying that your perceptual beliefs are justified. After all, we ordinarily take ourselves to live in a normal world in which perceptual beliefs are usually justified. Consequently, given that there is no phenomenally discernible difference between your actual perceptual experiences and those you have in the evil-demon scenario, we must take your beliefs in the evil-demon world to be justified as well.

What turns the scenario we are imagining into a difficulty for reliabilism is this: Your perceptual beliefs in the evil-demon world are all false, and thus *unreliably produced*. Put differently, for an evil-demon victim, perception is not a reliable cognitive process. Thus the perceptual beliefs in the evil-demon world are not produced by a reliable cognitive process. Yet they are justified. The conclusion to be drawn, then, is that reliability is not a necessary ingredient of justification.[12]

Could the premise that your perceptual beliefs in the actual world are justified be questioned? From a skeptical point of view, they could. However, Goldman explicitly states that process reliabilism is intended to be an account of our *ordinary* concept of justification.[13] The beliefs that are justified according to reliabilism are therefore expected to coincide roughly with those beliefs that turn out to be justified when we apply our ordinary concept of justification. But if we apply this concept to the evil-demon world, our verdict must be that the perceptual beliefs in this world are (by and large) as much justified as they are in the actual world. For according to our ordinary concept of justification, beliefs based on perceptual evidence are (by and large) justified.

THE CLAIRVOYANCE PROBLEM

Is reliable belief production *sufficient* for justification? The following case is intended to establish that it is not. Suppose Norman enjoys the power of perfectly reliable clairvoyance with respect to the whereabouts of the president.[14] At any given moment, he can tell where the president is located. Furthermore, his clairvoyance normally results in beliefs about the president's whereabouts only if Norman deliberately uses this power. Suppose Norman doesn't know that he has this power, and thus never uses it. On a rare occasion, he spontaneously comes to believe, on the basis of his clairvoyance, that the president is in New York. Let us suppose further that, according to a news report Norman heard on television, the president is supposed to be receiving senators in the White House that morning. (As a matter of fact, the meetings were canceled and the president is indeed in New York that morning.)

Ex hypothesi, Norman's belief is reliably produced. But is it justified? The news reports provide Norman with evidence against believing that the president is in New York. And since Norman has no other evidence concerning the president's whereabouts, we would have to say that Norman's belief is unjustified even though it is reliably produced. Reliable belief production by itself is not, therefore, sufficient for justification. Process reliabilism as intended by Goldman, however, involves an antidefeat clause. If amended with such a clause, it can handle the case we just considered. When Norman forms the belief that the president is in New York, there is a process available to him that he could and should have used: taking into account contrary evidence. Had he used that process, he would not have formed the belief that the president is in New York. Hence process reliabilism gives us the right result: Norman's belief is unjustified.

What is at stake in discussing process reliabilism, then, is not the claim that reliable belief production is sufficient for justification, but rather the claim that *undefeated* reliable belief production is sufficient for justification. In the example we considered, there is defeating evidence: the news reports according to which the president is receiving senators in the White House that morning. Thus in order for an objection from clairvoyance to produce a genuine challenge to process reliabilism, a different kind of example must be devised. First, the belief in question must be reliably produced. Second, it must be unjustified not because it is undermined by contrary evidence, but rather because the subject has no positive evidence in its support.

It's not so clear, however, that process reliabilism can't handle cases of that kind. For Goldman could say that when S believes something without supporting evidence, there is an available process S could and should have used: taking into account the absence of supporting evidence or, more generally, believing in accord with one's evidence. So Goldman's process reliabilism, if properly applied, implies what it should: that evidentially unsupported beliefs are unjustified.

Nevertheless, the clairvoyance problem does illuminate a feature of process reliabilism that advocates of naturalistic epistemology must view as a weakness. Process reliabilism is supposed to be a naturalistic theory—a theory that allows us to evaluate beliefs without applying evidentialist considerations. However, when process reliabilism is applied to particular cases, evidentialist considerations make their entry through the backdoor. In order to handle cases in which a reliably produced belief is defeated by contrary evidence, process reliabilists must introduce a process such as *taking into account contrary evidence*. And in order to handle clairvoyance cases in which supporting evidence is missing, they must appeal to a process such as *taking into account the absence of supporting evidence*. It could therefore be argued that, to get the right results, process reliabilists must ultimately employ evidentialist considerations. It could be doubted, therefore, that process reliabilism is in fact a genuine alternative to traditional evidentialist theories.

THE GENERALITY PROBLEM

To study the ins and outs of the generality problem, it is best to consider initially a simplified version of reliabilism (let's call it "simple reliabilism") and to turn at a later point to the more complicated version we discussed above. According to simple reliabilism, a belief's justification is solely a function of the reliability of the process that produced it. But a cognitive process that produces a belief in a particular case exemplifies many different *types* of cognitive processes. For example, when I look out my office window and see a dog on campus, the cognitive process that produces the belief "There is a dog over there" can be described thus:

(i)   Perception;

(ii)   Vision;

(iii) Vision during daylight;

(iv)   Vision during daylight through a pair of correcting lenses;

(v)   Visually perceiving a moving object during daylight and through a pair of correcting lenses at a distance of approximately forty feet.

We must, therefore, distinguish between the particular *token* of a cognitive process that produces a belief in a specific case and the various *types* of cognitive processes that that token exemplifies. This distinction is important because it is types, not tokens, of cognitive processes that can be said to be reliable or unreliable. In order for a process to be reliable, the tokens that instantiate that process must produce true beliefs most of the time. Hence the particular tokens of a cognitive process type do not themselves have the property of being reliable or unreliable, but rather determine whether that process type is reliable or not.[15]

Goldman himself points out that since process types can be described broadly or narrowly, a serious problem arises: that of how to describe process types in appropriate generality.[16] In order to examine the nature of this problem, let's introduce a belief that is both true and unjustified. Suppose my colleague Edith brought her dog on campus, and the dog ran away. Now she is looking for him, and spotting in the far distance a dog, she believes

(D)   There is my dog over there.

Since she doesn't recognize that dog very clearly, her visual evidence doesn't justify her belief, which is in fact an instance of wishful thinking. Thus (D) is unjustified. However, the dog she has spotted is in fact hers. Hence (D) happens to be true. Let's apply to this example simple reliabilism, which asserts:

Simple Reliabilism
    Belief B is justified if and only if the process token that produces B instantiates a reliable process type.

Edith's belief is a visual belief. Since vision is a reliable cognitive process, simple reliabilism implies that (D) is justified, when in fact it is not. Hence simple reliabilism doesn't give us the right result for the case we are considering.

A natural response to this problem is to demand *specification*. However, simple reliabilism suffers not only from too much generality but also from too much specificity. Consider the following process type, which makes reference to the identity of the perceiver (Edith N.), and the precise time and place at which the perceiver spots her dog: *Edith N. visually perceiving a dog at 3:15 p.m. on June 25, 1994, in front of Office 123 in Brown Hall.* This process type is instantiated by one, and only one, process token: namely, the one that leads my colleague to form belief (D). Let us call process types that are instantiated by one, and only one, process token "OTOPs" (one-token-only process types). What is remarkable about OTOPs is this: Whenever the unique token that instantiates an OTOP is true, that OTOP is an example of perfect reliability. For whenever an OTOP leads to a true belief, it isn't instantiated by a single process token that leads to a false belief.

The problem, then, is to describe the relevant process types in such a way that they are neither too broad nor too specific. Our example of a belief resulting from wishful thinking illustrates that since perception is, in general, a reliable process, without a specification device, process reliabilism implies that *all perceptual* beliefs are justified.[17] And the threat of OTOPs shows that unless the extent of permissible specification is limited, process reliabilism implies as well that *all true* beliefs are justified.

Simple reliabilism also implies that *all false* beliefs are *unjustified*. To see why, let's modify our example. Edith perceives the dog clearly and distinctly. The dog, which is in fact someone else's, is an exact look-alike of hers. Since Edith has no reason to suspect this, she is justified in believing (D). Alas, (D) is false. Now, just as in the previous case (where (D) was true) there was an OTOP perfect reliability, there is now an OTOP of perfect *unreliability*. The process type *Edith N. visually perceiving a dog at 3:15 p.m. on June 25, 1994, in front of Office 123 in Brown Hall* is instantiated by exactly one process token—the one that led my colleague to believe (D)—and that token leads to a false belief. This means that the process in question instantiates a perfectly unreliable process type. Hence simple reliabilism gives us the wrong result: Edith's belief is unjustified. Indeed, since *every* process token leading to a false belief instantiates some OTOP or other, simple reliabilism implies that a belief is unjustified *whenever* it is false.

In discussing the generality problem, we have thus far only considered a simplified version of reliabilism. It is now time to discuss whether process reliabilism is still vulnerable to the generality problem once it is amended with an antidefeat clause. (Let's refer to that version of reliabilism as "Goldman's process reliabilism.")

> *Goldman's Process Reliabilism (GPR)*
> *S*'s belief *B* is justified if and only if (i) *B* is produced by a reliable cognitive process; (ii) there is no alternative reliable process available to *S* that, had it been used by *S* in addition to the process actually used, would have resulted in *S*'s not forming *B*.[18]

GPR does not imply that a belief is justified whenever it is true. For sometimes when *S* forms a true belief, *S* ignores contrary evidence that undermines that belief. In such cases, condition (ii) will not be satisfied. However, GPR does imply that a belief is false whenever it is unjustified. As we saw above, for every such belief, there is a perfectly unreliable OTOP that produces it. Hence false beliefs can't satisfy condition (i), and thus are always, according to GPR, unjustified.[19]

RULE RELIABILISM AND THE EVIL-DEMON PROBLEM

In his 1986 *Epistemology and Cognition*, Goldman replaced process reliabilism with what we may call "rule reliabilism." Rule reliabilism makes a belief's justification a function of permission by a right system of epistemic rules—J-rules, in Goldman's terminology—and the rightness of a system of J-rules a function of reliability. Thus Goldman's 1986 proposal offers us a two-stage analysis of justified belief:

> J1 *S's* belief *B* is justified if and only if (a) *B* is permitted by a right system of J-rules, and (b) this permission is not undermined by *S's* cognitive state.[20]

> J2 A system of J-rules *R* is right if and only if *R* permits certain (basic) psychological processes, and the instantiation of these processes results in a sufficiently high truth ratio.[21]

One main difference between the process and rule frameworks is this: According to process reliabilism, the justification of a subject's beliefs in a world *W* is a function of the reliability of the subject's cognitive processes in *W*. As a consequence, process reliabilism is vulnerable to the evil-demon problem. In an evil-demon world, the subject's perceptual processes are unreliable, yet justified. According to rule reliabilism, in contrast, the rightness of a J-rule system does not vary among different possible worlds, but is rigidly fixed in what Goldman calls *normal* worlds. A world *W* is normal, according to Goldman, if our general beliefs in the actual world are true in *W*. For example, one of our general beliefs is that perception is a reliable cognitive process. Consequently, any world in which perception is not a reliable cognitive process—as is the case in an evil-demon world—is not a normal world.

This feature of rule reliabilism, which Goldman calls *normal-world chauvinism*, seems to allow for a neat solution to the evil-demon problem. Consider our J-rule system, which permits beliefs that are produced by undefeated perceptual processes. If we fix the rightness of this J-rule system for a world *W* by considering its output in *W*, it would not count as a right J-rule system in an evil-demon world, for in such a world it would permit beliefs that are mostly false. Thus we would get the result that perceptual beliefs in the evil-demon world are unjustified. However, Goldman's normal-world chauvinism demands that the rightness of our J-rule system be measured in normal worlds. And in normal worlds, the beliefs it permits are mostly true. Thus, when we apply our J-rule system to the evil-demon world, it rigidly remains a right J-rule system, which means our verdict must be that perceptual beliefs in that world are justified.

As Goldman himself has pointed out, however, his normal-world chauvinism faces a serious problem.[22] Although as a matter of fact there are no justified beliefs that result from clairvoyance, it is plausible to say that such beliefs are possible. The problem with normal-world chauvinism is that it makes such beliefs impossible. Consider a possible world in which clairvoyance is a known reliable cognitive process. Since clairvoyance is unreliable in normal worlds, rule reliabilism implies that clairvoyance beliefs are unjustified in this world. Indeed, since the lack of justification for clairvoyance beliefs is rigidly fixed by the fact that in normal worlds clairvoyance is unreliable, there *could* not be a world in which clairvoyance results in justified beliefs. Thus it turns out that rule reliabilism, as defined in *Epistemology and Cognition*, has an implausible consequence.[23]

STRONG AND WEAK JUSTIFICATION

In his 1988 paper "Strong and Weak Justification," Goldman proposes an alternative approach to the evil-demon problem. His new solution is based on a distinction between two ways in which beliefs can be justified: weakly and strongly. Weak justification results from not violating epistemic duties; strong justification, on the other hand, results from reliable processes and methods.[24] Beliefs produced by reliable processes or methods are strongly justified, whereas beliefs not thus produced are either not justified at all or weakly justified if they are held without violating epistemic duties.

For the purpose of illustrating the concept of weak justification, Goldman introduces the example of a culture in which people frequently base predictions on astrology, an instance of an unreliable method. The people of this culture cannot be blamed for believing these predictions, for they don't have the intellectual means to recognize that astrology is an unreliable method. As Goldman stipulates, "where outcomes reportedly go against the predictions [derived from using astrology], the community's astrology experts explain that the predictions had been based on misapplications of the method. The experts have techniques for 'protecting' their theory from easy falsification, and only sophisticated methodologies or astronomical theories would demonstrate the indefensibility of such tactics; but these are not available."[25] In this case, Goldman says, the beliefs in question are weakly justified, for the subjects cannot be blamed for trusting their astrology experts. But since the method the "experts" use is de facto unreliable, these beliefs do not enjoy strong justification.

Weak justification, then, is justification deriving from epistemic blamelessness. A second feature of weak justification is that weakly justified beliefs are unreliably produced, for Goldman wants weak justification to be the opposite of strong justification. Applying the distinction between strong and weak justification to the evil-demon problem, Goldman's solution is that the perceptual beliefs of the deceived subjects are weakly justified without being strongly justified. Since their perceptual experiences are just like those of perceivers in normal worlds, they can't be blamed for believing in the existence of a physical world; that's why their perceptual beliefs are free of epistemic blame and thus weakly justified. On the other hand, their perceptual beliefs are unreliably produced (because in the evil-demon world perception is not a reliable cognitive process); that's why their perceptual beliefs fail to be strongly justified.

In response to this maneuver, internalist critics of reliabilism would question the legitimacy of the distinction between weak and strong justification.[26] Advocates of a traditional, Cartesian-Lockean conception of epistemic duty could argue that there is nothing weak about the justification the deceived subjects in an evil-demon world enjoy. Their perceptual beliefs are supported by their evidence, and thus are justified fully and completely. From this internalist, traditional point of view, the unreliability of perceptual processes in the evil-demon world does not at all adversely affect the justification of perceptual beliefs. Internalist opponents of reliabilism would not, therefore, view Goldman's reconciliation offer—perceptual beliefs in the evil-demon world are weakly justified—as satisfactory. They would deny that just because these beliefs are unreliably produced, they are somehow deficient in justificatory status.

VIRTUE RELIABILISM

In his 1991 article "Epistemic Folkways and Scientific Epistemology," Goldman offers yet another solution to the evil-demon problem. In that paper, he distinguishes between two missions of epistemology. The first mission—descriptive in character—is to describe our commonsense epistemic concepts and norms, which Goldman calls "epistemic folkways." The second mission—normative in character—is to critically evaluate our folkways and, if necessary, to propose improvements.

Goldman's new approach to the analysis of justified belief, though still reliabilist, proceeds in terms of intellectual *virtues* and *vices*. Thus Goldman is now merging two different theoretical strands: reliabilism and virtue epistemology. According to the virtue approach to the analysis of justified belief, a belief is justified if it results from an intellectual virtue, and unjustified if it results from an intellectual vice.[27] What, however, are intellectual virtues and vices? According to Goldman, intellectual virtues are cognitive processes we deem reliable, and intellectual vices are cognitive processes we deem unreliable. The criterion for discriminating between intellectual virtues and vices, then, is that of reliability.[28]

Epistemic evaluators, so Goldman argues, inherit from their social and cultural background *lists* of cognitive virtues and vices. When they evaluate beliefs, they identify the psychological process by which a belief was produced and match it against the items on their list. At this point, three different evaluations are possible:

(i)   If the identified process matches virtues only, the belief is justified.

(ii)   If the identified process matches either completely or partly vices, the belief is unjustified.

(iii) If the identified process is not on the list at all, the belief is categorized as nonjustified. (A nonjustified belief is neither justified nor unjustified.)[29]

Recall the two cases of Edith and her runaway dog. Consider her justified but false belief that the dog she sees is hers. Neither wishful thinking nor any other nonvirtuous process is involved in the causal genesis of her belief. The relevant process matches virtues only; thus Edith's belief qualifies as justified. Next, consider Edith's unjustified but true belief that the dog she sees is hers. In this case, it is not only perception but also wishful thinking that leads her to form this belief. The relevant process, though it matches the virtue of perception, also matches the vice of wishful thinking. Thus her belief counts as unjustified. Finally, consider beliefs that have their genesis in telepathy. Since telepathy is not on our list of virtues, such beliefs turn out to be nonjustified.

What makes Goldman's virtue approach superior to the version of reliabilism he originally advocated, process reliabilism? To begin with, one might hope that virtue reliabilism is less susceptible to the generality problem than process reliabilism. This problem presents reliabilists with the challenge of describing cognitive processes in a way that is neither too broad nor too narrow. Now if some reliable processes count as virtues and others don't, then it will perhaps be possible to pin down the degree of generality appropriate to processes that produce justified beliefs. The future will show whether such an account of intellectual virtues can be success-fully developed. Secondly, Goldman's virtue reliabilism permits straightfor-ward solutions to the other two of our three standard problems: the evil-demon world and reliable clairvoyance. In the next section, we shall briefly discuss these solutions.

THE CLAIRVOYANCE PROBLEM
AND THE EVIL-DEMON PROBLEM REVISITED

Here is how Goldman's virtue approach to reliabilism affords him with a solution to the clairvoyance problem, the problem posed by a subject who possesses the faculty of perfectly reliable clairvoyance. Goldman distin-guishes between two kinds of clairvoyance problems: cases in which the subject ignores contrary evidence, and cases in which the subject has no evidence for or against the beliefs his clairvoyance produces. The verdict for the first kind of case is obvious. Since *ignoring contrary evidence* is on our list of intellectual vices, we are to say that beliefs resulting from perfectly reli-able clairvoyance, if undermined by contrary evidence, are unjustified.

The verdict for the second kind of case depends on whether or not we view clairvoyance as a vice. If we do, then we will say that the belief in question is unjustified. If we don't, then we must acknowledge that no intel-lectual vices are involved in the formation of the beliefs in question. So in that case there is no basis for saying that the beliefs in question are *unjusti-fied*. However, provided we don't view clairvoyance as an intellectual virtue, we could say that they are *nonjustified*.[30]

Next, let us turn to the question of how Goldman's virtue approach allows him to handle the evil-demon problem. Recall that in an evil-demon world, perception is not a reliable process. But since the deceived subjects have no reason to believe that they are deceived, we judge perceptual beliefs in an evil-demon world to be justified. The point of the evil-demon objection, therefore, is that beliefs can be justified even when they are unreliably produced. Goldman now agrees with this verdict. He writes:

> The account predicts that an epistemic evaluator will match the victim's vision-based processes to one (or more) of the items on his list of intellectual virtues, and therefore judge the victim's beliefs to be justified.[31]

But how does this solution to the evil-demon problem square with the fact that we are to discriminate between intellectual virtues and vices using reliability as a criterion? After all, in an evil-demon world, perception is unreliable. Are we not to judge, therefore, that in an evil-demon world, the deceived subject's perceptual beliefs are the result of exercising an intellectual vice?

Here we must take into account that Goldman assigns a new role to reliability. In virtue reliabilism, it is not *de facto* reliability that determines whether a cognitive process is virtuous or not, but rather *deemed* reliability. Consider Goldman's answer to the question of what the basis is for classifying some processes as virtues and others as vices:

> Belief-forming processes based on vision, hearing, memory, and ("good") reasoning are deemed virtuous because they (are deemed to) produce a high ratio of true beliefs. Processes like guessing, wishful thinking, and ignoring contrary evidence are deemed vicious because they (are deemed to) produce a low ratio of true beliefs.[32]

Given that it is deemed reliability that matters, Goldman's new account yields different results depending on which evaluators we consider. Evaluators in the evil-demon world don't know that they are deceived; they deem perceptual processes reliable. Hence they will judge perceptual beliefs in their own world justified. However, how should *we* judge perceptual beliefs in the evil-demon world? Of course, we deem perceptual processes in *our world* reliable, and thus consider perception an epistemic virtue. Yet, knowing that in the evil-demon world peception is unreliable, wouldn't we have to consider *perception in the evil-demon world* an epistemic vice? It would appear, then, that Goldman's theory gives us two responses to the problem of an evil-demon world: one for evaluators in the evil-demon world, and another one for evaluators in our world.

One crucial element of Goldman's solution to the evil-demon problem, then, is the transition from de facto to deemed reliability as a necessary condition for justification. Let's sum up Goldman's new theory as follows:

Goldman's Virtue Reliabilism

  B is justified if and only if B is produced by a cognitive process P such that P is an intellectual virtue and P does not involve any intellectual vice. A cognitive process P is an intellectual virtue if we deem P reliable, and an intellectual vice if we deem it unreliable.

One feature of this account is that $S's$ justification for B is dependent on, not what S deems reliable, but what *we* deem reliable. Hence we get one result if we adopt the point of view of evil-demon victims—for then we deem perception reliable, thus view perception a virtue, and hence judge perceptual beliefs in that world justified—and another one if we adopt our ordinary actual-world perspective—for then we deem perception in the evil-demon world unreliable, thus view perception in the evil-demon world a vice, and hence judge perceptual beliefs in that world unjustified. It is not so clear, therefore, that Goldman's virtue reliabilism offers a satisfactory solution to the problem of an evil-demon world.

Another feature of Goldman's new account is that it places no constraints on the reasons for which cognitivie processes are deemed reliable or unreliable. What if we were to fall victim to an outbreak of collective madness and deemed the most crazy processes reliable, and thus considered them intellectual virtues? Assuming such a scenario, Goldman's theory would give us manifestly wrong results.[3]

In response to these difficulties, we could decide to make $S's$ justification for B dependent on what S herself deems reliable on the basis of adequate evidence. This proposal can be formulated thus:

Evidentialist Virtue Reliabilism
> S is justified in believing that p if and only if $S's$ belief that p is produced by a cognitive process C such that (i) C instantiates an intellectual virtue and (ii) does not instantiate any intellectual vice. A cognitive process C is an intellectual virtue if S has adequate evidence for deeming C reliable, and an intellectual vice if S has adequate evidence for deeming C unreliable.

Evidentialist virtue reliabilism allows for easy solutions to the two standard challenges. In the evil-demon world, the subjects have adequate evidence for deeming perception reliable, for they have no reason to assume that they are being deceived by an evil demon. Consequently, perceptual beliefs in an evil-demon world are justified (provided condition (ii) is met as well). Beliefs resulting from clairvoyance are unjustified if undermined by contrary evidence, for such beliefs don't satisfy condition (ii). But beliefs resulting from clairvoyance where clairvoyance is known to be reliable meet condition (i), and thus qualify as justified (again, provided condition (ii) is met). In general, any belief known to have been produced by a given process—be it clairvoyance, telepathy, or extra sensory perception—counts as justified provided the subject has adequate evidence for taking that process to be reliable.

It could be objected, however, that evidentialist virtue reliabilism employs a strange understanding of epistemic virtues. Consider a cognitive faculty that produces wrong results more often than not. Do we really wish to say that such a faculty is an epistemic virtue just because there is evidence for taking the faculty to be reliable when in fact it is not? Consider a related question: Would we say that a person who tries very hard but mostly fails—a person who mostly does the wrong thing but for the right reasons—is a person who has achieved virtue?

Furthermore, evidentialist virtue reliabilism has a flaw, that is likely to be unacceptable to reliabilists: the term "evidence" occurs in its analysans. Evidentialist virtue reliabilism fails to satisfy the naturalistic caveat that an analysis of epistemic justification be carried out without the use of epistemic terms. However, as mentioned earlier, it is not so clear that this must really be considered a weakness. Notice that Goldman's virtue reliabilism shares the following feature with his earlier process reliabilism: in order to handle potential counterexamples involving defeating evidence, it must help itself to evidentialist considerations. According to virtue reliabilism, for a belief to be justified, there must not be any intellectual vices involved in the process that produced it. And among intellectual vices, we find a process such as *ignoring contrary evidence*. Unless this vice can be described in nonepistemic terms, virtue reliabilism is bound to be an evidentialist theory in any case. We may wonder, therefore, why it should be illegitimate to turn the covert appeal to the subject's evidence into an overt one.

STUDY QUESTIONS

1. What kind of difficulty motivates to supplement simple reliabilism with an antidefeat condition?
2. Why is reliabilism typically a version of naturalistic epistemology?
3. What are the three standard problems for reliabilism?
4. Why does simple reliabilism imply that a belief is justified whenever it is true?
5. Why does simple reliabilism imply that a belief is unjustified whenever it is false?
6. Can the generality problem be solved by supplementing simple reliabilism with an antidefeat clause?
7. What is Goldman's rule-reliabilist solution to the problem of an evil-demon world?
8. Why does a possible world in which clairvoyance is known to be reliable raise a problem for rule reliabilism?
9. According to Alvin Goldman, what's the difference between weak and strong justification?
10. Which role does reliability play in Goldman's virtue reliabilism?

EXERCISES

1. Using specific examples, explain the nature of the generality problem.
2. Give an account of what you take to be a successful solution to the generality problem.
3. Discuss whether virtue reliabilism can solve the evil-demon problem.
4. Discuss what you take to be the most plausible version of reliabilism.

NOTES

[1] Goldman (1979), p. 9.

[2] Ibid.

[3] The phrase "a belief's being *produced* by a given process" is meant to include both its being *formed* and then *sustained* by that process.

[4] See Goldman (1979), p. 18. The following example is a slight variation of Goldman's own example.

[5] For an interesting case study about the (un)reliability of memory, see Wright (1994).

[6] Goldman (1979), p. 20.

[7] See ibid.

[8] Ibid. pp. 19f.

[9] See Maffie (1990), p. 284. According to Maffie, the choice of reliability as a criterion for justification marks the difference between naturalistic and nonnaturalistic theories.

[10] See Goldman (1979), p. 1.

[11] For a brief discussion of the internalism/externalism distinction, see the last section of Chapter 2.

[12] For statements of the evil-demon problem, see Cohen (1984), pp. 281f, and Ginet (1985), p. 178.

[13] See Goldman (1979), p. 1.

[14] Clairvoyance counterexamples to reliabilism were proposed by Laurence BonJour. See BonJour (1985), chap. 3.

[15] See Goldman (1979), p. 11.

[16] See ibid., p. 12. See also Chisholm (1982), p. 29. A clear and penetrating account of the problem can be found in Feldman (1985).

[17] It also implies that all memorial and introspective beliefs are justified, for memory and introspection are, in general, reliable processes.

[18] See Goldman (1979), p. 20.

[19] One strategy for solving the generality problem is to restrict the domain within which cognitive processes are permitted. For example, we could stipulate that only neurophysiological processes count as genuine cognitive processes. The problem with this proposal is that there is little reason to assume that there can't be genuinely neurophysiological OTOPs. Since this objection can be raised against all similar proposals, it doesn't seem that that strategy is a successful one. See Goldman's reply to an objection of Chisholm's (based on the generality problem) in Goldman (1988), p. 55, and Chisholm's rebuttal in Chisholm (1989), p. 79.

[20] Goldman (1986), p. 63.

[21] Ibid., p. 106.

[22] See Goldman (1988), p. 62.

[23] For further objections to Goldman's 1986 version of rule reliabilism, see Goldman (1988); see also Swank (1988).

[24] Here is how Goldman explains the difference between processes and methods: "Processes are basic psychological processes, roughly, wired-in features of our native cognitive architecture. 'Methods' are learnable algorithms, heuristics, or procedures for forming beliefs, such as procedures that appeal to instrument readings, or statistical analyses." Goldman (1988), p. 53.

[25] Ibid., p. 57.

[26] Goldman's distinction between weak and strong justification is a version of the distinction between subjective and objective justification. This distinction can be drawn in a number of different ways. For example, subjective justification can be viewed in terms of duty fulfillment. However, since in some points of view duty fulfillment is a completely objective affair, it is doubtful that the distinction can be explained in terms of deontological versus nondeontolog-

ical justification. Another way of drawing the distinction is to characterize subjective justification as justification conferred by what the subject believes, and objective justification as justification conferred by what the subject believes on good grounds. It could be questioned, however, that a subject's beliefs, if not based on good grounds, can confer *any* degree of justification. One may doubt, therefore, whether the attempt to characterize subjective justification can succeed in marking a class of beliefs that are justified in any reasonable sense at all. For a critical examination of the distinction between subjective and objective justification, see Feldman (1988b).

27 For a useful brief account of virtue epistemology, see Greco (1992). See also Kvanvig (1992) and Greco (1994).

28 We don't have the space here to launch into an examination of intellectual virtues. Suffice it to say that the project of characterizing the nature of intellectual virtues is by no means an easy one. According to Alston (1993), an adequate definition of intellectual virtues must take the following point into account: "One may have a power or ability one infrequently exercises if at all. But a virtue is rather of the nature of a habit. It is a matter of what one *would* do under certain conditions rather than of what one is *able* to do" (pp. 202f.). If Alston is right here, then the reliability of a cognitive process would not be sufficient to make that process an intellectual virtue.

29 Goldman (1991), p. 157.

30 Goldman argues that he can account as well for the intuition of those who would say that the beliefs in question are unjustified. "For those evaluators who would judge [the beliefs in question] to be *un*justified, there is another possible explanation in terms of the theory. There is a class of putative faculties, including mental telepathy, ESP, telekinesis, and so forth, that are scientifically disreputable. It is plausible that evaluators view any process of basing beliefs on the supposed deliverances of such faculties as vices." Goldman (1991), p. 159.

31 Ibid.

32 Ibid., p. 160. In contrast, Sosa, who also advocates a version of virtue reliabilism, seems to require of an intellectual virtue that it enjoy de facto reliability. See his essays "Reliabilism and Intellectual Virtue" and "Intellectual Virtue in Perspective" in Sosa (1991), pp. 131–45 and 270–293.

33 Goldman's reply to these two objections would probably be that virtue reliabilism is intended to be descriptive epistemology: a mere descriptive account of our epistemic folkways. Its point is not to give us necessary and sufficient conditions for applying the concept of epistemic justification. Rather, its purpose is to predict which beliefs evaluators will classify as justified, and which beliefs they will classify as unjustified. Consequently, it does not count against the theory that evaluators under different circumstances will respond to the evil-demon world differently. Nor does it count against the theory that crazy evaluators will judge beliefs quite differently from the way we would judge them. In response to this reply, we may wonder, however, whether the pursuit of such descriptive epistemology allows us at all to address the questions we have formulated at the beginning of this book.

CHAPTER NINE

NATURALISTIC AND NONNATURALISTIC EPISTEMOLOGY

ARMCHAIR EPISTEMOLOGY

In recent decades, the program to "naturalize" epistemology has become increasingly popular. The idea is that since the subject matter of epistemology, properly understood, is certain aspects of *nature*, epistemology ought to be made a part of natural science and the methods used in epistemology ought to be the methods of empirical science. The implementation of this program would amount to no less than a revolutionary reorientation of epistemology as the discipline has traditionally been understood. In order to discuss the naturalization program, we must, therefore, begin with a brief review of traditional epistemological methodology.

Let's start with Descartes. In his *Meditations*, Descartes set out to determine how knowledge was possible, which led him to formulate a criterion of knowledge: clear and distinct perception. Furthermore, he tried to figure out the extent of what we can know. The answer at which he eventually arrived was nonskeptical: we do enjoy knowledge of the physical world, and thus know more or less what we think we know.

To determine criteria for judging whether we know and to delineate the extent of our knowledge, Descartes simply sat down in his armchair in front of the fireplace, began meditating and reflecting, and devised the following strategy: First he determined the strongest possible reason for doubt, and then permitted himself to accept only those propositions that were immune to that kind of doubt. The strongest possible reason for doubt was, of course, his assumption of being deceived by an evil demon. As a result of implementing this strategy, there were only two kinds of propositions he could use as premises: propositions about his own mental states, and those a priori propositions that were certain to him.

Let us consider two propositions that survived the evil-demon doubt. Descartes determined that although an evil demon might deceive him into believing that he had a body, such a demon could not deceive him into believing that he was thinking. Thus he took himself to know the following two propositions:

(1)   I am thinking.

(2)   I could not possibly be mistaken in believing that I am thinking.

(1) expresses introspective awareness of one of Descartes's own mental states, and (2) is an a priori proposition Descartes took to be certain for him.

There are two clearly recognizable methodological assumptions underlying Descartes's approach to epistemology: solipsism and rationalism. First, since Descartes decided that the premises available for his project had to be immune to the strongest possible doubt, he could assume the existence of nothing but his own mental states. This is the solipsistic element of his approach. Second, he assumed that those premises were permissible that he recognized clearly and distinctly. This is the rationalistic element of his approach: the reliance on reason as a source of knowledge.

It will be instructive to compare the Cartesian approach to epistemology with that of Roderick Chisholm. According to Chisholm, when we do epistemology, we are entitled to make three presuppositions:

> We presuppose, first, that there is something that we know and we adopt the working hypothesis that what we know is pretty much that which, on reflection, we think we know. . . .
>
>   We presuppose, second, that the things we know are justified for us in the following sense: we can know what it is, on any occasion, that constitutes our grounds, or reason, or evidence for thinking that we know. If I think that I know that there is now snow on the top of the mountain, then . . . I am in a position to say what ground or reason I have for thinking that there is now snow on the top of the mountain. . . .
>
>   And we presuppose, third, that if we do thus have grounds or reasons for the things we think we know, then there are valid general principles of evidence—principles stating the general conditions under which we may be said to have grounds or reasons for what we believe.[1]

The first of these presuppositions makes it clear that Chisholm disagrees with Descartes. Descartes thought that when we start out doing epistemology, we must not assume that there is anything we know. According to Chisholm, however, we may assume that we pretty much know what we think we know. Chisholm, then, rejects Descartes's solipsism.[2]

The second presupposition indicates that Chisholm takes the question

> Am I presently justified in believing that p, and if so, what is it that justifies me in believing that p?

to be a *Socratic* question. A Socratic question is different from other kinds of questions in the following respect: *whenever* we ask a Socratic question, the answer to it can be drawn from the body of evidence and knowledge we have at the time we are asking the question. Chisholm would say, therefore, that in order to answer the question displayed above, all I have to do is consider my present evidence.

Indeed, Chisholm would say that the four questions we considered at the beginning of this book

Q1   What is knowledge?
Q2   What do we know?
Q3   What is it for a belief to be justified?
Q4   Which of our beliefs are justified?

are all Socratic in this sense. In order to set out to find the right answers to these questions, we don't need any empirical information we don't yet have. All we have to do is sit down and reflect on our present body of evidence and knowledge and what is entailed by it. Compare questions Q1–Q4 with the following two questions:

Q5   How much money is in my bank account?
Q6   What caused Chairman Mao's death?

These are not Socratic questions. It might of course be that I learned just five minutes ago how much money there is in my account. If so, then in order to answer Q5, all I need to do is recall the information I got five minutes ago. However, it might also be that I don't yet have the needed information. In that case, I would have to call my bank in order to find out. It is not the case, therefore, that *whenever* one asks Q5, the answer can be drawn from reflecting on one's present body of evidence and knowledge; thus Q5 is not a *Socratic* question. Q6 is not a Socratic question either because the reason somebody died is not always available just by reflecting on what one knows already.[3] The answer to Q6 is that Mao Zedong died of Lou Gehrig's disease. This answer was the result of a scientific, medical examination of the ailment from which Mao suffered. No question that can be answered only by carrying out such an investigation is one that is Socratic in the sense we have defined that term.

The third presupposition indicates that Chisholm shares Descartes's rationalism. He believes that there are general principles of evidence—principles telling us under which conditions our beliefs are justified—and that reason enables us to figure out what these principles are. Chisholm takes these principles to be necessary truths, and he believes that they are knowable a priori.[4]

How, then, should we characterize traditional epistemology? Let us say that what makes an approach to epistemology traditional is a commitment to the following two claims:

(i) The questions of epistemology are Socratic: in order to answer them, no more is required than to reflect on one's present body of evidence and knowledge.

(ii) The answers to the two questions "What is knowledge?" and "What is it for a belief to be justified?" are a priori knowable necessary truths.[5]

Thus understood, traditional epistemology can be solipsistic, but it need not be. We shall leave it an open question, therefore, whether Chisholm is right in repudiating Descartes. But however epistemologists proceed with regard to the question of how much knowledge can be taken for granted to begin with, if they accept claims (i) and (ii), then they agree on the following: When we wish to do epistemology, we may do as Descartes did: sit down in an armchair in front of the fireplace in order to think, reflect, and meditate. In order to succeed, nothing else is necessary. We don't need to engage in any sociological or psychological research projects, and we don't need to put on white coats and join neurophysiologists in their laboratories to study the biochemistry of the brain. If we needed to do such things, then we would not yet be in the position to answer the questions we are asking. We would have to gather empirical data first, and perhaps at some later stage, once the necessary data are collected, we might be able to succeed in finding the answers we seek. Traditional epistemologists—armchair epistemologists—believe, however, that we are *already* in a position to find the answers we seek. They believe that their project is *autonomous*: one that can be successfully pursued by anyone wherever and whenever the conditions permit one to think, reflect, and meditate.

QUINEAN NATURALIZATION: NORMATIVE EPISTEMOLOGY ELIMINATED

In his famous and extremely influential paper "Epistemology Naturalized," Quine makes a case for transforming epistemology into a new and entirely different discipline by making it a part of natural science. He recommends this transformation on the ground that traditional epistemology, pursued from outside of science, turned out to be a complete failure. Let us first discuss Quine's reasons for this diagnosis, and then the remedy he prescribes.

In characterizing the old kind of epistemology that he thought ought to be abandoned, Quine distinguishes between a *conceptual* and a *doctrinal* project.[6] The latter project is that of justifying our beliefs about the physical world, the former that of providing the definitions that are needed to accomplish the intended justification. The justificatory project, for which Descartes introduced the modus operandi, is of a foundational nature: from *infallible* beliefs about one's own conscious states, beliefs about the physical world are to be derived via *deduction*. Hume remained skeptical about the prospects for success of this project, but he accepted the terms set by Descartes: without a foundation of infallible or indubitable beliefs, and without an ironclad deductive link between this foundation and the super-structure of beliefs about the physical world, the desired justification cannot be achieved. Quine conceives of traditional epistemology as foundationalist epistemology à la Descartes, and he sides with Hume. "The Humean predicament," says Quine, "is the human predicament."[7]

The conceptual project can be viewed as one particular way of carrying out the justificatory project. Quine describes it thus: "One could undertake to explain talk of bodies in terms of talk of [sensory] impressions by translating one's whole sentences about bodies into whole sentences about impressions. . . ."[8] This project is motivated by the following consideration.[9] Beliefs about physical objects are occasioned by sensory experience of those objects. However, sensory experience is never sufficient for proving that the objects apparently causing sensory experiences really exist. The task, then, is to bridge the logical gap between our sensory experiences and our beliefs about the physical world. Now, one way of solving this problem is simply to make the gap disappear: to translate beliefs about physical objects into a language that makes reference only to sensory experiences. According to Quine, this project is bound to fail, for the desired translations of sentences about physical objects into sentences about sensory experiences cannot be had.[10]

This, then, is Quine's *diagnosis* of the state of traditional epistemology: its search for justification in the form of Cartesian certainty is a "lost cause," and so is its attempt to translate talk about physical bodies into talk about sensory experiences. The *remedy* he proposes is to replace the traditional endeavor with another one:

> But why all this creative reconstruction, all this make-believe? The stimulation of his sensory receptors is all the evidence anybody has to go on, ultimately, in arriving at his picture of the world. Why not just see how this construction really proceeds? Why not settle for psychology?[11]

It is important to appreciate the import of what Quine is saying here. What does he mean when he proposes to study how the stimulation of our sensory receptors constructs our picture of the world? And how is the project Quine proposes different from the traditional project of *justifying* our beliefs about the physical world?

According to Quine, traditional epistemology's main concern is justification. Since this concern takes the form of a quest for certainty, it must be abandoned. Instead, epistemologists must study how we get from sensory stimulation to our picture of the world. In this study, justification is not the aim, but rather *scientific explanation*. What we want is a psychological (or perhaps neurophysiological) account of what happens in our brains when our sensory receptors are being stimulated. In this project, we study

> a natural phenomenon, viz., a physical human subject. This human subject is accorded a certain experimentally controlled input—certain patterns of irradiation in assorted frequencies, for instance—and in the fullness of time the subject delivers as output a description of the three-dimensional external world and its history.[12]

This kind of study differs radically from traditional epistemological endeavors. Epistemologists used to attempt to *justify* our picture of the world or, in the case of Hume, to show that it cannot be justified. They tried to show that we have (or don't have) *good reasons* for this picture, that we are (or are not) *reasonable* in believing in it. In Quine's naturalized setting, normative questions raising issues of justification or reasonableness are asked no longer. Instead, our concern is simply to discover the chain of causes and effects that leads from sensory stimulation to our beliefs about our physical environment.

While the concern of traditional epistemologists is *normative*, Quine's project is *nonnormative*, or *descriptive*.[13] Thus, if we naturalized epistemology in the way Quine suggests, epistemology would, in effect, be eliminated. The only thing the new, Quinean project would have in common with the old project would be its name.

What are the merits of Quine's recommendation to naturalize epistemology? In order to discuss this question, let us restate the essence of his argument:

Quine's Argument for Naturalization

(1)   Traditional epistemology aims at two tasks: (i) to justify our beliefs about the physical world by deducing them from infallible premises about sensory experiences and (ii) to translate sentences about physical objects into sentences about sensory experiences.

(2)   Neither of these two tasks can be accomplished.

(3)   If traditional epistemology aims at these two tasks and neither of them can be accomplished, then traditional epistemology must be abandoned.

Therefore:

(4)   Traditional epistemology must be abandoned.

(5)   If traditional epistemology must be abandoned, epistemologists should study psychology instead.

Therefore:

(6)   Epistemologists should study psychology instead.

Friends of traditional epistemology are unlikely to be swayed by this argument. First of all, even if they were to grant the truth of (4), it would not be so clear they would have to agree with (5). This has been pointed out by Jaegwon Kim. He wonders why Quine couples his recommendation with the rejection of normative epistemology. If the Quinean diagnosis is false, psychology would still be a worthwhile subject to pursue. And if the Quinean diagnosis is right, it would not follow that epistemologists *must* turn to psychology. After all, asks Kim, "if normative epistemology is not a possible inquiry, why shouldn't the would-be epistemologist turn to, say, hydrodynamics or ornithology rather than psychology?"[14]

But the main problem with Quine's argument is raised, of course, by premise (1). Those who don't wish to go along with Quine could object that we can find a much wider range of projects within traditional epistemology than Quine's characterization of it suggests. This is not to say that they would challenge the diagnosis of the Cartesian foundationalist project. As far as *that* kind of epistemology is concerned, they would not have to disagree with Quine. What they should find objectionable, however, is Quine's presupposition that the Cartesian foundationalist project is all there is to epistemology.

Consider, for example, minimal foundationalism as it was characterized in Chapter 5. Advocates of that view believe that the justification of our empirical beliefs ultimately rests on sensory experience, but they do not insist on the existence of a foundation of infallible beliefs. Nor do they take justification to be passed on from belief to belief via deduction. Furthermore, there are coherentists and reliabilists. The former believe that justification has its source in coherence relations, the latter that it has its source in reliable belief production. Neither of them adopts the Cartesian model of justification. Clearly, then, Quine's characterization of epistemology is unduly restrictive. Advocates of traditional epistemology, therefore, have no reason to accept the first premise of Quine's argument, and hence no reason to accept its conclusion.

EPISTEMOLOGICAL NATURALISM

Many philosophers are in favor of naturalizing epistemology, but not in favor of Quinean naturalization—a process that, as we have seen, renders the traditional normative questions irrelevant. Epistemologists who wish to answer these questions, but within a naturalized epistemology, are typically motivated by a view that we may call "epistemological naturalism." In this section, we shall examine this view.

In his book *The Nature of Morality*, Gilbert Harman writes that ethical naturalism

> is the doctrine that moral facts are facts of nature. Naturalism as a general view is the sensible thesis that *all* facts are facts of nature.[15]

This can easily be translated into a statement about epistemological naturalism. According to Harman, naturalists believe that all *normative* facts are facts of nature. Elsewhere, Harman elaborates the meaning of this point thus:

> What a naturalist wants is to be able to locate value, justice, right, wrong, and so forth in the world in the way that tables, colors, genes, temperatures, and so on can be located in the world.[16]

Of course, in epistemology, our concern is *epistemic* values, such as certainty, reasonableness, justification, and probability. According to Harman's suggestion, naturalists wish to locate such values "in the way that tables, colors, genes, temperatures, and so on can be located in the world."

Harman's characterization suggests that there are two sides to epistemological naturalism: a metaphysical one and an analytic one. First of all, epistemological naturalists make a claim about the ontological makeup of the world. They assert that epistemic facts are natural facts because whatever there is is something "natural," something that is of the same kind as tables, genes, temperatures, and so on. Second, naturalists aim at a certain analytic objective: they want, in Harman's terms, to *locate* epistemic values in the natural world. They want to show how epistemic facts fit into the natural world.

Combining both of these features, let us sum up the Harmanian conception of epistemological naturalism as follows:

> D1A Epistemological naturalism is the view that (i) epistemic facts are facts of nature, and (ii) epistemologists must locate epistemic facts in the natural world.

The problem with this conception of epistemological naturalism is that it doesn't tell us very much. For it to be meaningful, we would have to know what it is that an epistemological *nonnaturalist* asserts. Presumably, a nonnaturalist would deny the two propositions the epistemological naturalist asserts. Hence we may formulate epistemological nonnaturalism thus:

> D1B Epistemological nonnaturalism is the view that (i) epistemic facts are *not* facts of nature, and (ii) epistemologists need *not* locate epistemic facts in the natural world.

But what is it for an epistemic fact *not* to be a fact of nature? And what is it for an epistemologist to locate epistemic facts *without* locating them in the natural world? Naturalists believe that there are no nonnatural facts. All facts are natural ones. For this to be a meaningful claim, we would have to have an idea of what kind of fact a nonnatural fact is supposed to be. Furthermore, naturalists believe that values must be located in the natural world. But if we don't know what kind of world a nonnatural world is supposed to be, we can't know what it means to locate facts in the natural world.

To get a better grasp of what it is for an epistemologist to be a nonnaturalist, let us turn to a passage by James Maffie. Maffie writes that, according to epistemological naturalists,

> epistemic value is anchored to descriptive fact, no longer entering the world autonomously as brute, fundamental fact. . . .[17]

Maffie's proposal advances our understanding of the issue, for he tells us what naturalists and nonnaturalists disagree about: how *epistemic* facts, a certain kind of normative facts, are related to *descriptive* (nonnormative) facts. In Maffie's words, what is at issue is "anchoring." Naturalists believe that epistemic facts are *anchored to* descriptive facts. Given that they are thus anchored, they are not brute and fundamental. Maffie's formulation seems to suggest that nonnaturalists deny this—that they take epistemic facts to be brute and fundamental, which means they don't think epistemic facts are anchored to descriptive facts. And given their disagreement concerning the nature of epistemic facts, naturalists and nonnaturalists disagree about the task of epistemology. The former would say that epistemologists must explain in precisely which way epistemic facts are anchored to descriptive facts, whereas the latter would say that epistemologists need not do any such thing.

Following Maffie's proposal, let us characterize epistemological naturalism and nonnaturalism thus:

D2A *Epistemological naturalism* is the view that (i) epistemic facts are anchored to descriptive facts, and (ii) epistemologists must explain how epistemic facts are anchored to descriptive facts.

D2B *Epistemological nonnaturalism* is the view that (i) epistemic facts are not anchored to descriptive facts, and (ii) epistemologists need not explain how epistemic facts are anchored to descriptive facts.

Of course, Maffie's talk about "anchoring" is just a metaphor. What we need to know is what it is for epistemic facts to be anchored in descriptive facts. Here Alvin Goldman and Jaegwon Kim provide us with illumination. This is what Goldman says about the relation between evaluative and descriptive facts:

> Evaluative status does not enter the world autonomously. It always "supervenes," as philosophers sometimes put it, on purely factual states of affairs.[18]

Jaegwon Kim concurs. He writes, specifically addressing how a belief's evaluative status of being epistemically justified relates to descriptive fact:

> If a belief is justified, that must be so *because* it has certain factual, nonepistemic properties. . . . That it is a justified belief cannot be a brute fundamental fact unrelated to the kind of belief it is. There must be a *reason* for it, and this reason must be grounded in the factual descriptive properties of that particular belief.[19]

According to Kim, if a belief's being justified is related to descriptive facts as asserted in this passage, then it *supervenes* on descriptive facts. In this regard, then, there is complete agreement between Goldman and Kim; both believe that epistemic justification supervenes on factual grounds. If epistemic justification thus supervenes, it does not, in Goldman's words, "enter the world autonomously," and a belief's justification is not, as Kim remarks, a "brute fundamental fact." This coheres nicely with Maffie's characterization of the difference between naturalism and nonnaturalism. Let us change our definitions accordingly:

> D3A *Epistemological naturalism* is the view that (i) epistemic facts supervene on descriptive facts, and (ii) epistemologists must explain on which descriptive facts epistemic facts supervene.
>
> D3B *Epistemological nonnaturalism* is the view that (i) epistemic facts do not supervene on descriptive facts, and (ii) epistemologists need not explain on which descriptive facts epistemic facts supervene.

According to this conception of naturalism and nonnaturalism in epistemology, the crux of the matter is the supervenience of epistemic facts on descriptive facts. The concept of supervenience Kim operates with is that of strong supervenience: whenever a belief is justified, it exemplifies a set of descriptive properties that entails its justification.[20] For those epistemologists who agree that epistemic justification thus supervenes, the task of epistemology is clear: it is to identify *which* descriptive properties are such that, necessarily, any belief exemplifying these properties is a justified one.

Is this specific version of epistemological naturalism in line with the generic one we generated applying Harman's characterization of naturalism? According to William Lycan, if one holds a naturalistic conception of epistemology, that is, if one is inclined to think that there are no real differences that are not at bottom natural differences, then one must try to say what it is in nature that distinguishes reasonable belief from unreasonable belief.[21]

Naturalists think of natural differences as *descriptive* differences. Thus Lycan appears to view the task of epistemology as that of explaining what descriptive differences account for the normative differences between justified and unjustified beliefs. Now, to carry out the project Goldman and Kim recommend—to explain on which descriptive properties epistemic justification supervenes—is to do precisely what Lycan wants epistemologists to do: it is to give a descriptive account of the normative difference between justified and unjustified beliefs. D3A and D3B, then, fit the generic understanding, as reflected in the quotes from Harman and Lycan, of what it is to be an epistemological naturalist.[22]

In order to identify the descriptive properties on which epistemic justification supervenes, what kind of analysis must epistemologists produce? In Jaegwon Kim's words, the view that epistemic differences are ultimately natural—that is, descriptive—differences imposes the following constraint on the analysis of justified belief:

> the criteria of justified belief must be formulated on the basis of descriptive or naturalistic terms alone, without the use of any evaluative or normative ones, whether epistemic or of another kind.[23]

Goldman agrees. In *Epistemology and Cognition*, he says this about what kind of an analysis he is interested in:

> We want to know the factual, or substantive, condition on which [epistemic status] supervenes. Consider justifiedness. What has to be true of a belief for it to qualify as justified? What factual standard determines justifiedness?
>
> What kinds of answers to this question are legitimate? It is not admissible to answer by using other terms of epistemic appraisal, such as "rational," "well-grounded," or the like. We need nonevaluative terms or conditions.[24]

Goldman is as good a witness here as any, for he is widely regarded as one of the preeminent advocates of the naturalistic approach to epistemology. Let us agree, therefore, to characterize epistemological naturalism as the view that epistemic justification supervenes on nonnormative, or descriptive, properties, and that the task epistemologists ought to accomplish is to specify, in nonnormative terms, on precisely which properties it supervenes.

Further below, we shall see, however, that the metaphysical and the analytic element in naturalism are independent of each other. It will be useful, therefore, to have separate accounts of each. Hence we shall distinguish between naturalism about epistemic value, which is a metaphysical doctrine, and analytic naturalism, which is a certain attitude concerning the epistemological objective.

Naturalism About Epistemic Value

Every belief's epistemic status supervenes on its descriptive properties. (Whenever a belief is justified, it has a set of descriptive properties such that, necessarily, any belief having these properties is justified.)

Analytic Naturalism

The epistemological task is to specify in nonnormative terms on which nonnormative properties epistemic justification supervenes.

In the next section, we shall discuss the epistemological projects of two well-known epistemologists: Roderick Chisholm and Alvin Goldman. Goldman is typically viewed as an advocate, and Chisholm as an opponent, of epistemological naturalism. It will be instructive, therefore, to examine in which ways their theories differ.

CHISHOLMEAN NATURALISM
AND GOLDMANIAN NATURALIZATION

As we saw in Chapter 2, one of Chisholm's projects is to formulate epistemic principles of the following form:

Necessarily, if belief B satisfies condition N, then B enjoys epistemic status E.

In the antecedent of such principles, condition N is to be given a nonepistemic (and indeed nonnormative) description, while E would be replaced by a property such as being certain, justified, or beyond reasonable doubt. In Chisholm's terminology, condition N provides us with a "criterion" for the application of a term of epistemic evaluation. About such criteria, Chisholm says the following:

We want to find a criterion stating a non-normative situation that warrants the assertion of a normative statement—a non-normative situation upon which, as it is sometimes said, a normative situation "supervenes." . . . Such criteria will tell us something about the conditions under which S is *justified* in believing that there is an F. The conditions in question will not themselves be normative facts; they will be non-normative facts (say, being appeared to in certain ways) which constitute sufficient conditions for the existence of certain normative facts.[25]

According to Chisholm, epistemic value supervenes on nonnormative facts: whenever a belief is justified, it exemplifies a set of descriptive properties that are sufficient for its status of being justified.

Chisholm, then, is an advocate of what we have called *naturalism about epistemic value*. He does not hold that epistemic value enters the world "autonomously," that epistemic facts are brute and fundamental. To the contrary, Chisholm believes that there is a very strong logical connection between epistemic value and nonnormative facts: whenever a belief is justified, it meets a nonnormative condition that is sufficient for epistemic justification. In short, epistemic justification supervenes on nonnormative properties. And since Chisholm attempts to formulate principles whose antecedents are nonnormative conditions, he even endorses what we have called *analytic naturalism*: he thinks that the criteria of justified belief should be formulated in nonnormative language.

Next, let us compare Chisholm's project with Alvin Goldman's. In the previous section, we saw that Goldman asserts the supervenience of epistemic status on nonnormative grounds and that he wants to state criteria of epistemic justification in nonnormative terms. Here, then, we don't find any disagreement between Chisholm and Goldman. Thus in order to find out what it is that sets Chisholm and Goldman apart, we have to look elsewhere. What attracts our attention, of course, is Chisholm's opposition to, and Goldman's advocacy of, reliabilism. Goldman holds that what makes a belief justified is reliability, appropriately qualified. Chisholm disagrees.[26] Their disagreement, though, is not about the epistemological objective at which both of them aim: an analysis of justified belief in nonnormative terms. Rather, their disagreement is merely about specifically which nonnormative base properties epistemic justification supervenes upon.

Yet Goldman is one of the main advocates of naturalistic epistemology. Much of his magnum opus *Epistemology and Cognition* is devoted to establishing the relevance of cognitive science to epistemology. Chisholm, on the other hand, is well known for his reluctance to naturalize epistemology. How can this discrepancy be explained, given that both of them pursue the same analytic objective? Illumination can be found in a response Goldman wrote to rebut a criticism of Richard Feldman's. Feldman argues that Goldman's reliabilism is, from the naturalistic point of view, conceived in sin: it is the offspring of an a priori methodology, and thus an example of armchair epistemology.[27] In reply to this charge, Goldman distinguishes among three stages in his theory of justification:

> The first state is to indicate the relationship between a belief's being justified and its conforming with a right system of justificational rules (J-rules). The second stage is to specify a criterion of rightness for a system of J-rules. My proposed criterion is a process-reliabilist one. The third stage of the theory of justification is to say, in detail, what the content of a right J-rule system (for human beings) would be. It would answer the question: which specific processes are in the human cognitive repertoire, and are such that their (joint) use would lead to a high truth ratio? It is only the third state of the theory, I claim, in which cognitive science would play an important role.[28]

At the first state of this project, Goldman formulates an equivalence: *B* is justified if and only if *B* is permitted by a right system of J-rules. This equivalence does not yet do the job, for the right-hand side contains a normative concept. At the second state, this concept—the rightness of a system of J-rules—is given a nonnormative analysis in terms of reliability. In the introduction to *Epistemology and Cognition*, Goldman remarks explicitly that, up to and including the second state, his methodology is "squarely within philosophy by anyone's conception."[29] Thus it turns out that Chisholm and Goldman have much in common: both believe that we can determine *a priori* on which nonnormative properties justified beliefs supervene.

An important difference between Chisholm and Goldman does emerge, however, at the third stage. Goldman argues that it is

> not the reliability feature, but rather the (cognitive) process feature of [his] theory that creates the special role [of calling for cooperation between epistemology and cognitive science]. What is crucially unavailable to introspection is what cognitive processes people use in belief formation, and what processes are available for their use. It is the nature of these processes that can only be revealed by (or with the help of) cognitive science. This is why my epistemological theory—or any other process oriented theory—creates a special role for the empirical sciences of cognition.[30]

According to Goldman, then, reliabilism as a theory of justification involves two altogether different projects: first, an a priori analysis of the nonevaluative entailing grounds of epistemic justification; second, an empirical investigation into which reliable belief-producing processes are available to humans. Since the latter investigation cannot be accomplished with the armchair method, cooperation with cognitive science is called for. Goldman's conception of naturalistic epistemology, then, is somewhat conservative: while within the first two stages of his project, the armchair remains the epistemologist's home, it is only during the third stage that it must be left behind, for then it is time to proceed to the cognitive science laboratory and learn about "what processes people use in belief formation."

This conception of naturalistic epistemology is a far cry from Quine's. In "Epistemology Naturalized," what Quine recommends to his colleagues is to abandon the concern for normative questions, to leave the epistemologist's armchair behind and let it collect dust. He urges his colleagues to put on white lab coats and study causes and effects, inputs and outputs, "patterns of irradiation in assorted frequencies," for instance. Goldman, too, favors putting on white lab coats, but only after epistemologists have spent an appropriate amount of time in the armchair. For otherwise, in Goldman's view, epistemologists would be wandering about in the cognitive science laboratory without knowing what to look for. (How could they possibly know that their task was to gather information about cognitive processes unless they had determined in advance that what makes beliefs justified is their origin in reliable cognitive processes?) Thus while for Quine naturalization means the *elimination* of normative epistemology, for Goldman it means *cooperation* between epistemology and cognitive science. Quinean naturalization heralds the end of epistemology as we know it; Goldmanian naturalization leads epistemology as we know it in new directions.

Let us sum up. Chisholm and Goldman share the same analytic objective: they want to answer the question, What are the criteria of epistemic justification? or, On which nonnormative properties does epistemic justification supervene? Furthermore, they share the methodology employed in answering this question. They believe that whatever the answer turns out to be, its justification is a priori. They do, however, propose different criteria. While Goldman's criterion is a reliabilist one, Chisholm proposes a number of criteria in which reliability plays no role. This disagreement over the relevance of reliability extends into a further disagreement about the naturalization of epistemology. Because of his advocacy of reliabilism, Goldman favors a conservative concept of naturalization. He thinks that epistemology can benefit from cooperation with cognitive science because cognitive science can tell us what reliable cognitive processes are available to human beings. Chisholm, on the other hand, thinks that reliable belief production is neither necessary nor sufficient for justification, and shows no interest in Goldmanian cooperation.

EPISTEMOLOGICAL PESSIMISM
AND GOLDMANIAN ANALYTIC NATURALISM

As we have seen, epistemological naturalism combines a metaphysical with an analytic element. The analytic element we characterized thus:

> *Analytic Naturalism*
> The epistemological task is to specify in nonnormative terms on which nonnormative properties epistemic justification supervenes.

Both Chisholm and Goldman endorse analytic naturalism in this sense. Yet there is an interesting difference in the way they attempt to meet this objective. Chisholm aims at formulating a number of epistemic principles that specify nonnormative conditions that are sufficient for justification. However, he does not aspire to a complete list of *all* such conditions. His list is incomplete, and thus does not identify a set of nonnormative core properties that every justified belief must exemplify. In short, it doesn't tell us what is necessary for justification.[31]

Goldman's analysis, on the other hand, is supposed to do precisely that. It is supposed to tell us not only what is sufficient but also what is necessary for justification. Unlike Chisholm, Goldman aims at formulating an analysis that states a condition (or set of conditions) that is both necessary and sufficient for justification: a belief *B* is justified if and only if *B* meets condition *C*. According to Goldman, condition *C* has to be spelled out, of course, in terms of reliable belief production. A Goldmanian analysis, if correct, would tell us that there is a core property that is necessary for a belief's justification: reliability. Since Chisholm's list of criteria is incomplete, it involves no such claim; it merely gives us a number of distinct conditions each of which is sufficient for a belief's justification.

Nevertheless, Chisholm and Goldman agree that in formulating criteria of justification, normative terms must not be used. But if epistemological pessimism—the view that conditions sufficient for justification cannot be formulated without using epistemic terms—is correct, then that constraint cannot be met, and neither Chisholm's nor Goldman's project can succeed. In what follows, we shall first consider the reasons pessimists are skeptical about Goldman's project. Then we will consider why they think that Chisholm's project, too, is unlikely to succeed.

First, there is the *problem of infinity*: there might be an infinite number of distinct nonnormative, justification-entailing base properties. If so, the sheer fact of infinity would stand in the way of identifying conditions that are necessary for justification. In that case, we could formulate a number of Chisholmian principles, but we could not formulate a Goldmanian equivalence.[32]

Second, there is the *problem of magnitude*: even if the number of base properties is finite, it might still be so enormous that listing them all would be an endless task. If so, there would in principle be a set of necessary and sufficient conditions of epistemic justification, but practically it would not feasible to identify that set. Again, in that case, a limited number of Chisholmian principles would still be possible, but a Goldmanian equivalence would not.

Third, there is the *problem of unity*. Let's suppose the number of base properties is relatively small. Indeed, let's suppose there are only three: P1, P2, and P3. Once we are sure there are no further base properties, we can formulate an equivalence:

E1   *B* is justified if and only if *B* exemplifies P1 or P2 or P3.

But does E1 tell us anything of significance in addition to what we know already: that there are no base properties other than P1 and P2 and P3? The answer is that it does not. If there were something that *unites* our three base properties, something that could truly be said to be the one core property *P** that is both necessary and sufficient for justification, then we could formulate a different, more powerful equivalence:

E2   *B* is justified if and only if *B* exemplifies *P**.

Identifying such a core property would be of paramount interest. If we succeeded in doing that, we would then have formulated a truly interesting equivalence. In the absence of such a core property, however, the exercise of offering an analysis with a disjunctive analysans is not very informative. It would tell us nothing over and above the information needed in order to know that E1 is true: that in addition to P1, P2, and P3, there are no further base properties.[33]

Fourth, there is the *problem of certitude*: having proposed an equivalence, could we ever be certain that there are no further justification-entailing base properties—peculiar rogue properties that, hiding in the niches and crevices of metaphysical complexity, are extremely difficult to spot? If we cannot rule out the existence of such properties, then we can never be completely confident in asserting an equivalence that identifies what is necessary for justified belief.

EPISTEMOLOGICAL PESSIMISM
AND CHISHOLMIAN ANALYTIC NATURALISM

Next, let's see what misgivings pessimists have regarding Chisholm's project of producing a limited criteriological list. This project faces, so they would argue, what we might call the *problem of complexity*. Consider the property *being grounded in perception* as a candidate for a nonnormative, justification-entailing base property. Obviously, this property is a bad candidate: there are many beliefs that are grounded in perception and unjustified. Hate, haste, impatience, avarice, bias, pompousness, wishfulness, and despondency are but some of the psychological conditions that can defeat perceptual evidence. Suppose, looking for my runaway dog, I clearly see a dog not far away that somewhat looks like mine. Overcome by impatience and wishful thinking, I believe that the dog is mine. This belief is unjustified because of the way I *use* my perceptual evidence. Being impatient and thinking wishfully, I ignore the fact that the similarity between my own dog and the one I see is not close enough to justify me in taking the dog to be mine.

It is necessary, then, to modify the property *being grounded in perception* further. We can do this by adding the requirement that the belief must not be defeated by things such as impatience and wishful thinking, which would give us the following property: *being grounded in perception in an undefeated way*. Now, it is arguably true that whenever a belief exemplifies this property, it is justified. However, this property is not the kind of property we are looking for because it has a normative component. The belief must be grounded in perception in a way that is *undefeated*. The question arises, therefore, whether we can come up with a descriptive condition that, in one fell swoop, rules out all possible ways in which psychological conditions such as impatience, wishful thinking and the like can render beliefs grounded in perception unjustified.

The crux of the matter, then, is that it is not easy to come up with a nonnormative property, or conjunction of such properties, that is really sufficient for a belief's justification. It seems that for almost all candidates for such a property, we can imagine circumstances under which a belief has the property but fails to be justified.[34] Should it be impossible to specify such a property, then there is hope neither for Chisholmian principles with nonnormative antecedents nor for a Goldmanian analysis with a nonnormative analysans. Pessimists believe that it is indeed impossible to do specify such a property.[35]

EPISTEMOLOGICAL PESSIMISM AND NATURALISM

How plausible is epistemological pessimism? In this book, we examined both the Chisholmian and the Goldmanian way of analyzing on what epistemic justification supervenes. As we have seen, neither can be said to have met with unqualified success. Concerning Chisholm's project, the problem is that very few nonnormative properties are plausible candidates for nonnormative base properties. And concerning Goldman's project, there are two problems: First, is reliability really necessary for justification? Second, it would appear that it isn't reliability by itself, but at best undefeated reliability, that is sufficient for justification. The concept of undefeated justification, however, is a normative one.[36] We would have to say, therefore, that epistemological pessimism enjoys at least some measure of plausibility.

What is the relation of epistemological pessimism to naturalism? Pessimism does not imply naturalism; neither does it preclude it. And since there are good reasons for naturalism, we may even say that pessimists ought to be naturalists.[37] If they adopt naturalism, their position can be described as follows: Whenever two beliefs differ in epistemic status, there must be a natural—that is, nonnormative—difference between them that explains the epistemic difference. However, the nonnormative differences on which epistemic status supervenes do not manifest the kind of regularity and unity that would allow us to identify necessary and sufficient conditions. In short, we know *that* epistemic justification supervenes on nonnormative base properties, but we can't say very much about *how* it supervenes on such properties.

But this is not to say that, according to pessimists, there is nothing we can say about the natural groundings of epistemic justification. Here is a brief account of the kind of analysis they would propose about justification based on perceptual evidence:

> Perception, a natural process that can be analyzed by cognitive science, is one source from which justified beliefs arise. But perceptual processes do not invariably result in justified beliefs. Perceptual evidence can be defeated. Hence the relation between perception and justification is this: If one has perceptual evidence

E for a belief, and *E* is not defeated by further evidence *E**, then one is justified in holding that belief. Analogous points can be made about introspection, memory, and reason.

In proposing an analysis along these lines, pessimists cover *some* ground in locating epistemic justification in the natural world. They assert that justification is generated through natural sources such as perception, introspection, memory, and reason. They doubt, however, that we can formulate necessary and sufficient conditions of epistemic justification without supplementing them with at least one normative component.

NATURALIZED EPISTEMOLOGY AND ANTIAPRIORISM

There are two different attitudes toward cooperation between epistemology and cognitive science, and the difference between these two attitudes concerns the role of a priori epistemology. The first attitude is Goldman's. According to him, there is a legitimate purpose for a priori epistemology: its purpose is to determine on what epistemic justification supervenes. Once we know that justification supervenes on certain properties of cognitive processes, we must then go on and do cognitive science in order to learn more about the nature of cognitive processes.

The second view is held by James Maffie and Hilary Kornblith. According to these philosophers, a priori epistemology does not have a legitimate purpose. In this section, we shall discuss Maffie's view; in the next section, Kornblith's.

Maffie rejects the a priori methodology employed by Chisholm and Goldman on the basis of the following argument:[38] Since a priori methods are discontinuous with science, a priori epistemology leaves us with an epistemological dualism of facts and values. Such a dualism is unacceptable.[39] Hence a priori epistemology must be rejected.

In order to evaluate this argument, we must discuss what Maffie might mean by the term "epistemological dualism." Perhaps a reasonable guess is this: Armchair epistemology implies that we know about values in *one* way and about facts in *another* way. The idea here is that our knowledge of the nature of epistemic value is a priori, whereas our knowledge of facts is a posteriori, or empirical.[40]

Why, however, should this be such a bad idea? Well, it would be a bad idea if a priori methods were a rather dubious way of coming to know something. Now, while this is indeed what some advocates of naturalization want to argue, it must be said that a broad assault on a priori knowledge in general would be quite an uphill battle. Consider mathematics, geometry, deductive logic, the probability calculus, and, most basically, our grasp of the difference between valid and invalid arguments. The received view is that our knowledge of such matters is a priori. For each of these, the skeptic about apriority must establish that those items that appear to be clear instances of a priori knowledge are really instances of empirical knowledge. The radical skeptic about apriority, then, has to prove a negative—that for any *p*, knowing *p* a priori is impossible—which is a notoriously difficult thing to accomplish.[41] While lifetimes may be spent in pursuit of such an endeavor, a decisive and compelling attack on the possibility of a priori knowledge has yet to emerge from the philosophical literature.

But if the view that a priori knowledge is possible is not in such bad shape, then there is no reason to worry about the dualism Maffie complains of: that the way we know about values is different from the way we know about facts. It is just about as worrisome as saying that the way in which we know truths of mathematics is different from the way in which we know about the mating habits of rats. Traditional epistemologists, then, would agree with Maffie that armchair epistemology implies an epistemological dualism. But while Maffie thinks that such a dualism is bad, armchair epistemologists will see no reason to agree, for they don't share Maffie's doubts about the possibility of a priori knowledge.

THE DARWINIAN ARGUMENT

Kornblith characterizes the naturalistic approach to epistemology by introducing three questions:

Q1   How ought we to arrive at our beliefs?

Q2   How do we arrive at our beliefs?

Q3   Are the processes by which we do arrive at our beliefs the ones by which we ought to arrive at our beliefs?

In order to answer Q1, we need to formulate criteria that allow us to distinguish between good and bad cognitive processes, that is, between processes that lead to justified beliefs and processes that lead to unjustified beliefs. Traditional epistemologists believe that such criteria can only be known a priori. In order to answer Q2, we have to consult psychologists or cognitive scientists, for they study how we actually go about the business of forming beliefs. According to Kornblith, what separates naturalists from friends of the armchair is how each of these two camps views the relation between Q1 and Q2. Armchair epistemologists would say that knowing the answer to Q2 is of no help for finding an answer to Q1. However, Kornblith, who advocates naturalistic epistemology, thinks we can't answer Q1 without first knowing the answer to Q2. He writes:

> I take the naturalistic approach to epistemology to consist in this: question 1 cannot be answered independently of question 2.[42]

So according to Kornblith, in order to answer Q1, we must engage in an empirical study: we must analyze what procedures we actually follow in arriving at our beliefs. But how could such a study help us find out how we *ought* to arrive at our beliefs? Here is Kornblith's solution to this puzzle: If we can answer Q3 with "yes," then we know the answer to Q1 once we know the answer to Q2. And if our affirmative answer to Q3 is based on empirical evidence, then we are able to answer Q1 through empirical means. Kornblith sums this method up as follows:

> If we know in advance, however, that we arrive at beliefs in just the way we ought, one way to approach question 1 is just by doing psychology. In discovering the processes by which we actually arrive at beliefs, we are thereby discovering the processes by which we ought to arrive at beliefs. The epistemological enterprise may be replaced by empirical psychology.[43]

Here is an example to illustrate Kornblith's suggestion. Suppose there were empirical evidence for answering Q3 with "yes":

(1)   The processes by which we do arrive at our beliefs are the ones by which we ought to arrive at our beliefs.

Next, we determine a partial answer to Q2:

(2)   Perceptual processes are one way in which we arrive at our beliefs.

Clearly, (1) and (2) imply

(3)   Perceptual processes are one way in which we ought to arrive at our beliefs.

The main problem with an argument of that nature, of course, is this: What empirical evidence could there possibly be for accepting premise (1)? According to Kornblith, an example of such evidence is the theory of evolution. Let us call the argument based on that evidence "the Darwinian argument."

The Darwinian argument begins with an observation of Quine's: "There is some encouragement in Darwin."[44] What is supposed to be encouraging here is this: The process of Darwinian evolution has resulted in the successful propagation of the human species. But that means we must have plenty of true beliefs, for beings that don't can't successfully reproduce. So from the fact that we are here, having emerged from successful reproduction in the past, and are fully engaged in propagating our species into the future, we can infer that nature has equipped us with what Kornblith calls "a bias in favor of true beliefs." And from here we can, according to Kornblith, reason thus: "If nature has so constructed us that our belief-generating processes are inevitably biased in favor of true beliefs, then it must be that the processes by which we arrive at beliefs just are those by which we ought to arrive at them."[45]

Let's have a look at a formal representation of this argument.

The Darwinian Argument

(1)   Nature has endowed our cognitive processes with a bias toward true beliefs.

(2)   If nature has endowed our cognitive processes with a bias toward truth, then the processes by which we form our beliefs are the ones by which we ought to form our beliefs.

Therefore:

(3)   The processes by which we form our beliefs are the ones by which we ought to form our beliefs.

The first premise expresses the encouragement that we can, according to Quine and Kornblith, find in Darwin. The second premise restates the Kornblithean observation we quoted above. From (1) and (2), (3) follows by modus ponens. And once we know (3), all we have to do in order to get an answer to Q1 is to consult psychologists. They will tell us by which processes we actually form our beliefs. In this way, we would have answered Q1 with empirical means.

Kornblith's argument involves two problems. First of all, we might wonder how premise (2) could be justified. The answer is that, for (2) to be plausible, we need a normative presupposition: the processes by which we form our beliefs ought to have a bias toward truth. If a bias toward truth is not viewed as something to be valued, then we have no reason to prefer (2) to

> If nature has endowed our cognitive processes with a bias toward truth, then the processes by which we form our beliefs are *not* the ones by which we ought to form our beliefs.

Since, therefore, a normative presupposition is needed for the justification of the second premise, we may wonder how we know that this presupposition is true. Do we know that empirically or a priori?

The second problem has to do with the *extent* to which nature has endowed our cognitive processes with a bias toward truth. Surely it is not the case that *all* of our cognitive processes exhibit such a bias. To a lamentably large extent, the processes by which people form their beliefs are not the processes that exhibit such a bias. Wishful thinking, hasty generalization, false appeal to authority, appeal to pity, appeal to ignorance, false dichotomy, and other fallacies abound in ordinary belief formation. In short, premise (1) severely lacks plausibility, and must be replaced with:[46]

(1*)   Nature has endowed *some* of our cognitive processes with a bias toward truth.

Of course, once (1) is replaced by (1*), (2) must be replaced with

(2*)   If nature has endowed *some* of our cognitive processes with a bias toward truth, then *some* of the processes by which we form our beliefs are the ones by which we ought to form our beliefs.

And the conclusion we get from (1*) and (2*) is rather weak compared with (3):

(3*)   *Some* of the processes by which we form our beliefs are the ones by which we ought to form our beliefs.

The situation, then, is this: Although many of our cognitive processes are quite good, many are quite bad. Which of the processes we actually use are the good ones and which the bad ones? Though there may be encouragement to be found in Darwin, evolutionary theory just doesn't tell us which cognitive processes are good and which ones are bad.

At the beginning of this chapter, we characterized armchair epistemology as a project that rests on two assumptions: (i) The questions we are asking when we do epistemology are Socratic in nature: in order to answer them, we don't depend on information we don't yet have, information that could be acquired only through empirical research. (ii) The answers to the questions of epistemology are knowable a priori. According to Quine, if epistemology is to succeed, it must become a part of science. If that is so, then epistemologists will have to forgo the comfort they have long found in the armchair. Quine's argument, however, rests on an unduly narrow conception of what traditional epistemology is all about, and thus is less than compelling.

Unlike Quine, Alvin Goldman accepts that epistemological insight can be found in the armchair. He recommends, however, that a priori armchair research be supplemented with scientific research. According to him, epistemologists can benefit from cooperation with cognitive scientists and psychologists. This proposal poses no threat to traditional epistemology. Indeed, if it seems at all likely to be fruitful, traditional epistemologists should welcome such cooperation. Yet there are some grounds for skepticism about whether the cooperation between epistemology and science is likely to be fruitful. After all, Goldmanian cooperation depends on the success of reliabilism. Those who don't think that reliabilism is true won't see much reason to join in this cooperative enterprise.

Finally, there is Kornblithean cooperation between epistemology and science. According to Kornblith, to naturalize epistemology is to answer normative questions through empirical means. We have considered one such attempt—the Darwinian argument—and judged it to be a failure. This does not mean, of course, that other attempts might not succeed. Indeed, we should not display a preconceived, dogmatic hostility to the idea of empirically resolving normative issues. Why foreclose possible avenues of philosophical knowledge? Yet it must be said that no one has as yet succeeded in demonstrating to the philosophical world how that feat can be accomplished.

STUDY QUESTIONS

1. What is meant by calling the questions of epistemology "Socratic" questions?
2. In which sense does Quine suggest "naturalizing" epistemology, and what is his argument for its naturalization?
3. How could advocates of traditional epistemology reply to Quine's argument?
4. What is the difference between naturalism about epistemic value and analytic naturalism?
5. In which sense can Roderick Chisholm be called a "naturalist"?
6. In which sense does Alvin Goldman suggest "naturalizing" epistemology?
7. How would epistemological pessimists view the project of analytic naturalism?
8. How does Hilary Kornblith characterize naturalized epistemology?
9. What is the point of the Darwinian argument?
10. What are the weaknesses of the Darwinian argument?

EXERCISES

1. Discuss epistemological naturalism by contrasting it with epistemological *nonnaturalism*. Precisely what is it that an epistemological nonnaturalist asserts?
2. Critically discuss the thesis: Epistemology can benefit from cooperation with cognitive science and psychology. Explain how such cooperation could be fruitful, and what can be said for and against this thesis.
3. Do you think that epistemology is a discipline that is independent of science in the following sense: In order to answer the questions of epistemology, we do not depend on information that can be gained only through a scientific investigation? Defend what you take to be the right answer to this question.

NOTES

[1] Chisholm (1977), pp. 16f.

[2] See ibid., p. 18.

[3] But on occasion it may be thus available. Suppose I see right in front of me a drive-by shooting in which a passer-by is hit in the head by a stray bullit. In such a situation, knowing the cause of the passer-by's death does not require any further investigation but is evident upon reflection.

[4] See Chisholm (1990), p. 210. For a somewhat different take on the question of whether epistemic principles are a priori, see Chisholm (1989), pp. 72f.

[5] The answers to the two questions "What do I know?" and "What am I justified in believing?" are neither knowable a priori nor necessary truths. They are not a priori because in order to know what I know empirically and which of my empirical beliefs are justified, I depend on empirical evidence. And they are not necessary truths because what at a particular time I happen to know and to be justified in believing is an entirely contingent affair.

[6] See Quine (1969), p. 71.

[7] Ibid., p. 72.

[8] Ibid.

[9] The view in question here is often referred to as "phenomenalism." For a short and instructive article on phenomenalism, see Fumerton (1992).

[10] Quine's reason for taking such translations to be impossible is his doctrine of the indetermiacy of translation. See ibid., pp. 78 ff., and Quine (1960).

[11] Ibid., p. 75.

[12] Ibid., p. 83.

[13] For an excellent discussion of this point, see Kim (1988).

[14] Ibid., p. 391.

[15] Harman (1977), p. 17.

[16] Harman (1984), p. 33.

[17] Maffie (1990), p. 284.

[18] Goldman (1986), p. 22.

[19] Kim (1988), p. 399.

[20] For the distinction between strong and weak supervenience, see Kim (1984) and Chapter 2, pp. 31 ff.

[21] Lycan (1988), p. 128.

[22] Not all naturalists, however, would endorse D3A and D3B. For an overview of various epistemological "naturalism," see Maffie (1990).

[23] Kim (1988), p. 382.

[24] Goldman (1986), p. 23.

[25] Chisholm (1989), pp. 42f.

[26] See Chisholm (1989), pp. 77ff.

[27] See Feldman (1989).

[28] Goldman (1989), p. 315.

[29] Goldman (1986), p. 9.

[30] Goldman (1989), p. 314.

[31] See Chisholm (1977), pp. 84f.

[32] It is important to see that the skepticism in question here is not directed toward the *existence* of an infinity of nonnormative properties on which epistemic justification supervenes. Rather, the point is an epistemological one: if there is such an infinity, then we cannot *tell* on what epistemic justification supervenes.

[33] The problem at issue here is the so-called scatter problem. See Chapter 2, p. 38.

[34] Certain introspective properties, appropriately specified, might be the exception. See Chisholm's self-presentation principle in Chisholm (1989), p. 62.

[35] We can distinguish between extreme and less extreme pessimists. An extreme pessimist would deny that there are any justification-entailing base properties. A less extreme pessimist would allow for a limited number of introspective base properties, but deny that there are any such properties that entail the justification of beliefs about nonintrospective matters.

[36] See Chapter 1, pp. 39, and Chapter 8.

[37] Given that we have characterized naturalism as the view that epistemic justification supervenes on descriptive properties, the reasons in favor of naturalism are the same as those in

favor of the claim that epistemic facts supervene on nonnormative facts. See Chapter 2, pp. 31–36.

38 Maffie (1990), p. 289.

39 Maffie does not make this premise explicit, but it is clearly implicit in his argument.

40 The claim that what we know about epistemic value we know a priori should not be confused with the claim that we can know a priori whether a particular belief is justified or not. The claim here is merely that general principles about justification can be known a priori, not that epistemic value judgments about particular beliefs can be known a priori.

41 Moreover, there is the question of whether it is possible at all to *argue coherently* that a priori knowledge is not possible. See Chapter 3, pp. 64ff.

42 Kornblith (1987), p. 3.

43 Ibid., p. 5.

44 See Kornblith (1987), p. 4, and Quine (1969), p. 126.

45 Kornblith (1987), p. 5.

46 Kornblith is aware of this problem. He writes: "If psychological investigation is to be able to replace epistemological theorizing, there must be a perfect match between the processes by which we do and those by which we ought to acquire beliefs. Without such a perfect match, the results of psychological theorizing will only give an approximate answer to question 1, and epistemology will be called on to make up the slack." Kornblith (1987), p. 5. It may be assumed, therefore, that he doesn't take the Darwinian argument to be sound, but views it merely as an example illustrating how one might attempt to reach a normative conclusion on the basis of empirical evidence.

CHAPTER TEN

SKEPTICISM

THE EVIL DEMON AND THE MAD SCIENTIST

In his first Meditation, Descartes introduces the evil-demon argument, perhaps the most prominent skeptical argument in the history of philosophy. Suppose an evil demon deceives you into believing that you have a body and that there is a world of physical things, when in fact you do not have a body and there is no such world. It merely *appears* to you that you have a body and there is a physical world. Because of the evil demon's trickery, your perceptual experiences are exactly the same as they would be if the world were what you take it to be. Relying on your experiences, you cannot, therefore, tell whether or not you are deceived in this manner. How, then, can you know anything about the world of physical things?

Nowadays, mad scientists are more credible philosophical villains than evil demons. Thus in contemporary epistemology we often find demonology replaced with brain surgery and computer technology. Suppose, then, that last night as you were sleeping, a mad scientist kidnapped you, removed your brain from your skull, put it in a vat with a nutrient solution to keep it alive, and hooked it up to a powerful computer. This computer deciphered your complete stock of memories, determined your character traits, and then constructed an eminently plausible biography for you. You are going to experience, to "live," this biography, but only in your mind. Through direct stimulation of the nerve endings in your brain, the computer will make you have the exact sensations you would have if you were able to continue to live your normal life. So the morning after you were kidnapped, it will seem to you as though you are getting up out of bed. You are sleepy, you brush your teeth, you have your customary breakfast, and then leave your house to go to your epistemology class. Frequently, you used to be late for class. The computer takes that habit into account and stimulates your brain accordingly. You arrive late to class and find the instructor discussing Descartes's evil-demon argument. As is your custom, you participate actively in the discussion. You enthusiastically defend the view that you know with certainty that you are not a brain in a vat. Alas, you *are* a brain in a vat. You are not actually in the classroom, and when you seemed to wake up, you were not actually in your bed. The fact of the matter is that you (or rather, what's left of you) have been floating the entire time inside a vat on a shelf in the mad scientist's laboratory. Thus you merely had the experience of waking up in your bed, and now you merely have the experience of being in a classroom on campus. In our hypothetical scenario, these experiences are, sadly, nothing but computer-generated hallucinations that are indistinguishable from real life.

Arguments that appeal to Descartes's evil demon or to its modern equivalent, the mad scientist who collects brains in vats, are supposed to establish that you don't know what you ordinarily think you know. Can you tell whether or not you are deceived by an evil demon or whether you are a brain in a vat? Skeptics would argue that you cannot, and that since you cannot, you don't know what you normally think you know—for example, that you have a body, that you are reading a book, and that you are wearing shoes.

SKEPTICAL ARGUMENTS

In the debate over what we know and what we don't know, what is at issue is typically whether the propositions we take ourselves to know are based on good reasons—that is, whether they are justified. Skeptical arguments, therefore, are often arguments to the effect that we are not *justified* in believing what we ordinarily think we are justified in believing. Such arguments are bound to be restricted in their scope, for unrestricted skepticism is self-refuting. Suppose a skeptic were to assert

(1)   There is nothing we can be justified in believing.

Obviously, if (1) is true, then (1) itself is a proposition we cannot be justified in believing. If the skeptic were to assert (1), he would be asserting something that, by his own admission, he would not be justified in believing. Thus extreme skepticism, as expressed by (1), is a self-defeating position. The moral to be drawn from this is that a skeptical argument must be formulated in such a way that it leaves intact the kind of justification the skeptical argument itself requires.

Coherently argued skepticism, then, must be restricted in its scope. It asserts that knowledge and justification, though possible in that area in which the skeptical argument itself is located, are not possible in certain other areas. The brain-in-the-vat argument, for example, has as its target the possibility of empirical knowledge about the physical world. Consequently, it is not itself intended to be an empirical argument, but rather rests on the presupposition that its premises can be known a priori.[1]

Skeptical arguments that attack knowledge by attacking justification involve two essential steps. In order to demonstrate that knowledge in a certain area cannot be had, such arguments must establish that (i) knowledge requires justification to a degree N, and (ii) propositions in the area in question cannot be justified to degree N. For example, the skeptic could argue that knowledge of the physical world requires certainty, and that propositions about the physical world are never certain. Or he could argue that such knowledge requires probability, and that what we believe about the physical world is not even probable.

The attack on knowledge need not establish that beliefs about the physical world are not justified to *any* degree. Rather, what is at issue is whether they are justified to *degree N*: the degree required for knowledge. Suppose empirical knowledge requires certainty. A moderate skeptic could reason that our empirical beliefs can't amount to knowledge because they can't be certain, but allow for the possibility that they can be justified to *some* degree. A more radical skeptic, however, would go further than that. He would argue that the arguments he can muster support the conclusion that our beliefs about the physical world are not justified to any degree.

Skeptical arguments directed against the possibility of knowledge in a certain area have the following form (let *p* stand for propositions in the area in which the claim to knowledge is challenged):

The Attack on Knowledge

(1)   In order to know that *p*, *p* must be justified to degree N.

(2)   *p* is not justified to degree N.

Therefore:

(3)   We do not know that *p*.

The function of the first premise is to establish a common ground between the skeptic and the nonskeptic. What's at issue here is a definitional question: Does knowledge require justification, and if so, how much of it? Once the skeptic and the nonskeptic agree that knowledge requires justification to a degree N, the debate moves on to the second premise, the defense of which will constitute the hard core of the attack on knowledge.

How does the skeptic attempt to establish that beliefs in a certain area are not justified to degree N, the degree necessary for knowledge? In order to simplify the issue, we shall ask how a skeptic can attempt to show that beliefs in a certain area are not justified to any degree. This has the advantage of avoiding getting tangled up in a discussion of premise (1). For except for those who deny that knowledge requires justification at all, nobody would deny that knowledge would require justification to at least some degree. Hence, if the skeptic succeeds in showing that in a certain area justification is impossible to any degree, then, provided it's agreed that knowledge requires justification, it must be conceded that knowledge in that area is not possible. If, on the other hand, it turns out that in the area under consideration justification *is* possible after all, we can return to the question of how much justification is required for knowledge and examine whether the type of justification possible in that area is sufficient for knowledge.

How, then, can the skeptic establish that a certain class of beliefs doesn't enjoy any degree of justification? This brings us to the skeptical argument against the possibility of justification. In order to attack justification, skeptics first implicitly or explicitly appeal to what we may call the *transmissibility principle*. This principle may be stated thus:

> *The Transmissibility Principle*
> If I am justified in believing *p* and am justified in believing that *p* entails *q*, then I am justified in believing *q*.

The reason this is called the "transmissibility principle" is that it asserts that justification is transmitted via justifiably believed entailments.² For example, if I am justified in believing that the president is in Washington, and am justified in believing that the president's being in Washington entails his not being in Idaho, then I am justified in believing that the president is not in Idaho.

Second, the skeptics introduce a *skeptical hypothesis* that, via the transmissibility principle, leads to the conclusion that empirical beliefs cannot be justified: for example, the hypothesis that you are a brain in a vat (the BIV hypothesis), that you are dreaming, or that you are deceived by an evil demon. Each such hypothesis is of the following type: (i) it is incompatible with the truths of (almost all) beliefs in the area in question; (ii) it is perfectly compatible with the evidence you have for the beliefs in that area. Using such a hypothesis and appealing to the transmissibility principle, the skeptic can argue thus:

> *The Attack on Justification*
> (1)   If you are justified in believing *p* and in believing that *p* entails the denial of the skeptical hypothesis, then you are justified in denying the skeptical hypothesis.
> (2)   You are justified in believing that *p* entails the denial of the skeptical hypothesis.
> (3)   You are not justified in denying the skeptical hypothesis.
> Therefore:
> (4)   You are not justified in believing *p*.

In order to discuss this argument, let the skeptical hypothesis be the BIV hypothesis and let *p* be the proposition "I am reading a book." If you are a BIV, then you don't have hands to hold a book and you don't have eyes to look at any print. So if you are a BIV, then you can't read. You can only have the experience as though you were reading. Thus the proposition

> *A*   I'm reading a book

entails that the skeptical hypothesis

B   I'm a BIV

is false. The first premise tells us that if you are justified in believing that *A* entails the negation of *B* and in believing that you are reading, then you are justified in denying the BIV hypothesis.

The second premise asserts that you *are* justified in believing that *A* entails *B*. Given the obviousness of the entailment, this premise is certainly plausible. But if you must accept premises (1) and (2), then you face the following situation: either you are justified in believing you are reading, and thus justified in denying the skeptical hypothesis that you are a BIV, or you are not justified in denying the skeptical hypothesis, and thus not justified in believing you are reading. According to the skeptic's argument (the BIV argument, for short), the latter of these two options is the one that is true.

The skeptic's main task is defending premise (3). In order to do that, he will appeal to a feature that is built into the skeptical hypothesis. Consider the possibility of your being a brain in a vat. The mad scientist makes sure that your brain is stimulated in such a way that your computer-generated life is, as far as your experiences go, *indistinguishable* from your actual life. Whatever you point to that you think is a sign of a normal life will, according to the skeptical hypothesis, also be a feature of your life in the vat. Hence your experiences don't seem to be of any help whatever for distinguishing between what you take to be your normal existence and the existence in the vat. Therefore, the skeptic reasons, you cannot possibly be justified in believing that you are not a BIV. And since you are not, it follows that you are not justified in believing that you are reading a book.

A GENERAL POINT ABOUT DEBATING THE SKEPTIC

How can nonskeptics reply to the BIV argument? We shall address this question shortly, but before we do so, we must first think about what it takes to rebut any skeptical argument. Suppose you believe a proposition *A*, and the skeptic believes that *A* is false. Suppose further the skeptic's reason for taking *A* to be false is *B*. So the skeptic argues thus:

> Skeptic: I'm justified in believing that *B* is true. Therefore, I'm justified in believing that *A* is false.

If you are convinced you're justified in believing *A*, you can reply as follows:

> You: I'm justified in believing that *A* is true. Therefore, I'm justified in believing that *B* is false.

Whether it is reasonable of you to rebut the skeptic in this way depends on what you can reasonably determine about the epistemic competition between *A* and *B*. And here there are three possibilities. After careful consideration, you could decide that:

(i)   Your reasons for *A* are better than the skeptic's reasons for *B*.

(ii) Your reasons for *A* are just as good as the skeptic's reasons for *B*.

(iii) The skeptic's reasons for *B* are better than your reasons for *A*.

In the first situation, you have successfully rejected the skeptic's challenge, and you will be fully justified to continue believing *A*, and rejecting *B* on the basis of *A*, as you do in the argument displayed above. In situation (ii), however, you lose the debate. To see why, suppose you wonder whether drinking coffee is unhealthy because it causes cancer. The two propositions competing with each other are these:

D   Drinking coffee is risk-free.

C   Drinking coffee causes cancer.

Having researched the issue, you determine that the reasons for *C* are just as good as the reasons for *D*. In that case, you should *believe* neither *D* nor *C*, and you should *disbelieve* neither *C* nor *D*. Rather, what you should do is *suspend judgment* concerning both propositions. A parallel conclusion must be drawn for situation (ii): though you wouldn't have to believe *B*, it would be your intellectual duty to stop believing *A*. And this means that in situation (ii) you lose the debate, for what the skeptic aims at establishing is precisely that you should not believe *A*.

In situation (iii), however, you lose even more badly. For in that situation, you should not only *not believe A*, but indeed *believe that A is false*. Suppose you determine that there are better reasons for believing *C* than for believing *D*: then you should believe that *D* is false. Let's apply this to the debate with the skeptic. The skeptic argues against your belief *A* on the basis of *B*. You determine that the reasons for *B* are better than the reasons for *A*. Well, that means you ought to believe that *A* is false.

Let us see how all of this works out in debating the BIV argument. The two propositions competing with each other are these:

J   I'm justified in believing I'm reading.

T   I'm not justified in denying the skeptical hypothesis.

The skeptic's reason for rejecting *J* is *T*. Let's now run again through the three situations we considered above. After careful consideration, you determine that:

(i)   There are better reasons for *J* than there are for *T*. You win the debate, for you can reject *T* on the basis of *J*.

(ii) The reasons for *J* are just as good as the reasons for *T*. You lose the debate, for you ought to refrain from believing *J*.[3]

(iii)   The reasons for *T* are better than the reasons for *J*. You lose the
       debate badly, for you ought to believe that *J* is false.

It must be said, then, that in any debate between skeptics and nonskeptics,
the skeptics have the advantage. In order to win, they must merely show
that their reasons for skepticism are *at least as good* as your reasons for
nonskepticism. However, for you to win, you must show that your reasons
for nonskepticism are *better* than their reasons for skepticism.

THE ANTISKEPTICISM OF G. E. MOORE

G. E. Moore is famous for having argued that, in debating the skeptic, the
nonskeptic wins. More specifically, Moore argued that the premises of skeptical arguments are less plausible than the propositions such arguments are
designed to attack.[4] To see how Moore's strategy works out when applied to
the BIV argument, let's consider the following two propositions:

A   I'm justified in believing I'm not a brain in a vat.

B   I'm justified in believing I'm reading.

Moore would agree with the skeptic that if *A* is false, then *B* is false. Consequently, the issue is whether -*A* can be rejected on the basis of *B*, or whether
B can be rejected on the basis of -*A*. The skeptic uses modus ponens to do
the latter, that is, to derive -*B* from -*A*:

The Skeptical Argument
(1)   If -*A* then -*B*.
(2)   -*A*.
Therefore:
(3)   -*B*.

Moore, however, would say that the skeptic's premise—I'm not justified in
believing I'm not a brain in a vat—is less credible than the proposition the
skeptic wants to deny—I'm justified in believing I'm reading. Moore, then,
would argue that it's more reasonable to assert *B* than to deny *A*, and thus
would use modus tollens (an argument of the form: if *p*, then *q*, not *q* , therefore not *p*) to derive *A* from *B* (that is, to reject -*A* on the basis of *B*).

Moore's Counterargument
(1)   If -*A*, then -*B*.
(2)   *B*.
Therefore:
(3)   *A*.

Now when we evaluate the epistemic competition between -*A* (the skeptic's
premise) and *B* (the nonskeptic's premise), it is not exactly obvious that the

skeptic is right in claiming that -*A* is at least as reasonable as -*B*.[5] He needs, therefore, to employ a further consideration in support of -*A*. Let us abbreviate this consideration using the letter *C*. This allows us to formulate the skeptical argument thus:

The Expanded Skeptical Argument
(1)   *C*.
(2)   If *C*, then -*A*.
Therefore:
(3)   -*A*.
(4)   If -*A*, then -*B*.
Therefore:
(5)   -*B*.

But once the issue involves epistemic competition not only between *B* and -*A*, but also between *B* and premises (1) and (2), the skeptical position becomes more vulnerable. Now the nonskeptics need not necessarily resort to the Moorean countermove (to reject -*A* on the basis of *B*), for they might be able to find independent reasons against (1) or (2). In the next few sections, we shall examine whether there are such independent reasons.

REBUTTING THE BIV ARGUMENT AGAINST JUSTIFICATION

Let us return to the skeptical attack on justification that we considered in the section on skeptical arguments, and let us restate it in the specific form of the BIV argument:

The BIV Argument Against Justification
(1)   If you are justified in believing yourself to be reading and in believing that that belief entails the denial of the BIV hypothesis, then you are justified in denying the BIV hypothesis.
(2)   You are justified in believing that that belief entails the denial of the BIV hypothesis.
(3)   You are not justified in denying the BIV hypothesis.
Therefore:
(4)   You are not justified in believing yourself to be reading.

As we saw in the previous section, as the argument stands, it invites a G. E. Moore response: the response of inferring the denial of (3) from the denial of (4)—of saying that since I'm justified in believing myself to be reading, I'm justified in denying the BIV hypothesis.[6] In order to avoid this type of response, the skeptic must offer an additional argument in support of (3). He must justify his assertion that I'm not justified in denying that I'm a brain in a vat.

Now one reason in support of (3) the skeptic can cite is that, from one's subjective point of view, one cannot distinguish between being and not being a BIV. Jonathan Dancy puts this point this way:

> Since you have only your own experience to appeal to, and that experience is the same in either situation, nothing can reveal to you which situation is the actual one.[7]

In order to state Dancy's point as clearly as possible, let us fix the two situations under consideration as follows:

The Normal Situation
I'm just what I think I am, and I'm reading a book.

The BIV Situation
I'm a brain in a vat, and I only think I'm reading a book.

In fact, I have neither eyes nor arms, and thus can't be reading a book.

Dancy's point is that nothing can reveal to me which situation is actual: the normal one or the BIV situation. The skeptic argues that since this is so, I am not justified in believing I am not a BIV. Let us formulate the argument accordingly.

The Argument for the Third Premise
(1) Nothing can reveal to you which situation obtains.
(2) If nothing can reveal to you which situation obtains, then you're not justified in denying the BIV hypothesis.
Therefore:
(3) You are not justified in denying the BIV hypothesis.

How can the nonskeptic reply to this line of reasoning? The nonskeptic will be well advised to take a closer look at the claim that nothing can "reveal" to me which situation obtains. For some state of affairs P to be "revealed" to me, I need evidence for believing that P is the case. For example, what reveals to a detective that X killed Y is evidence that incriminates X: evidence in support of "X killed Y." Let us, then, interpret (1) in this way:

(1a) You don't have any evidence in support of a belief about which situation obtains.

But is (1a) plausible at all? It would not appear it is. After all, we have plenty of evidence against believing that medical technology has reached a stage at which it's feasible to keep a brain alive for an extended period of time, let alone stimulate it in such a way that the impression of a normal life is generated. Perhaps neuroscience will accomplish such feats at some point in the future, but surely in light of all the relevant evidence available to us, we may say that at present neuroscience isn't anywhere near that point. So as far as my evidence is concerned, there is a good reason for me to believe that I'm not a brain in the vat—that is, that the normal situation obtains. We must conclude, therefore, that (1a) is false.[8]

Perhaps, then, premise (1) must be interpreted as saying the following:

> (1b) You don't have *conclusive* evidence in support of a belief about which situation obtains.

If I have conclusive evidence for a proposition *p*, then my evidence logically guarantees that *p* is true.[9] It would be impossible to have that evidence for *p* when *p* is false. Now I must certainly concede to the skeptic that my evidence for not taking myself to be a BIV is less than conclusive. After all, it might be that the mad scientist who feeds me through his powerful computer whatever reasons I have for not believing myself to be a BIV. So no matter how well my evidence justifies me, it can't justify me to the point where I can say that it logically guarantees to me that I'm not a BIV.

The nonskeptic must, therefore, accept (1b). However, she must accept the skeptical conclusion only if she must also accept the second premise, appropriately modified:

> (2b) If you don't have any conclusive evidence in support of a belief about which situation obtains, then you're not justified in denying the BIV hypothesis.

Now when the nonskeptic claims she is justified in believing herself not to be a BIV, she is operating with what we might call our *ordinary* concept of justification. And according to that concept, being justified in believing that *p* does not require having conclusive evidence for believing that *p*. Hence the nonskeptic need not agree with (2b). This means that if what is at issue is justification in the ordinary sense of the word, then the skeptic's argument fails to lend compelling support for its conclusion. If, on the other hand, the skeptic's aim is to show that we lack a different kind of justification—the kind of justification that requires conclusive evidence—then the nonskeptic need not disagree with that conclusion. For she never claimed to have justification in *that* sense of the term.

In order to pin down the result of our discussion, let us distinguish between *fallible* and *infallible* justification. The skeptic appeals to premise (1) in order to establish that I cannot be justified in believing I'm not a BIV. But this premise itself is ambiguous. If interpreted as (1a), it suggests that I can't have fallible justification for believing that I'm not a BIV. As we have seen, this is false. If, on the other hand, premise (1) is interpreted as (1b), then we don't get the result that I'm not justified to any degree in believing that I'm not a BIV. So in that case, the issue is merely whether, given that I have justification for denying the skeptical hypothesis, that justification is good enough for *knowing* that I'm not a BIV.

THE BIV HYPOTHESIS AND DEFEASIBILITY

In the previous section, we argued that my evidence justifies me in believing that I am not a BIV. However, perhaps the skeptic could argue that the skeptical hypothesis, or some related proposition, *factually defeats* my evidence for believing that I am not a BIV. Recall our definition of *knowledge* from Chapter 1; there, we defined knowledge as justified belief that is factually undefeated—that is, not defeated by any true proposition.[10] Thus, the skeptic's argument could be viewed as an attempt to show that there are true propositions that factually defeat our empirical beliefs.

But let us see precisely what, according to this line of reasoning, the defeater is supposed to be. Let's begin with the skeptical hypothesis itself. The claim in question is that

D1   I am a BIV

factually defeats my justified belief

R   I'm reading a book.

In order to determine whether D1 does indeed factually defeat R, we must distinguish between two cases: (i) D1 is true; (ii) D1 is false. Suppose D1 is true. If so, there is no issue to debate, for if D1 is true, R is false, and thus the nonskeptic would agree that R isn't known simply because what's known must be true. Now suppose D1 is false. In that case, D1 fails to factually defeat R, for factual defeaters must be true.

A second suggestion is that what factually defeats R is the *possibility* that I am a BIV:

D2   It is logically possible that I am a BIV.

The nonskeptic must admit that D2 is true. But she need not concede that it is a factual defeater for R. For a true proposition to be a factual defeater for R, it must be such that, if added to S's body of evidence, S loses her justification for believing R. And certainly D2 does not meet this condition.[11]

It would appear, therefore, that D2 must be strengthened. Let us consider the following proposal:

D3   It is probable that I am a BIV.

The problem with D3 is obvious: it is false. Hence it does not qualify as a factual defeater. Let's consider one final proposal. The skeptic might argue that what does the defeating here is this:

D4   I cannot distinguish between being and not being a BIV.

This claim suffers from the same ambiguity as the claim that nothing can reveal to me whether I'm a BIV or not. In order to be able to distinguish between two states of affairs, one needs evidence indicating which of the two states of affairs obtains. Thus in judging what to make of D4, we must decide between:

D4a   Concerning the question of whether or not I'm a BIV, I don't have any *evidence* either way.

D4b   Concerning the question of whether or not I'm a BIV, I don't have any *conclusive evidence* either way.

For the reasons we discussed in the previous section, D4a is false, and thus doesn't qualify as a factual defeater. D4b, on the other hand, is true, but it doesn't qualify as a factual defeater either. Suppose, having evidence E for believing that p, you are informed that E does not guarantee the truth of p. That information would not pose a threat to your justification, for being justified in believing that p does not require having a guarantee for the truth of p.[12]

It is time to put our discussion of the BIV hypothesis in its larger context. The purpose of the skeptical attack on my justification for believing that I'm not a BIV is to undermine the possibility of ordinary empirical knowledge. The initial step is to argue that if I don't know I'm not a BIV, then I don't know whatever entails that the skeptical hypothesis (my being a BIV) is false. The next step is to establish that I can't know I'm not a BIV because of a lack of justification for believing this. Above, we distinguished between two ways in which the skeptic can attempt to establish this. He can argue either that I don't have *any* justification for believing I'm not a BIV, or that, although I have some justification for believing I'm not a BIV, I don't have *enough* justification for knowing it. Above, we have argued that the BIV argument does not succeed in doing the former. Next, let's see whether it succeeds in doing the latter.

THE BIV HYPOTHESIS AND THE CONCEPT OF KNOWLEDGE

Recall that in order to argue against the possibility of knowledge of the physical world, the skeptic starts out with a claim about how knowledge is connected to justification. Since, as we have seen, I have fallible justification for believing I'm not a BIV, the skeptic must assert that knowledge requires *infallible* justification. Once this premise is agreed on, the skeptic can derive the desired conclusion as follows:

The Brain-in-the-Vat Argument Against Knowledge

(1)   In order to know that I am not a BIV, I must be infallibly justified in believing that I'm not a BIV.

(2)   I am not infallibly justified in believing I'm not a BIV.

Therefore:

(3)   I don't know that I'm not a BIV.

Once this conclusion is established, the skeptic can appeal to the transmissibility principle in order to argue that for any proposition *p* that entails that I am not a BIV, I don't know that *p*.

The nonskeptic could rebut this argument by attacking premise (1). She could try to neutralize the first premise, and thus the entire argument, with the following consideration: The issue between the skeptic and the nonskeptic concerns the extent of knowledge. And the extent of knowledge is a function of the nature of knowledge, of how knowledge is defined. Unfortunately there isn't a ready, universally agreed upon definition of knowledge available to both parties to the debate. Rather, at the outset of the debate the skeptic and the nonskeptic must come to an agreement on how to define the concept of knowledge. And here there are two possibilities. The skeptic and the nonskeptic can agree on operating with either our *ordinary* or a *revised* concept of knowledge.

Our ordinary concept of knowledge manifests itself in our customary epistemic practice, and this practice is *nonskeptical*. We take ourselves to have an enormous body of knowledge about our physical environment. At the same time, however, we don't take the kind of evidence that enables us to acquire such knowledge to be conclusive. Rather, the fallibility of our senses is a generally acknowledged ingredient of our epistemic practice. So according to our ordinary concept, knowledge does not require infallible, but only fallible, justification.

Now recall that the skeptic's attack on justification is not entirely successful. He cannot show that our ordinary empirical beliefs don't enjoy *any* degree of justification. He only succeeds in showing that they are not infallibly justified. Consequently, if the skeptic wishes to deny that we can have knowledge of physical objects, he must replace our ordinary concept with a revised one, according to which only *infallible* justification is good enough for knowledge.

This very move, however, means the skeptic loses the debate. For the skeptic set out to show that we don't know what we *ordinarily* think we know. But if this is what he wishes to accomplish, he must demonstrate that we don't have empirical knowledge in the *ordinary* sense of "knowledge." As we have seen, he cannot do this. He can only demonstrate that we don't have empirical knowledge in the *revised* sense of knowledge. But if this is what he establishes, then he does not meet the objective he set out to met. And in that case, the nonskeptic can respond: "Well, what you have established is that if knowledge requires infallible justification, then we don't know what we ordinarily think we know. And with that I agree. However, that's not much of a concession on my part, for I never claimed that we have empirical knowledge if *that* is what we mean by 'knowledge.' Rather, what I claimed all along is that we have empirical knowledge given our ordinary understanding of that concept. And certainly you haven't shown me that that claim is false."[13]

Let us consider what the nonskeptic's point is specifically with regard to the argument displayed above. The nonskeptic can argue that the transition from premise (1) to the conclusion involves an equivocation. Let "$know_0$" refer to knowing in the ordinary sense, and "$know_r$" to knowing in the revised sense. For the first premise to be correct, it must be about knowledge in the revised sense, or else the nonskeptic need not agree with it:

(1′)   If I'm not infallibly justified in believing I'm not a BIV, then I don't $know_r$ that I'm not a BIV.

But for the conclusion of the skeptical argument to be disturbing, for it to have the intended import of undermining our *ordinary* knowledge claims, it must be about knowledge in the ordinary sense:

(3*)   I don't $know_0$ that I'm not a BIV.

However, (3*) does not follow from (1′) and (2). If the first premise is about knowledge in the revised sense, and the conclusion is about knowledge in the ordinary sense, the argument is invalid. For it to be valid, the conclusion, too, must be about knowledge in the revised sense:

(3′)   I don't $know_r$ that I'm not a BIV.

Unlike (3*), (3′) follows from (1′) and (2). But, as we saw above, (3′) is an innocuous conclusion, one over which the nonskeptic need not lose any sleep. The conclusion that does pose a genuine threat to our ordinary knowledge claims is (3*). *That* conclusion, however, does not follow from any premises the nonskeptic is obliged to accept.

THE ARGUMENT FROM ERROR

The BIV argument is intended to undermine the possibility of empirical knowledge by undermining the possibility of empirical justification. However, sometimes skeptics try to undermine the possibility of empirical knowledge without making an attack on justification. In this section, we shall discuss such an argument.

Surely you know that you have made errors in numerous situations. These are some examples: you thought you knew you had already paid the electricity bill, but you had not; you thought you knew you had more than ten dollars in your wallet, but you did not; you thought you knew there was still milk in the refrigerator, but there was not. A skeptic could ask you whether you have any reason to believe, with regard to your *present* claims to knowledge, that you are not again mistaken in attributing knowledge to yourself. He could argue that if you don't have any such reason, then you cannot now reasonably claim to have empirical knowledge.

Here is an example to illustrate how this argument goes. Suppose you have a dog and have frequently taken yourself to know "There's my dog over there." There were a few situations, though, when your knowledge claim turned out to be mistaken. On these occasions, you mistook your dog for someone else's. Now you are again walking your dog. For a while, he was out of sight, but now he is back, and you again you take yourself to know "There's my dog over there." Here are the two situations we must compare:

S1   You took yourself to know "There's my dog." Later it turned out it was someone else's. Your knowledge claim was mistaken.

S2   Now you take yourself again to know "There's my dog."

The problem is that since you did not know in S1, and since S2 is analogous to S1—in both situations, it is perceptual evidence that seemingly puts you in a position to know—it is unclear how you could know in S2. Dancy gives a lucid account of the problem:

> Nothing you can point to in your present situation tells you that this situation is not one in which you are mistaken. For all you can tell, it is relevantly similar to situations in which you have made mistakes. Since you clearly did not now then, how can you say that you know now?[14]

What is at issue here is whether you can reasonably claim to know in S2. According to the skeptical argument, you cannot unless you can show a *relevant difference* between the two situations.[15] The skeptic would argue that you can't show that there is such a difference. Consequently, you don't know in S2 that there is your dog over there.

The Argument from Error

(1)   If I can't show that there is a relevant difference between S1 and S2, then I can't reasonably claim I know that *p* in S2.

(2)   I can't show that there is a relevant difference between S1 and S2.

Therefore:

(3)   I can't reasonably claim I know that *p* in S2.

In order to reply to this argument, I must show that there is a relevant difference between the two situations. According to the skeptic, I can't do that. However, the nonskeptic will argue that I can. Here is how. My present total evidence indicates two things: First, in S1, my belief was false. Back in S1, I mistakenly thought the dog I was looking at was mine. But later I found out that it was someone else's. This is an additional piece of evidence that I did not have in S1. But it is part of my total evidence *now*. Furthermore, part of the total body of evidence I have now is perceptual evidence indicating that I'm seeing my dog over there. Thus, from my present perspective, there is a difference between the two situations: regarding S1, I now have evidence for taking *p* to be *false*, but regarding S2, I now have evidence for taking *p* to be *true*. Hence premise (2) is false, and I can reasonably insist on my present knowledge claim.

The skeptic arrives at a different conclusion because he compares what evidence I have *in S1* with what evidence I have *in S2*. And when looking at the matter in that way, there would not appear to be any relevant difference. In both cases, my evidence consists in a certain body of perceptual experience. The nonskeptic will argue, however, that it is a mistake to look at the matter in that way. For the question at hand is not

Q1 Is there a relevant difference between the evidence I had in S1 and the evidence I now have in S2?

but rather

Q2 Is there a relevant difference between my present evidence regarding S1 and my present evidence regarding S2?

Why is Q2 and not Q1 the relevant question? Consider again our problem. In S1, I claimed I knew that *p*. It turned out I was mistaken. Now I claim again I know that *p*. Given that I was mistaken in S1, and given the similarity between S1 and S2, the skeptic challenges me to defend my present claim to knowledge. The difficulty I face is to justify my present knowledge claim vis-à-vis the error I committed in S1. Now, in order to meet this challenge, I must *now* come up with a difference between the two situations. I must be able to explain why I can, on my *present* evidence, claim that I now know although I didn't know in S1. But this means that I must address not Q1 but Q2.

As we saw above, there is a satisfactory answer to Q2. I now have evidence for the *falsehood* of *p* in S1, and also evidence for the *truth* of *p* in S2. Hence I can reject the argument from error, as displayed above, on the ground that premise (2) is false.

A REVISED ARGUMENT FROM ERROR

The argument we discussed in the previous section derives its force from comparing the present situation with a *past* one in which a mistake was made. According to the skeptic, I can't come up with a relevant difference between the two situations, and thus can't reasonably claim that I know in the present situation. In reply, we argued that my evidence regarding the present and the past situations is different. With regard to the past situation, my present evidence suggests that *p* was false; with regard to the present situation, it suggests that *p* is true. Hence I can reasonably claim that, although I did not know that *p* then, I do now.

To avoid exposing himself to this line of reasoning, the skeptic could replace the first-person perspective of his argument with a third-person, or God's eye perspective. In the previous argument, the issue is whether, on the basis of the evidence I now have, *I* can justify my claim that I know in the present situation although I didn't know in the past situation. Above, we saw that I can. In a revised version of the argument from error, the skeptic could instead raise the issue of what, having constructed a hypothetical case, *we would say about the subject in that case*. In order to construct an appropriate hypothetical case, let us introduce propositions *p* and *q*, for which our hypothetical subject has equally good evidence, and then simply stipulate that *p* is false and *q* true. Then the question will not be whether the subject himself would claim to know, but whether *we* would say that the subject knows.

The following case proposed by John Tienson is suitable for constructing a skeptical argument from error of that kind. Consider a detective investigating Black and White, who are suspected of embezzling. "After a lengthy and painstaking investigation he has exactly the same evidence that Black is not the embezzler and that White is not the embezzler. Suppose that Black is in fact the guilty party, and that White is perfectly innocent. Now, given the assumption that [the detective's] evidence is exactly the same in both cases, . . . no matter how good that evidence is, he does not know that White is innocent."[16]

Let us pin down the essential elements of this case. The two propositions in question are these:

p   White is innocent.

q   Black is innocent.

Concerning these propositions, the following conditions obtain:

(i)   The detective's evidence for believing *q* is as good as his evidence for believing *p*.

(ii)   *p* is true.

(ii)   *q* is false.

On the basis of (i), (ii), and (iii), Tienson concludes that the detective doesn't know *p*, however good his evidence for *p* is. The underlying reason for this verdict would appear to be this: Given that the detective's evidence misleads him regarding Black, and given that his evidence regarding White is no better than his evidence regarding Black, we can't reasonably claim the detective knows that *p*. If we turn this consideration into a principle, we can formulate the following argument:

The Revised Argument from Error
(1) If *S* doesn't know that *p*, and *S*'s evidence for *q* is no better than her evidence for *p*, then *S* doesn't know that *q*.
(2) *S* doesn't know that *p*.
(3) *S*'s evidence for *q* is no better than her evidence for *p*.
Therefore:
(4) *S* doesn't know that *q*.

This is an argument from error because of premise (2); the reason *S* does not know that *p* is that *S* is mistaken in believing *p*. Although it initially looks as if the argument has a skeptical implication only for the specific case in question, further reflection reveals that its skeptical implications concern empirical knowledge in general. For any proposition *q* you believe on the basis of empirical evidence, there is a possible situation in which you believe a false proposition *p* on the basis of evidence that is exactly like your evidence for *q*. Hence the argument displayed above applies for any proposition that you believe on the basis of empirical evidence.

What can the nonskeptic say in response to this argument? Since (2) and (3) are true ex hypothesi, she must attack premise (1). Here is a case she could cite in order to undermine the plausibility of that premise.

It's Tuesday 10:00 A.M., and the philosophy faculty at St. Cloud State University get together for the regular department meeting. Around the conference table, *S*'s colleagues are gathered. Across from her, there is JB, or so it looks to her. What she doesn't know is that JB has an identical twin brother, TB, who is capable of perfectly impersonating JB. And it so happens that it is not JB, but TB, who came to today's department meeting. Hence when *S* believes "There's JB over there," she is mistaken in that belief. Next to TB, there sits MA, and thus *S* also believes "There's MA over there."

Using the following argument, the nonskeptic can argue thus (let *p* be "That's JB over there" and let *q* be "That's MA over there"):

The Nonskeptic's Counterargument
(1) *S* knows that *q*.
(2) *S*'s evidence for *q* is no better than her evidence for *p*.

(3) *S* does not know that *p*.

Therefore:

(3) It is false that if *S* doesn't know that *p*, and *S's* evidence for *q* is no better than her evidence for *p*, then she doesn't know that *q*.

This counterargument is a good example of G. E. Moore's strategy of dealing with the skeptic. The confrontation between the two arguments shows that we must choose between ordinary knowledge claims of the most basic and elementary nature, such as

K I know that this is my colleague MA over there

and the skeptical principle

P If *S* doesn't know that *p*, and *S's* evidence for *q* is no better than her evidence for *p*, then she doesn't know that *q*.

And here the nonskeptic faces the kind of choice we discussed earlier in this chapter. She must determine whether she thinks that

(i) the reasons for *K* are better than my reasons for *P*;

(ii) the reasons for *K* are just as good as my reasons for *P*;

(iii) the reasons for *P* are better than my reasons for *K*.

As we pointed out above, for the nonskeptic not to lose the debate, her verdict must be that (i) is correct. Here we shall leave it open whether that verdict would be right, but not before adding one further consideration. *P* is a general and abstract principle, *K* is a particular and concrete proposition. The risk involved in accepting general and abstract principles is greater than the risk involved in accepting particular and concrete propositions. This consideration ought to supply the nonskeptic with hope, for it nourishes the suspicion that it may not be so easy for the skeptic to show that the reasons for *P* are at least as good as the reasons for *K*.

STUDY QUESTIONS

1. Why can't skeptical arguments be unrestricted in their scope?
2. How do skeptics attack knowledge claims?
3. How do skeptics derive the conclusion that for a proposition *p* in a given area, one is not justified in believing that *p*?
4. In order not to lose the debate with the skeptic, what must the nonskeptic accomplish?
5. How does G. E. Moore argue against skepticism?

6. One what grounds can the nonskeptic object to the skeptical premise "Nothing can reveal to me whether or not I'm a BIV"?
7. How would nonskeptics reply to the skeptical argument that because I might be a BIV, my justification for believing I'm not a BIV is factually defeated?
8. What is the "argument from error"?
9. How could the nonskeptic reply to that argument?

EXERCISES

1. Discuss the argument: "You can't rule out that you are a BIV. Therefore, you are not *justified* in believing that you are reading a book."
2. Discuss the argument: "You can't rule out that you are a BIV. Therefore, you do not *know* that you are reading a book."
3. Discuss the argument: "I can clearly perceive that I have a body. Therefore, I'm not a BIV."
4. What do you think is the best reason for taking yourself not to be a brain in a vat?
5. Discuss the revised argument from error, which is stated on page 000. Explain what you take to be the best way to reply to this argument, and whether you take that reply to be successful.

NOTES

[1] In addition to empirical knowledge of physical objects, areas of knowledge skeptics would challenge are knowledge of the past, of the future, and of other minds. For a brief overview of skepticism about different areas of knowledge, see Fred Feldman (1986), pp. 23ff.

[2] Gettier uses a similar principle in his famous 1963 article, albeit not for skeptical purposes. The transmissibility principle is also referred to as the "closure principle." See Klein (1992) and Dancy (1985).

[3] If (ii) is the case, *J* might be true after all. The point is that even if, as a matter of fact, *J* were true, you wouldn't be justified in believing it to be true.

[4] See Moore (1922), p. 228, and (1953), pp. 120–126.

[5] On the other hand, it isn't obvious either that a Moore-type nonskeptic would be right in asserting that *B* is more reasonable than -*A*, which is why Moore's argument has failed to produce unanimous consent.

[6] An alternative way of rebutting the skeptic that can't be discussed here is to reject the transmissibility principle—that is, premise (1). For a brief discussion of that strategy, see Klein (1992a).

[7] Dancy (1985), p. 10.

[8] This passage should not be misunderstood as suggesting that there are no other reasons against (1a). In fact, I have plenty of reasons to disbelieve that I'm a BIV. The scenario in question involves severe scientific, legal, financial, and practical difficulties which make its actual occurrence extremely unlikely.

[9] See Chapter 1, pp. 11f.

[10] See Chapter 1, pp. 17f.

[11] If the skeptics were to press their point here, we could repeat the concluding argument in the previous section.

[12] A further question that could be raised is the following: Do D1, D2, D3, or D4 *evidentially* defeat the evidence for my empirical beliefs? If they do, then the brain-in-the-vat argument establishes after all that my empirical beliefs are unjustified. In order to answer this question, we must, for each of the potential defeaters under consideration, ask a further question: if that defeater is added to my evidence, do I lose my justification for my empirical beliefs, for example, for a belief such as "I'm reading a book"? Consider first

> D1   I'm a BIV

D1 is not a proposition I have evidence for. Hence it doesn't defeat the evidence I have for believing I'm reading. The same applies to D3, the proposition that it's probable that I'm a BIV. On e other hand,

> D2   It is logically possible that I am a BIV

is a proposition that is evident to me. But surely D2's epistemic effect is not to defeat the evidence I have for believing I'm reading D2 merely has the effect of preventing that evidence from being conclusive, that is, of preventing it from providing me with infallible justiication. The same reasoning applies to D4b, the proposition that concerning the question of wheter I'm a BIV, I don't have any conclusive evidence. It would not appear, then, that there are propositions having to do with the possibility of my being a BIV that defeat my justiciation for believing I'm reading.

[13] See Fred Feldman (1986), pp. 33–35.

[14] Dancy (1985), p. 12.

[15] Ibid., p. 13.

[16] Tienson (1974), pp. 289f.

References

ALSTON, WILLIAM
  1989 *Epistemic Justification: Essays in the Theory of Knowledge* (Ithaca, N.Y. Cornell University Press).
  1992 "Foundationalism," in Dancy and Sosa (1992), pp. 144–147.
  1993 Review of Ernest Sosa, *Knowledge in Perspective: Selected Essays in Epistemology* (Cambridge: Cambridge University Press, 1991).

ARMSTRONG, DAVID
  1973 *Belief, Truth and Knowledge* (Cambridge: Cambridge University Press).

AUDI, ROBERT
  1988 *Belief, Justification, and Knowledge* (Belmon, Cal.: Wadsworth).
  1993a "Contemporary Foundationalism," in Pojman (1993), pp. 206–213.
  1993b "Fallibilist Foundationalism and Holistic Coherentism," in Pojman (1993), pp. 263–279.

BENDER, JOHN W.
  1989 *The Current State of the Coherence Theory: Critical Essays on the Epistemic Theories of Keith Lehrer and Laurence BonJour, with Replies* (Dordrecht: Kluwer Academic Publishers).

BLANDSHARD, BRAND
  1939 *The Nature of Thought* (London: Allen and Unwin).

BONJOUR, LAURENCE
  1985 *The Structure of Empirical Knowledge* (Cambridge, Mass: Harvard University Press).
  1989a "Reply to Steup," *Philosophical Studies 55*: 57–63
  1989b "Replies and Clarification," in Bender (1992), pp. 276–292.
  1992 "A Rationalist Manifesto," *Canadian Journal of Philosophy*, Suppl. Vol. 18, ed. Philip Hanson and Bruce Hunter, pp. 53–88.

BRADLEY, RAYMOND, AND SWARTZ, NORMAN
  1979 *Possible Worlds* (Indianapolis: Hackett).

CASULLO, ALFRED
  1992 "A Priori—A Posteriori," in Dancy and Sosa (1992), pp. 1–3.

CHILSHOLM, RODERICK
1966 "Freedom and Action," in K. Lehrer (ed.), *Freedom and Determinism* (Atlantic Highlands, N.J.: Humanities Press), pp. 11–44.
1977 *Theory of Knowledge*, 2nd ed. (Englewood Cliffs, N.J. Prentice Hall).
1982 *The Foundations of Knowing* (Minneapolis: University of Minnesota Press).
1989 *Theory of Knowledge*, 3rd ed. (Englewood Cliffs, N.J.: Prentice Hall).
1990 "The Status of Epistemic Principles," *Nous 209*: 209–215.

CHURCHLAND, PAUL
1984 *Matter and Consiousness* (Cambrdige, Mass.: MIT Press).

COHEN, STEWART
1984 "Justification and Truth," *Philosophical Studies 46*: 279–295.

CONEE, EARL, AND FELDMAN, RICHARD
1985 "Evidentialism," *Philosophical Studies 48*: 15–44.

CLAY, MARJORIE, AND LEHRER, KEITH
1989 *Knowledge and Skepticism* (Boulder, Colo.: Westview Press).

DANCY, CHRISTOPHER, AND SOSA, ERNEST
1992 *A Companion to Epistemology* (Oxford: Blackwell).

DANCY, JONATHAN
1985 *Introduction to Contemporary Epistemology* (Oxford: Blackwell).

DAVIDSON, DONALD
1983 "The Coherence Theory of Truth and Knowledge," in Dieter Henrich (ed), *Kant oder Hegel* (Stuttgart: Klett Cotta), pp. 423–438.

FELDMAN, FRED
1986 *A Cartesian Introduction to Philosophy* (New York: McGrawHill).

FELDMAN, RICHARD
1985 "Reliability and Justification," *Monist 68*: 159–174.
1988a "Epistemic Obligations," *Philosophical Perspectives 2*: 235–256.
1988b "Subjective and Objective Justification in Ethics and Epistemology," *Monist 71*: 405–419.
1989 "Goldman on Epistemology and Cognitive Science," *Philosophia 19*: 197–208.
1993 "Proper Functionalism," *Nous 27*: 34–50.

FIRTH, RODERICK
1967 "The Anatomy of Certainty," *Philosophical Review 76*: 3–27.

FOLEY, RICHARD
1987 *The Theory of Epistemic Rationality* (Cambridge, Mass.: Harvard University Press).
1992 "Roderick Chisholm," in Dancy and Sosa (1992).

FUMERTON, RICHARD
1980 "Induction and Reasoning to the Best Explanation," *Philosophy of Science 47*.
1988 "The Internalism/Externalism Controversy," *Philosophical Perspectives 2*: 443–459.
1992 "Phenomenalism," in Dancy (1992), pp. 338–342.
1993 "A Critique of Coherentism," in Pojman (1993), pp. 241–245.

GETTIER, EDMUND
1963 "Is Justified True Belief Knowledge?" *Analysis 23*: 121–123.

GINET, CARL
1975   *Knowledge, Perception, and Memory* (Dordrecht: Reidel).
1985   "Contra Reliabilism," *Monist 68*: 175–187

GOLDMAN, ALVIN
1979   "What is Justified Belief?" in Pappas (1979), pp. 1–23.
1986   *Epistemology and Cognition* (Cambridge, Mass.: Harvard University Press).
1988   "Strong and Weak Justification," *Philosophical Perspectives 2*: 51–69.
1989   "BonJour's *The Structure of Empirical Knowledge*," in Bender (1989), pp. 105–114.
1991   "Epistemic Folkways and Scientific Epistemology," in *Liaisons: Philosophy Meets the Cognitive and Social Sciences* (Cambridge, Mass.: MIT Press).

GRECO, JOHN
1992   "Virtue Epistemology," in Dancy and Sosa (1992), pp. 520–522.
1993   Review of John Bender (ed), *The Current State of the Coherence Theory: Critical Essays on the Epistemic Theories of Keith Lehrer and Laurence BonJour, with Replies* (Kluwer 1989), *Nous 27*: 111–113.
1994   Review of Jonathan Kvanvig, *The Intellectual Virtues and the Life of the Mind* (Savage, Md.: Rowman and Littlefield, 1992), *Philosophy and Phenomenological Research 54*: pp. 973–976.

GRICE, H. P., AND STRAWSON, P. F.
1956   "In Defense of a Dogma," *Philosophical Review 65*. Reprinted in Sleigh (1972), pp. 73–88.

HARE, RICHARD
1952   *The Language of Morals* (Oxford: Oxford University Press).

HARMAN, GILBERT
1977   *The Nature of Morality* (New York: Oxford University Press).
1984   "Is There a Single True Morality," in David Copp/David Zimmerman (eds.), *Morality, Reason and Truth* (Totowa: Rowman and Allanheld).

HEIL, JOHN
1992   "Belief," in Dancy and Sosa (1992), pp. 45–48.

HETHERINGTON, STEPHEN CADE
1992   *Epistemology's Paradox: Is a Theory of Knowledge Possible?* (Savage, Md.: Rowman and Littlefield).

HORGAN, TERENCE (ED.)
1983   Spindel Conference on Supervenience, *Southern Journal of Philosophy 22*: supp.

HORWICH, PAUL
1992   "Theories of Truth," in Dancy and Sosa (1992), pp. 509–515.

JAMES, WILLIAM
1909   *The Meaning of Truth* (New York: Longmans Green).

KANT, IMMANUEL
1781   *The Critique of Pure Reason*, trans. N. Kemp Smith (London: Macmillan, 1964).

KIM, JAEGWON
1984   "Concepts of Supervenience," *Philosophy and Phenomenological Research 45*: 153–177.
1988   "What Is Naturalized Epistemology?" *Philosophical Perspectives 2*: 381–405.

KLEIN, PETER
1985 "The Virtues of Inconsistency," *Monist 68*: 105–135.
1992a "Contemporary Scepticism," in Dancy and Sosa (1992), pp. 458–462.
1992b "Certainty," in Dancy and Sosa (1992), pp. 61–64.

KORNBLITH, HILARY
1987 *Naturalizing Epistemology* (Cambridge, Mass. MIT Press).
1989 "The Unattainability of Coherence," in Bender (1989), pp. 207–214.

KRIPKE, SAUL
1972 *Naming and Necessity* (Cambridge: Cambridge University Press).

KVANVIG, JONATHAN L.
1992 *The Intellectual Virtues and the Life of the Mind* (Savage, Md.: Rowman and Littlefield).

LEHRER, KEITH
1974 *Knowledge* (Oxford: Oxford University Press).
1989 "Coherence and the Truth Connection: A Reply to My Critics," in Bender (1989), pp. 253–275.
1990 *Theory of Knowledge* (Boulder, Colo.: Westview Press).

LEHRER, KEITH, AND PAXSON, THOMAS
1969 "Knowledge: Undefeated Justified True Belief," *Journal of Philosophy 66*: 225–237.

LEWIS, C. I.
1929 *Mind and the World-Order* (New York: Charles Scribner's Sons).
1946 *An Analysis of Knowledge and Valuation* (LaSalle, Ill.: Open Court).

LOCKE, JOHN
1959 *An Essay Concerning Human Understanding*, ed. A. C. Fraser (New York: Dover).

LUPERFOY, STEVEN
1992 "Knowledge and Belief," in Dancy and Sosa (1992), pp. 234–247.

LYCAN, WILLIAM
1988 *Judgment and Justification* (Cambridge: Cambridge University Press).

MAFFIE, JAMES
1990 "Recent Work on Naturalizing Epistemology," *American Philosophical Quarterly 27*: 281–293.

MOORE, G. E.
1912 *Ethics* (Oxford: Oxford University Press).
1922 *Philosophical Studies* (London: Routledge and Kegan Paul).
1953 *Some Main Problems of Philosophy* (London: Allen and Unwin).

MOSER, PAUL
1985 *Empirical Justification* (Dordrecht: Reidel).
1989 *Knowledge and Evidence* (Cambridge: Cambridge University Press).
1992 "Gettier Problem," in Dancy and Sosa (1992), pp. 157–159.

NEURATH, OTTO
1932 "Protokollsätze," *Erkenntnis 3*: 204–214.

PAPPAS, GEORGE (ED.)
1979 *Justification and Knowledge* (Drodrecht: Reidel).

PLANTINGA, ALVIN
  1993a *Warrant: The Current Debate* (Oxford: Oxford University Press).
  1993b *Warrant and Proper Function* (Oxford: Oxford University Press).

POJMAN, LOUIS P. (ED.)
  1993 *The Theory of Knowledge: Classic and Contemporary Readings* (Belmont, Cal.:
        Wadworth).

POLLOCK, JOHN
  1986 *Contemporary Theories of Knowledge* (Savage, Md.: Rowman and Littlefield).

POST, JOHN F.
  1992 "Infinite Regress Argument," in Dancy and Sosa (1992), pp. 209–212.

PUTNAM, HILARY
  1981 *Reason, Truth, and History* (Cambridge: Cambridge University Press).
  1983 "There Is At Least One A Priori Truth," in *Realism and Reason, Philosophical
        Papers, Volume 3* (Cambridge: Cambridge University Press).

QUINE, W. V.
  1953 "Two Dogmas of Empiricism," in *From a Logical Point of View* (New York:
        Harper and Row), pp. 20–46.
  1960 *Word and Object* (Cambridge, Mass.: MIT Press).
  1969 "Epistemology Naturalized," in *Ontological Relativity and Other Essays* (New
        York: Columbia University Press), pp. 69–90.

ROSS, W. D.
  1988 *The Right and the Good* (Indianapolis: Hackett).

RUSSELL, BERTRAND
  1912 *The Problems of Philosophy* (Oxford: Oxford University Press).

SACKS, OLIVER
  1987 *The Man Who Mistook His Wife for a Hat and Other Clinical Tales* (New York:
        Harper and Row).

SAINSBURY, R. M.
  1988 *Paradoxes* (Cambridge: Cambridge University Press).

SCHLICK, MORITZ
  1959 "The Foundation of Knowledge," in A. J. Ayer (ed.), *Logical Positivism*,
        (Glencoe, Ill.: The Free Press). Appeared originally in 1934 in *Erkenntnis 4*,
        as "Über das Fundament der Erkenntnis."

SELLARS, WILFRID
  1963 "Empiricism and the Philosophy of Mind," in *Science, Perception and Reality*
        (London: Routledge and Kegan, Paul), pp. 127–196.

SHOPE, ROBERT K.
  1983 *The Analysis of Knowing: A Decade of Research* (Princeton, N. J.: Princeton
        University Press).
  1992 "Propositional Knowledge," in Dancy and Sosa (1992), pp. 396–401.

SKYRMS, BRIAN
  1986 *Choice and Chance* (Belmont, Cal.: Wadsworth).

SLEIGH, R. C.
  1972 *Necessary Truth* (Englewood Cliffs, N. J.: Prentice Hall).

SOSA, ERNEST
  1986 "Presuppositions of Empirical Knowledge," *Philosophical Papers 15*: 75–87.

1991 *Knowledge in Perspective* (Cambridge: Cambridge University Press).

STEUP, MATTHIAS
1989 "The Regress of Metajustification," *Philosophical Studies 55*: 41–56.

STROUD, BARRY
1989 "Understanding Human Knowledge in General," in Clay and Lehrer (1989), pp. 31–50.

SWANK, CASEY
1988 "A New and Unimproved Version of Reliabilism," *Analysis 48*: pp. 176–177.

TIENSON, JOHN
1974 "On Analyzing Knowledge," *Philosophical Studies 25*: 289–293.

VAN CLEVE, JAMES
1985 "Epistemic Supervenience and the Circle of Beliefs," *Monist 68*: 90–104.
1990 "Supervenience and Closure," *Philosophical Studies 58*: 225–238.

WRIGHT, LAWRENCE
1994 *Remembering Satan: A Case of Recovered Memory and the Shattering of an American Family* (New York: Alfred A. Knopf).

NAME INDEX

SUBJECT INDEX